HEALING
THE
NATIONS

Other Books

From John Loren Sandford
Why Some Christians Commit Adultery

From John Loren Sandford and Paula Sandford
The Elijah Task
Restoring the Christian Family
The Transformation of the Inner Man
Healing the Wounded Spirit

From John Loren Sandford and Loren Sandford
The Renewal of the Mind

From John Sandford and Mark Sandford
The Comprehensive Guide to Deliverance and Inner Healing

From Paula Sandford
Healing Victims of Sexual Abuse
Healing Women's Emotions

HEALING
THE
NATIONS

A CALL TO
GLOBAL
INTERCESSION

JOHN LOREN SANDFORD

Foreword by Cindy Jacobs

Chosen Books

A Division of Baker Book House Co
Grand Rapids, Michigan 49516

Published by Chosen Books
A division of Baker Book House Company
P.O. Box 6287, Grand Rapids, MI 49516-6287

Printed in the United States of America

Library of Congress Cataloging-in-Publication Data

Sandford, John Loren.
    Healing the nations : a call to global intercession / John Loren Sandford ; foreword by Cindy Jacobs.
       p.   cm.
    Includes index.
    ISBN 0-8007-9276-9 (pbk.)
      1. Intercessory prayer—Christianity. 2. Spiritual Warfare. 3. Salvation outside the church. I. Title.
    BV220.S26 2000
    269—dc21   99-053976

For current information about all releases from Baker Book House, visit our web site:
http://www.bakerbooks.com

CONTENTS

To all the intercessors
who prayed for this book
and who will respond to its summons

FOREWORD

You are about to open the pages of an amazing book. This is no mindless, easy-read material; rather, it is life-changing and groundbreaking. God has used John Sandford and his wife, Paula, to pioneer the area of inner healing, which has brought wholeness and release to thousands of people around the world. In fact, it was after I did a study of some of John's books on inner healing that the Holy Spirit gave me the first revelations I ever received on how to heal a nation.

Since this book is about the healing of nations, I think it is pertinent to write what the Holy Spirit spoke to me when I asked Him, "How do you heal a nation?" His reply to me was, *Cindy, how do you bring healing to an individual's life?* Since I had gone to school on John and Paula's books, I could easily begin to make the leap in my mind to apply the messages of forgiveness and reconciliation to nations (see chapter 11).

The insights John shares in this book are not new to him. He has been waiting for this hour and time to share them. I have personally walked with him through some of the processing of his thoughts and know how he has labored to share revelation that he is aware might be controversial. I believe he does this with integrity.

Cindy Jacobs, co-founder
Generals of Intercession

ACKNOWLEDGMENTS

My first thanks, of course, is to God. At times the Holy Spirit poured in ideas and words so fast I could hardly type them into the computer before the next were crowding the first out of my mind.

Thanks, too, to our friends Frank and Rosemary Miller, whose invitation to Paula and me to spend the last of April 1999 and all of May in their lovely home on the shore in Kailua-Kona gave me the combination of privacy and beauty that made inspiration and labor, for the most part, a joy. No thanks to the old devil, who plagued me with attacks on my health, on the computer and on my desktop printer, especially while I was trying to write chapter 9, "Defeating the Devil's Devices"!

Thanks to our son Mark, who read the rough draft and challenged me to add or delete and to justify scripturally many thoughts and concepts.

To our daughter Ami and husband, Tony, who live with us and had to join Paula in wielding the head-knockers that called out to me, "Earth to John," many times when deep thoughts spaced me out of their world. And Tony's editing here and there in the book was a great help.

To our Elishas, a group of friends with the same ministry as ours, who came by for a visit. Their reading and listening to chapters brought welcome encouragement, especially when the labor and warfare were getting me down.

ACKNOWLEDGMENTS

Most of all I am grateful to Jane Campbell, our editor. I marvel at her ability to take scrambled writings that did not say what I meant them to, and turn them into readable, understandable chapters. I am afraid the possibly controversial material in parts of this book must have driven her to more research and struggle to rewrite than most books she edits for Chosen! She did a great job, and for that I am grateful and appreciative.

Finally, thanks to our board and staff at Elijah House, who took the financial step of faith to put us on paid sabbatical for all of 1999 so we could write. They had to trust that God would supply while we brought in no income—and they have done it with grace and joy.

I say "we" because, although this time the writing has been more mine than ours, Paula's advice and continual support have made this as much a joint adventure as all the rest of the books we have co-authored more directly. She had to carry a lot of the burden-bearing and warfare so I could be free in heart and mind to write.

May God bless all who read and who are called to His purposes.

INTRODUCTION

In November 1973 the Lord called my wife, Paula, and me out of the pastorate into the ministry that has become Elijah House. At that time He ordered us to write seven books and gave us the titles: *The Elijah Task, Restoring the Christian Family, The Transformation of the Inner Man, Healing the Wounded Spirit, The Renewal of the Mind, Healing the Nations* and *The Healing of the Earth*. All of these books, plus six others we have written, are pioneering works in the application of the blood and cross and resurrection life of our Lord Jesus Christ to the deep wounds and practices of the heart that prevent Christians from becoming who they are in Christ.

Each of the first five books, which have been written and published, concern the maturation and sanctification of individual Christians. The last two books present a departure from individual (perhaps even self-centered) concerns to corporate, altruistic, others-minded service to the Lord, to mankind and to earth. These call for forgetting about one's self and one's own sanctification and laying down one's life for others.

The earlier five books direct our gaze inward, then outward. This new book and the next call us to look inward only when we find our flesh interfering, and then merely enough to get the flesh out of the way. Those who come looking for something for themselves had better put this book and its sequel down until they are ready to serve others unmindful of their own needs.

Don't get me wrong. There is a time for introspection. If there were not, Paula and I—and many others—have wasted a lot of time and energy! But we are to be healed and transformed in order to be wiser and stronger servants of Jesus for the sake of others. If sanctification and transformation do not issue in selfless service, we have missed the mark.

The earlier five books plunge us into the pain of facing personal sin and dying to ourselves on the cross of Christ. This book and the next call us to the pains and joys of bearing the burdens of others as we stand in the gap for a hurting world. God has been preparing us to be a people for Himself—bloodwashed, cross-crucified, resurrection-transformed children of God who are becoming mature sons and daughters, warriors for others. There is a call on our lives. God has been preparing us to answer it.

John Loren Sandford, co-founder
Elijah House

ONE

THE CALL TO THE NATIONS

The LORD stretched out His hand and touched my mouth, and the LORD said to me, "Behold, I have put My words in your mouth. See, I have appointed you this day over the nations and over the kingdoms, to pluck up and to break down, to destroy and to overthrow, to build and to plant."

Jeremiah 1:9–10

No longer can we get away with relegating Jeremiah's calling solely to him or to Old Testament times. That is the revelation and call of this book: *Jeremiah's calling is ours for the consummation of history.* We have been raised to sit with Christ in heavenly places (see Ephesians 2:6). "To sit" means "to rule." We have been given the keys of the Kingdom (see Matthew 16:19) as well as authority over the nations:

Jesus came up and spoke to them, saying, "All authority has been given to Me in heaven and earth. Go therefore and make disciples of all the nations, baptizing them in the name of the Father and the Son and the Holy Spirit, teaching them to observe all that I commanded you; and lo, I am with you always, even to the end of the age."

Matthew 28:18–20

We are ambassadors for Christ (see 2 Corinthians 5:20)—and, if we comprehend our authority, ambassadors plenipotentiary! And we are all called to be intercessors. Hebrews 7:25 says that the Lord Jesus "always lives to make intercession for [those who draw near to God]." Our great High Priest is always interceding before the Father on our behalf. But where does Jesus live? In our hearts. This means that if we let Jesus live His life in us, we must constantly be in intercessory prayer. The very life breath of a Christian is intercession! If we do not spend ourselves daily in intercession, the Lord may indeed be *in* our hearts, but we are not allowing Him to *live His life in us*, because intercession is what He is always doing. (More about this in chapter 7.)

What Does Intercessory Spiritual Warfare Do?

Intercessory spiritual warfare, more than anything else, breaks up, overthrows, tears down and upbuilds the kingdoms of the world. In less than three hundred years the prayers and lifestyle of Christians overcame the mightiest kingdom of that day, Rome.

In the mid-1980s my wife, Paula, and I spoke in Altensteig, Germany, to Intercessors for Germany, headed by Berthold Buecker. We taught that if German people would repent together, East and West, they could destroy the strongholds of division that were keeping the Berlin Wall in place. Herr Buecker took that message behind the Iron Curtain to teach East Germans how to join West Germans in unity, repentance and intercessory prayer.

Later, though no one orchestrated it, East Germans began to come to a great church in Leipzig, interceding fervently for their country—at great risk, because the Stasi (the secret police) were watching and recording. Thousands gathered in the church and throughout the city. Let me quote from an article in the *Zeitung Rheinischer Merker*, a newspaper in Augsburg, Germany, dated September 23, 1999:

> In the evening of November 9, 1989, a crowd of thousands of citizens . . . gathered at the checkpoint of Bornholmer Street [in East Berlin]. Hour after hour the masses increasingly pushed

against the gate. Obersleutnant Harold Jager hoped to get an answer from above. But the paralyzed leadership made no answer to his repeated warnings. Shortly before midnight the Obersleutnant, on his own, lifted the first barrier of the iron curtain in Germany.

An endless stream of excited people poured into the festival city of joy in the west, leaving Jager behind, with a feeling as though his stomach were in revolt. His colleagues and superior officers were unable to handle or stop it, as citizens swung bottles of champagne—and hugged the border police. A whole world came to a collapse.

It was too late to stop the pendulum of history; it had swung to freedom, and in November 1989 the Berlin wall was torn down.

The intercessors did not let up, and the greatest bloodless revolution in modern history followed, as Communism fell out of power, the Soviet Union was dissolved and, miracle of miracles, Germany was reunited. So we see the power of intercessory prayer and spiritual warfare for the nations of the world.

Believers also have the power to overthrow kings and rulers. A prophetic intercessor Paula and I knew (who has since passed on) became more and more disgusted with the way things were going during the presidency of Lyndon Baines Johnson. At last she retired into council with the Lord, and subsequently marched out to announce with finality, "Johnson is through!" To everyone's surprise, perhaps even his own, the President announced a few months later that he would not run for reelection.

This is not to say that President Johnson was more evil than other men, nor is it to impugn one party over another. The country has gone in wrong directions under both parties—witness the attempted impeachment of Republican President Andrew Johnson. And perhaps this woman's prophetic intercession had little to do with Lyndon Johnson's decision. But listen to God's Word:

> "Who has stood in the council of the LORD, that he should see and hear His word? Who has given heed to His word and listened?"
>
> Jeremiah 23:18

"If they had stood in My council, then they would have announced My words to My people, and would have turned them back from their evil way and from the evil of their deeds."

Jeremiah 23:22

The voice of the LORD is upon the waters; the God of glory thunders, the LORD is over many waters. The voice of the LORD is powerful, the voice of the LORD is majestic.

Psalm 29:3–4

What God purposes will be done. That is the power of prophetic intercession. Every Christian has power, and God will hear and accomplish for any one of us. But prophets have been raised to hear and proclaim with God's authority, and to give direction to intercessors' prayers. When prophets intercede, and others with them, power is magnified and God's highest purposes are accomplished with finality, exactly as He intended. (More about prophetic intercession in chapters 5 and 7, and about the councils of God in chapter 8.)

Truly we have power to overthrow kingdoms, even as Jeremiah did.

I met in Odessa, Michigan, in the early 1970s with a woman with a prophetic gift, in order to pray for America. In a vision the Lord took us high above Washington, D.C., and showed us a vision of government buildings, and the White House itself, being discolored by defilement and corruption. It actually increased as we watched. Then God's voice said, *What shall we do about this?*

Multitudes of possibilities flooded our minds—mostly forms of drastic judgment. We consulted together a moment, then asked whether repentance might cleanse and prevent judgment.

The Lord gave us four specific prayers for repentance and cleansing to be said each day, and commanded that at the end of the six months we were to cease praying, to release all to Him and to forget the prayers. He would move to expose the corruption and purify the White House.

We said those prayers faithfully every day for six months, then asked the Lord obediently to enable us to forget them. Strangely, though I said those special appointed prayers doggedly each day for half a year, today I cannot remember even one of them!

At the end of six months, the first inklings of the scandal began to emerge that came to be known as Watergate. And, astonishingly, the first break in the wall of secrecy came during a speech that one of President Richard Nixon's advisors gave in Odessa, Michigan. President Nixon resigned in 1974.

I am sure my prophetic friend and I were not the only ones praying. Among others, Paula's and my prayer group at home participated, and saw a vision of a skeleton in a White House closet. Many other groups also prayed. That is precisely the point. When many join their prayers—especially with those who are specifically called and given direction from the council of God—authorities are (in the words of Jeremiah 1:10, quoted at the beginning of this chapter) plucked up and broken down, destroyed and overthrown, built and planted.

Is it enough? Are we clear and certain that we have both the calling and the authority and power to dispossess nations and to resurrect righteousness and justice among the nations?

God Has Speeded Things Up

But here is the problem: ignorance. Truly,

My people are destroyed for lack of knowledge.

Hosea 4:6

It is to overcome that lack that I write. Often we Christians have not understood how or what to pray for. Historically we have often been like blind fencers frantically swinging swords that turned out to have the power of wet noodles. And we have been isolated, many of us fighting all alone. Now at last, just at the Lord's own right timing, He is giving back to the Church the fivefold gifts He named in Ephesians 4:11–12, including prophets and teachers sent to equip the Church for ministry and to call for unity in intercession and warfare.

Is it any surprise, considering God's faithful providence and planning, that at the climax of history, when His fivefold gifts are needed so desperately, television and radio, audio and video-tapes, books and magazines, telephone and faxes, Internet and e-mail are for the first time in history ready at hand the world over? Now, quickly, the Body can be readied for war.

And the war is on. Make no mistake, it is not now as it has been. Previous generations had time—sometimes centuries—to stumble along, learning by the often long and tedious school of trial and error. Opinions and ways sometimes did not change for centuries. A man could count on his father's knowledge and wisdom to be up to date and appropriate for his own time.

In many aspects of life today, except in the core matters of faith, Dad's knowledge no longer seems to be wisdom. Before the Second World War, except for some so-called holy rollers, few knew anything about the Holy Spirit, to say nothing of heal-ing, deliverance, intercessory prayer and spiritual warfare. Almost the entire Church lay in the valley of dry bones, scat-tered and dead (see Ezekiel 37:1–10).

When I was a child—on hot August days, especially—time seemed to stand still. Hours seemed to last for days, and days for eternity. Now it is as though the Lord's giant hand has spun the earth faster and faster, like a basketball twirling on the tip of an athlete's finger. Time and change seem to whistle by, faster than we can keep up.

We have all watched as the Church has rediscovered the nine gifts of the Holy Spirit; the fivefold offices of apostles, prophets, evangelists, pastors and teachers; and the offices of exorcism, intercession and warfare. We have seen the power of the Holy Spirit fall on worship services with miracles happening—in some ministries, regularly. At the turn of the century we thought demons were mere superstitions of a less advanced age. We thought the age of rationality and science would dispel them as easily as the noonday sun burns away morning fog. Now, we have learned, they are real!

New converts today, filled with the Holy Spirit, seem to be born anew with knowledge and skills it took us oldies years to learn. Again and again the Lord is taking us all on Emmaus walks, opening to us long-hidden Scriptures and understanding. Divine insights are falling like huge snowflakes swirling down out of heaven and covering the earth with soft, new cleanliness.

Revelations bring decisions, so it is also a time of division. Division, I hope, and not divisiveness. Revelations break the controls of the old; they let God out of the box in which we have tried to hold Him. Heavenly insights free Him to lead us onward "for the prize of the upward call of God in Christ Jesus" (Philippians 3:14).

Rediscovering Ancient Paths

There are always those—perhaps all of us, at times—who want to sit down and rest awhile, content with what we have. A cowboy in the musical *Oklahoma* sang, "They've gone about as fur as they kin go." That may be what all of us in moments, and some of us a lot of the time, would like to cry: "I've gone about as fur as I kin go!"

But it is not a time to sit down and celebrate what we have. The call is upon us to move forward and tackle issues and embattlements far beyond what we in our fledgling years ever thought we would face.

God is calling the Body to rediscover ancient paths in which to walk (see Isaiah 58:12). It is a time of relearning, perhaps more intensely than ever before, the new-old ways of God's Kingdom.

One problem (or blessing), besides ignorance, is that the call to heal cities, tribes and nations comes to a Church already struggling to keep up with the new, struggling to adapt and yet to hang onto what should never be changed. Revelations calling for change keep pouring in—for example, the Toronto Blessing; "Catch the Fire" conferences; a new understanding of multiple personality disorder (already changed to dissociative identity disorder); victims of Satanic ritualistic abuse; teachings about spiritual mapping, identificational repentance and much more.

Time to Expand Our Stakes

Churches are stretched to expand their stakes to take in and raise the ever-increasing influx of babes in Christ. Pastors are having to leap the credal walls of denominational lines to pray together. In our town, every Tuesday morning at seven A.M., about 25 pastors meet to pray together for one another's churches. This is happening in many places throughout the land. Countless churches are banding together to support ever-larger crusades. In March 1995, for example, Billy Graham held the largest TV crusade ever in the history of the world.

Some of these developments stretch us far beyond our comfort zones. Certain rituals and doctrines—long-held practices and beliefs that seemed to work well all our lives—are bashing up against what our brothers and sisters are doing. We are having to crack out of our safe shells. Some of us feel like Tevye in that wonderful movie "Fiddler on the Roof," when his third daughter, his beloved little Havilah, wanted his permission to marry a Gentile, and Tevye cried out, "If I bend any farther, I'll break!"

Time for Maturity

At present a rash of critics—men and women who consider themselves apologists—feel called to defend the faith, as in Jude 3 and 4. Some truly are. Correction is sorely needed, and many strange new revelations have come so fast that the Body is being tossed to and fro, in danger of being carried away "by every wind of doctrine" (Ephesians 4:14). We need balance and wisdom. Those of us in the vanguard especially must learn to consider the warnings of all apologists, wise or foolish.

Unfortunately some of the Lord's apologists lack depth of scholarship, grace of compassion, magnanimity of mind and heart, and maturity in the Lord. Too often they cause greater confusion and divisiveness in the Body than the imbalance they are trying to prevent.

Time for Unity

The Holy Spirit is calling the Lord's Body into unity. God the Father is answering His Son's prayer recorded in John 17. Satan copies whatever he sees God doing, so he is trying to establish his own kind of unity—an apostate, one-world, one-church organization. Some fail to distinguish between unity—Christ's attempt to unite His Body as one and prepare her as His beautiful Bride—and Satan's attempts at false unity. So they tear up the good seed with the bad.

John Dawson helped organize the first World Christian Gathering of Indigenous People, held November 7–17, 1996, at Rotorua, New Zealand. (More about this in chapter 10.) It was a marvelous time of celebrating the glory of the Lord together. Midway through, when a few of us shared lunch together, John told me his e-mail box was full of hate letters from Christians who were sure he was trying to establish the Antichrist's one-world church! I grieved for those so blinded by fear that they could not see and celebrate what God is doing.

Behind many of the critiques, both fair and unfair, is often fear—fear of losing control, of being swamped by waves not from the Holy Spirit. Much criticism is an attempt to retreat to the ostensible safety of the familiar, to grasp what seems to be solid amid violently tossing storms of revelation and consequent change, to attempt to hold onto the past, fearing to lurch into the future in simple trust of God.

Time to Step Out Boldly

But this is not a time to quit or to retrench in the familiar. It is a time to step out boldly in faith. Revelation 21:8 tells us that the first to be rejected and thrown into "the lake that burns with fire and brimstone" are not the "abominable and murderers and immoral persons" but the "cowardly and unbelieving"! *It is time for courage, for risk-taking, for moving out from the familiar into the unknown, into the seemingly uncharted waters of spiritual warfare—no longer for personal petty concerns, but for the sake of tribes and vast nations of peoples.*

21

Every once in a while we will be called to act on the flimsy ground of knowledge that we believe is inspired by the Holy Spirit but that cannot be proven historically or factually or scientifically. Today is heart-in-the-throat, simple raw obedience time. We must be willing to be fools if what seems to be guidance turns out to be delusion, trusting that God is able to turn all our dirty water into the best of wines.

Time to Confirm What We Hear

I am not calling for irresponsibility. We need to check everything we think we hear from God with brothers and sisters and with the Word of God itself. We need to act within the best wisdom and common sense we can muster.

At a large conference on spiritual warfare, Cindy Jacobs received a word from God that frightened her. She was told to tell God's people that if they did not repent, the terrorist bomb blast that destroyed the Murrah Federal Building in Oklahoma City and killed many innocent children would be only the first of many disasters that would harm many more innocent children, and that our sins as a nation would cause God to remove His hand of protection.

There was more to the message, but that alone sent her to the elders present at the meeting, who could confirm or deny the word and give her wise counsel. Peter Wagner, Dutch Sheets, Larry Lea, Jean Steffenson and others told her they thought the word was truly from God, and they counseled her to present it.

Not satisfied and still gripped by fear, she called me for further ratification. I not only confirmed her word but added to it several particulars the Lord had given me. In obedience and fear and trembling, she gave the word. The conference attendees responded in repentance and prayer.

Fear is good. Counsel is better. Cindy handled her responsibility rightly. But despite all the precautions we can and should take, there will be occasions in the coming days when obedience demands steps off mental cliffs that appear to have no safe landing places!

Are You Willing?

Are you willing to enlist in the Lord's end-time army? Are you able to trust His headship blindly? Habakkuk 2:4 says that "the righteous will live by his faith."

I want to be willing. I pray that He will make our fearful hearts more trusting. I choose to enlist out of sheer obedience, but haltingly, fearing the blindness, trying to trust. And I hope that the fear and reticence in many of us will spawn a prerequisite humility that will help keep us out of presumption. The coming warfare is neither light nor easy. A little holy fear will stand us all in good stead.

TWO

WHAT DOES "HEALING" MEAN?

In the last chapter we identified two of the problems facing the Church: ignorance and isolation. Now let's define our terms. If we are called to pray for the healing of the nations, who is meant by "we"? And what does "healing" mean—and not mean?

Second Chronicles 7:14 tells us,

> "[If] *My people* who are called by My name humble themselves and pray and seek My face and turn from their wicked ways, then I will hear from heaven, will forgive their sin and will *heal their land.*"

> emphasis added

Using this Scripture as a guide, let's consider these two questions in turn.

1. Who Are "My People"?

Since it is unlikely that *all* God's people will hear and respond in any given endeavor, and if unanimity is required, a cynic

24

could say it is a safe promise for God to make, if He knows that at no time will His people ever respond unanimously. He would never have to heal any land!

Perhaps *My people*, therefore, was never intended to mean *all* God's people, maybe not even a majority. God is no manipulative trickster, so *My people* cannot mean everyone in every land who calls himself a Christian. If only ten righteous people could have been found, God would have spared Sodom and Gomorrah (see Genesis 18–19). How many is "ten righteous" for any nation? For any region, state or province? For any church? For any group of people anywhere?

I think *My people* begins with whomever God specifically calls. God wanted to save Nineveh, so He called Jonah, who at first demurred—and wound up in the belly of the whale. One could say Jonah experienced a sudden change of perspective! When he obeyed, God moved on the king's heart, who called the entire city to repent in sackcloth and ashes, and Nineveh was saved. Note that in this case "My people" was initially only one man: reluctant Jonah. We would not normally think of the Ninevites, a heathen population, as God's people, yet their repentance and unity enabled God to save their city. When one specific member of God's people responded in obedience, their salvation commenced.

Can any nation today be said to be truly Christian, fully *My people*? How many Christians does it require for a land to be justly called "Christian"?

Not all the people in Israel—a nation given by covenant to God, a people consecrated to Him in what was supposed to be a theocracy—were believers. So many turned to idolatry and apostasy that judgment fell repeatedly on the nation, until finally destruction and exile resulted. Whom, then, could the Lord have meant by "My people who are called by My name"? In Elijah's time it meant only seven thousand who had not bowed the knee to Baal (see 1 Kings 19:18). Whom does it mean today?

I do not know that, short of sitting down with the Lord in heaven, after all is said and done, we could find a satisfactory answer. But the point is definitive: We must stop thinking all-inclusively. *My people* cannot mean all Christians praying in unity—that will never happen before the Lord returns! It may not even mean a majority in any nation or in any group of people.

I think *My people* must mean *those specifically called to pray in any given situation*. Perhaps *My people who are called by My name* does not refer solely to "Christians," but simply to "those who are called." Literally the Hebrew of that text indicates "the people over whom My name is called." Could it mean those over whom God calls His name, which in biblical custom means "what God stands for"? People called to duty, then? People called to stand?

This is to say to Christians who may lose courage at the enormity of the task of calling nations to repentance, "Take heart." *My people* most likely does not mean that everyone in any nation will have to respond, or else the nation is doomed. It means first our own personal obedience, and then the obedience of who knows how many others the Holy Spirit may enlist. Who knows how many obediences may be required for any nation or group to be saved? Or if sufficient numbers will respond? Or how long it will take for the Lord to muster enough praying people?

Ours is neither to guarantee success nor to quail at enormity, but only to obey. *The rest is up to God.* And sooner or later His purposes will be accomplished. We are on the winning side.

2. How Will God "Heal Their Land"?

As we consider the second question, let's look again at 2 Chronicles 7:14:

> "[If] My people who are called by My name humble themselves and pray and seek My face and turn from their wicked ways, then I will hear from heaven, will forgive their sin and *will heal their land*."

> emphasis added

Maybe we have misunderstood when we have read this passage, or maybe we have reduced it to less than it means. Note that the text does not say *heal their nation* or *heal their country*

26

politically or *heal their country morally*. It says *heal their land*. In verse 20, in fact, the Lord warns that if His people do not respond, but continue to turn away from His statutes, "then I will uproot you from My *land* which I have given you" (emphasis added).

To God, land and nation are as one. What a people do in a land either defiles and destroys that land or else blesses it with fertility and increase. God's promise to "heal their land," then, is more inclusive than had He merely said He would heal their nation. It means He will heal them politically and morally, cleanse their hearts and restore them so fully that their actions no longer defile and ruin the beautiful land He has given them. The promise actually includes the healing of *land*, physical earth.

Farmers and native people the world over can feel this in their bones. They know in the depths of their hearts the intimacy and delicacy of the interrelationship between men and women and the land they inhabit. What good news it is to my own Indian nature to hear that God will respond to our repentance by healing our land as well as our people!

People affect lands, but lands also greatly affect the people who live on them. Who has walked onto a battlefield such as Gettysburg and not felt the groaning and suffering still resident within the land? What Holy Spirit–filled Christian has not discovered that if he is to be able to rest in a motel or hotel room, he must first cleanse it by prayer?

A returned missionary from China told me that pagan Chinese often invited Christians to house-sit when they went on vacation, or if death and sorrow had occurred. They knew that when they returned, their homes would be clean and fresh again because of the Christians' prayers.

In New Zealand Paula's and my host took us for a drive through the beautiful countryside. Suddenly it seemed as though we had driven into a sheet of rain on a clear day. Pouring all about us was defilement—hatred, vengeance, sickness in the spirit and sexual debasement.

"Have we just driven onto a battlefield between the English and the Maoris?" I asked.

"Oh, yes," he said, "this was one of the major battlefields." And he went on to explain that all living in that beautiful farmland were afflicted. Neighbors feuded. One set of brothers refused to repair the fence between them for fear they would encounter one another and have to speak to each other! Sexual problems erupted in many families. I knew from having counseled one resident farmer that he often fell into bestiality with his cattle. No matter how they prayed, our host said, they had been unable to cleanse the land. (In chapter 10 we will speak more about evil descendancies from the sins of our forefathers that have not been brought under the blood of Christ.)

The history of a place, then, affects its present inhabitants.

A young married couple came to me for counseling. They had never fought, and now could not understand why for many months they could not stop quarreling about every little thing. Their biographies made the quarreling an unanswerable conundrum. They had few dysfunctional behavioral patterns from their childhoods, and none so intense as to account for what was happening.

Then the Holy Spirit prompted me to ask, "How long have you lived in your present house?"

"Two years," replied one of them.

"And how long have you been quarreling?"

"Two years."

Subsequent research revealed that the house had been inhabited by three previous couples, all of whom had fought bitterly and divorced. A spiritual "deposit" of rancor in the house had given the demonic access to disrupt. We cleansed the house by prayer and the couple "lived happily ever after."

Is it enough? Do we see that God has said He will heal the land because if the land we live on is not healed, corruption and wounding can seep back into our lives?

The healing of the nations must first be a call to heal the history of those nations, much as inner healing restores the hearts of individuals. But the healing of the nations must also include *healing their lands*, which includes *healing the history of their lands*, or troubles will most likely recur. We who are called into the healing of the nations must learn the fullness of our calling. The Lord who calls will accomplish it. Again, our part is only to obey.

THREE

THE FIRST STEP: HUMILITY AND REPENTANCE

Our Lord Jesus Christ has called many prophets, teachers and intercessors to lead His army into the great end-time war for the saving and healing of the nations. He will call more. This is, I believe, that long-prophesied time for all the world to hear the Gospel and for all nations to come to Him seeking truth:

> It will come about that in the last days the mountain of the house of the LORD will be established as the chief of the mountains, and will be raised above the hills; *and all the nations will stream to it.* And many peoples will come and say, "Come, let us go up to the mountain of the LORD, to the house of the God of Jacob; that He may teach us concerning His ways and that we may walk in His paths." For the law will go forth from Zion and the word of the LORD from Jerusalem. And He will judge between the nations, and will render decisions for many peoples; and they will hammer their swords into plowshares and their spears into pruning hooks. *Nation will not lift up sword against nation, and never again will they learn war.*
>
> Isaiah 2:2–4, emphasis added

29

Because the hill of Zion is "up" geographically from any direction—north, south, east or west—one had to go up to come to the house of God, the Temple in Jerusalem. Isaiah was saying that in the end times the Lord will exalt the worship of the God of the Israelites, and that from that holy mountain (which most Christians believe symbolizes our Hebraic-Christian faith) will go forth to all the world the sacred and wonderful teachings of the laws of God. All the nations of the world will recognize this anointing and come streaming "up" to the house of God.

This prophecy antedates the Church by seven hundred years. The vision for the healing of the nations at the end of time was never solely a command for Christian evangelism, but was always a vital part of Hebraic-Christian mentality and calling. The clarion to the nations is neither a modern invention nor solely a Christian ambition for the world. It has been part of the plan of God from before the foundation of the world.

When the War Began

The war between Hebraic-Christian people and the forces of darkness was prophesied as early as Genesis 3:15:

> "I will put enmity between you and the woman, and between your seed and her seed; he shall bruise you on the head, and you shall bruise him on the heel."

Most Christian scholars believe the woman spoken of here is a type of the Church, and we are the seed of the Church. The war was engaged from the first moments of temptation, from the first sin of Adam and Eve in the Garden. All the separate and sinful nations of the world descend from that moment.

Throughout all of pre-history and the annals of history, that war has raged unabated. Listen to Jesus in Matthew 13:37–43:

> "The one who sows the good seed is the Son of Man, and the field is the world; and as for the good seed, these are the sons of the kingdom; and the tares are the sons of the evil one; and the enemy who sowed them is the devil, and the harvest is the end

of the age; and the reapers are angels. So just as the tares are gathered up and burned with fire, so shall it be at the end of the age. The Son of Man will send forth His angels, and they will gather out of His kingdom all stumbling blocks, and those who commit lawlessness, and will throw them into the furnace of fire; in that place there will be weeping and gnashing of teeth. Then THE RIGHTEOUS WILL SHINE FORTH AS THE SUN in the kingdom of their Father. He who has ears, let him hear."

Thus the war between God's people and the forces of darkness will continue until mankind has fulfilled our part in the final warfare and the angels of God complete the last glorious cleansing of the earth.

Before the World Was Created

But the struggle between heaven and Satan began before the earth was created. Lucifer had fallen but had not yet been cast out of heaven. He could still come among the sons of God (even as late as Job 2:1), but his rebellion had begun. Darkness, therefore, "was over the surface of the deep" (Genesis 1:2). *Darkness was present through Satan's rebellion even before God spoke the holy words of creation.*

When God commanded, "Let there be light" (Genesis 1:3), He saw to it that the light was pure and good, separated from the darkness of rebellion and hate that extended over the face of the deep. And "God saw that the light was good; and God separated the light from the darkness" (verse 4).

Look at another familiar passage. The apostle John, informing us that darkness is hate, says prophetically that since Jesus brought His kind of love into the world, the age-old battle between darkness and light is beginning to be won:

> Beloved, I am not writing a new commandment to you, but an old commandment which you have had from the beginning; the old commandment is the word which you have heard. On the other hand, I am writing a new commandment to you, which is true in Him and in you, *because the darkness is passing away and the true Light is already shining.* The one who says he is in the Light and yet hates his brother is in the darkness until now.

31

The one who loves his brother abides in the Light and there is no cause for stumbling in him. But the one who hates his brother is in the darkness and walks in the darkness, and does not know where he is going because the darkness has blinded his eyes.

1 John 2:7–11, emphasis added

The entire warfare of heaven and earth, of mankind and the forces of darkness, is encapsulated in these wondrously inspired few words. Satan's jealousy, born of hatred for the Son of God who was the Logos and who would become our Lord Jesus Christ, had spawned the darkness of hate across the surface of the deep.

God moved, then, to create anew through the Word, who would become incarnated as Jesus, the only begotten Son of God (see John 1:1–3; Colossians 1:15–16; James 1:18). In this new creation God would place the children with whom He desired to have fellowship throughout eternity. Satan knew God's hope and moved to thwart it, tempting Adam and Eve into sin. *Thus the warfare that already existed in the heavens entered mankind and the earth, becoming the root of sin behind all succeeding generations and nations.*

In these fundamentally simple words from John, the essence of the war is distilled. Satan's hatred could be overcome only by love—the longsuffering, crucified love of our Lord Jesus Christ. There on the cross God's love through the sacrifice of Jesus began to blot out the darkness of hate once for all. Truly "the true Light is already shining."

This means that however we pray, whatever actions we take, whatever sacrifices we make to win this war, none shall have heaven's effect or find victory unless it is an example of our Lord's love manifested once again on the earth, in the sight of heaven and hell (see Ephesians 3:9–10). The war is simply and only a warfare between love and hate, and "love never fails" (1 Corinthians 13:8). Our Lord, by His sacrificial, dying love, has won the war. Only by love, no matter what our knowledge and tactics, can we also win.

The Loss of Ability to Commune with God

In the Garden Adam and Eve could visit freely with God—in the words of an old Latvian hymn, they could "walk and talk and jest, as good friends should and do." Their hearts and minds were tuned perfectly to His. Love rested in trust. They read God's thoughts and moods in perfect harmony. There was no confusion, no misunderstanding to mar communication. All was harmony and meeting—spirit to Spirit, their hearts to His heart, their minds to His mind.

Then came temptation and sin, which caused immediate separation. Always before, when God came in the cool of the evening, Adam and Eve had rushed to embrace Him, like children running with open arms, exclaiming, "Daddy's home!" But now their spirits had been infected with Satan's distrust. The very God of love and forgiveness came and they fled from Him. They could no longer trust His merciful nature. (For a full exposition of what happened in the Garden, see chapters 2–4 of my book with my son Loren, *The Renewal of the Mind*.)

Adam and Eve could no longer read God's heart. His words of love, calling them to reconciliation, appeared to them only as threats of condemnation. Rather than simply offering a confession—"Father, we sinned. We ate of the tree You commanded us not to eat. Father, forgive us"—they lied and passed the buck. They could not trust God's motives, so they could no longer comprehend what He said, even if they could hear His words. Communication was broken. Fellowship had shattered like the shards of a once-beautiful window.

Since then, whenever God has approached His fallen children anywhere across the earth, they cannot hear Him. They might catch a bit here, a line there, but none can see who God is or hear the loving heart behind His words. None can see Reality as He is (see 1 John 3:1–3).

He came to His children in China, and they caught the idea of His wisdom—and nothing else of His nature. He came to His own in India, and they perceived correctly that the Godhead is triune—but the third person of that trinity was Shiva the Destroyer, not our gentle, loving Holy Spirit. He came to the red men of the isthmus of America, and they foretyped the blood sacrifice of Jesus the Son of God—and slew thousands of young men!

Wherever God came, mankind caught only warped pieces of His reality. Theologically the entire world had become mentally ill.

Exposing Two False Teachings

Lest some react and leave us at this point, let me clear up two false teachings that have held captive the hearts and minds of many.

1. No Other Religion Contains Any Truth

The first false doctrine is that no other religion contains any truth, that every other faith has been spawned by none other than the devil, and that God has had nothing to do with anyone except Jews and born-anew Christians. *In whatever degree Christians have held this three-pronged wrong belief, to that degree we have failed to sanctify the nature of God and have not believed the witness of Scripture.* Listen to the Word:

> "Are you not as the sons of Ethiopia to Me, O sons of Israel?" declares the LORD. "Have I not brought up Israel from the land of Egypt, *and the Philistines from Caphtor and the Arameans from Kir?*"
>
> Amos 9:7, emphasis added

God is not merely the God of Abraham, Isaac and Jacob; He is the God of the universe, the God of all peoples, who moves tribes and nations wherever He wills. He has not confined His activities to Jews and Christians. I am not espousing the heresy of universalism; it is only by grace through our Lord Jesus Christ that we are saved. The Lord has acted electively, distinctively, purposefully through His Hebrew children to prepare the way for the coming of His Son. But it is insupportable hubris—spiritual pride and elitism—to believe He has acted only among Jews and Christians.

In that day Israel will be the third party with Egypt and Assyria, a blessing in the midst of the earth, whom the LORD of hosts has blessed, saying, "Blessed *is Egypt My people, and Assyria the work of My hands*, and Israel My inheritance."

Isaiah 19:24–25, emphasis added

Is Israel, then, the only chosen people? Has God worked only through Hebraic-Christians? Obviously not. Would it sanctify God's nature to think He has rejected and neglected every other people ever since the Fall? "For God so loved the *world*, that He gave His only begotten Son. . . ." He has not left Himself without witness in any age—or in any place, among any people.

Let's be clear that God has attempted to inspire all men and women in nearly every religion. In the book *Eternity in Their Hearts* (Regal, 1981) Don Richardson says that parallels to familiar Bible stories can be found in ninety percent of the world's religious cultures. But let's be just as clear that what many have received has become warped and twisted. Only in Hebraic-Christian history has the Lord acted electively and decisively to preserve and protect a clean deposit of faith for salvation. Others remain a mixed bag.

Our friends Frank and Rosemary Miller were assigned, as part of their Youth With A Mission outreach, to assist in an orphanage owned and operated by members of a fundamentalist branch of Hinduism. Unwanted, handicapped and deformed children were dumped into the orphanage at birth or soon after. Left uncared for, perhaps diapered but otherwise nearly naked, they were unwashed, unloved and fed a mere subsistence diet. Most of the orphans, even those approaching teen years, were tiny and underdeveloped and actually could not speak. They had been taught nothing and spoken to by no one.

The people of that faith believed in reincarnation and saw these unfortunate children as reaping the evil they had sown in some previous incarnation. Neither the children's parents nor the patrons of the orphanage, therefore, did anything for them other than keep them alive so they could suffer their "karma"—the ostensible effect of their conduct that had determined their destiny. In that belief system, to do anything to help the children would be to postpone and possibly worsen the suffering of the karma they had to endure.

The members of this sect had caught hold of the concept that every person must reap what he or she has sown. But they had little notion of the operation of mercy, and no notion that God in Jesus reaped our evil for us on the cross.

How painful to see that the lost children of God have heard His truths only in part, often missing His grace! What Paul said of the Jews can be applied to those of other faiths as well:

> I testify about them that they have a zeal for God, but not in accordance with knowledge. For not knowing about God's righteousness and seeking to establish their own, they did not subject themselves to the righteousness of God. For Christ is the end of the law for righteousness to everyone who believes.
>
> Romans 10:2–4

Frank and Rosemary began to minister the love and mercy of the Lord Jesus Christ in that orphanage, serving to cleanse and help and pray for the youngsters with the laying on of hands. This upset the administrators, who believed the YWAM staffers were interfering with the children's karma.

Not all adherents of any Eastern religion are that devoid of compassion and love, even as some fundamentalist Christians exalt laws above mercy and compassion but they do not represent all Christians. Still, this one example among thousands demonstrates that truth is often caught from God only in part, without counterbalancing aspects of our Father's loving nature. All over the world, in every religion, Satan has worked to twist and warp what could have been true revelation (see 2 Corinthians 4:1–4). But to say that God has not spoken into any religion other than Hebraic-Christianity cannot be justified scripturally.

2. Only Christians Are Sons and Daughters of God

The second false teaching we need to address is one that many teachers and evangelists have advanced: "Anyone who has not received Jesus Christ as Lord and Savior has never been anything but a son of the devil." But can it be justified scripturally to say that non-Christians have *never* been sons or daughters of God?

Some readers may be disconcerted by this discussion because I use language that may seem universalistic. I assure you I am no universalist! There is only one way to heaven, which is through accepting Jesus Christ as our Lord and Savior. Scripture is equally clear that not all will receive Him (see Matthew 7:13–14 for one of many texts). Others may become upset at my willingness to speak of people around the world who have not yet been born anew in Jesus as "children of God," as though that were heretical or that it somehow diminishes our uniqueness as those who have been given "the right to become children of God' (John 1:12). But please read with an open mind and hear what I have to say, both scripturally and logically. To me this is an important area of spiritual pride and elitism that we in the Body of Christ need to see and repent of.

Texts and statements may convince you as you read. But for openers, think about this: What if the elder brother of the prodigal had added to his objections about "this son of yours" (Luke 15:30) that his younger brother had never been a son to his father anyway? That he had never had a right to be called a son? This is what we have often done in the way we think and speak about everyone who has not yet accepted Jesus as Lord and Savior. I think you will see, if you read with an open mind, that we have been in error, both scripturally and theologically, and arrogant in heart, unnecessarily offensive to the very people our Lord has sent us to love and win.

We must be careful to rightly divide the Word of God. Listen to Jesus, speaking to the Jews:

> "Has it not been written in your Law, 'I SAID, YOU ARE GODS'? If he called them gods, to whom the word of God came (and the Scripture cannot be broken), do you say of Him, whom the Father sanctified and sent into the world, 'You are blaspheming,' because I said, 'I am the Son of God'?"
>
> John 10:34–36

Jesus was quoting Psalm 82:6—"I said, 'You are gods, and all of you are sons of the Most High'"—to Jews who did not even believe in Him!

The Word of God makes it evident beyond dispute that we were all created as sons and daughters of God. *Every person on the face of the globe was created as a child of God.* But all of us fell and died to our status as children of God, even as the father of the prodigal said: "For this son of mine was dead and has come to life again" (Luke 15:24). For this reason, to the same people to whom Jesus said, "You are gods," He also said, "You are of your father the devil, and you want to do the desires of your father" (John 8:44).

When we fell into sin and died, we entered into the ways of the world and became sons of the devil. Ezekiel 18:4 says, "The soul who sins will die." It is not merely that we died; we became captive to do the will of Satan (see 2 Timothy 2:26). We became, therefore, the children of our father the devil, "by nature children of wrath" (Ephesians 2:3).

But all of us, anywhere in the world, began as children of God. If all mankind had been created sinful, sons of the devil, there could have been no Fall, because there would have been nothing to fall from! We would only have acted out the sinful natures with which we were created. But it was from the high image of God that we fell into death and became sons of the devil.

To be sure, we were all infected with original sin, even from before our birth. But we cannot solely blame Adam and Eve for our fall into sin and need of a Savior. We are responsible. All of us turned aside and fell by our own choosing (see, for example, Psalm 14:3; Romans 3:12).

This theological point is one over which many stumble. Unconsciously we want to blame Satan, Adam and Eve (original sin), our parents, God—anyone!—rather than admit our own responsibility for our fallen condition. But if blame can justly be laid anywhere other than mainly on ourselves, then there is no real guilt or fall. The cross becomes only a manipulative gimmick by God to trap us into loving Him, even as some mothers play the noble martyr role: "Oh, how I've suffered for you!"—the message being, "Now you have to love me."

No, the cross was necessary because of Adamic sin and because of our own sin.

By the same token, it is wrong theologically and biblically to posture as though no one else has ever been a child of God. We are not erring theologically or biblically to say that God has come to the children He has created all over the world. They are dead children, to be sure, which makes John 1:11–12 so meaningful:

> He came to His own, and those who were His own did not receive Him. But as many as received Him, to them He gave the right to become children of God, even to those who believe in His name.

But it is important to acknowledge that God has moved by His Holy Spirit in most religious expressions in the world.

When Christians say, quoting Jesus, "No one comes to the Father but through Me" (John 14:6), we are caught in a necessary elitism and exclusivism. Jesus was saying that no one in any other religion comes successfully to God our Father. If His statement were a figment of our own imaginations, we should justly be called arrogant, spiritually prideful and exclusivistic. But this is God's own Word—divine revelation, not human arrogance.

Romans 9:33 says (quoting Isaiah 8:14 and 28:16), "I lay in Zion a stone of stumbling and a rock of offense, and he who believes in Him will not be disappointed." Christian faith is an offense to every other faith simply because, believing Jesus, we say there is no other way to come to the Father but through Him.

Nevertheless we do not have to add to that offense our own carnal arrogance, by believing and proclaiming our own specialness in God's sight beyond what His Word says.

That we have done this, and that we have often spoken of every other religion as demonic, with nothing of God in it, brings great shame on us as Christians. By our arrogance and judgmentalism we have turned away countless millions who otherwise would have received Christ. This was not what St. Paul modeled to us as the way to win souls to Christ, as we will see.

The First Step in the Salvation and Healing of the Nations

Rabbi Ernst Jacob, my beloved professor of Old Testament and Prophets at Drury College in Springfield, Missouri, answered the question as to why the Jews were God's chosen people by alluding to Amos 9:7. "Gott luffs effryvone," he replied in his heavily accented English. "He choss de Philistines und de Egyptians, too. De difference iss, ve choss Him back."

But perhaps that is not a sufficient answer. Christians, too, chose God when He called. So did Hindus and Buddhists and all others who believe in God by whatever name. They just do not, as Paul said, know Jesus.

If we would win the many lost souls from other religions, we must stop denigrating their beliefs and denouncing all or most of what they believe as nothing but demonic. We earn the right to win them by our humility and by our willingness to hear and cherish what is good in what they know and believe.

Herein lies the first step in the salvation and healing of the nations. We Christians must repent deeply for the arrogance and exclusivism we have trumpeted (or strumpeted) beyond what our Lord stated. In the end we do have to assert, "Yes, but no other faith has the truth of God in Jesus Christ." That is harmful enough for others to hear without our adding insult to injury.

I repeat, because it is crucial to the healing (and evangelization) of the nations: We do not need to injure people of other faiths more than the revelation of the uniqueness of Christ already does. We must learn to respect men and women of other faiths and cherish what God has done in their midst. We must earn our right to be heard, respecting people of whatever faith.

Paul modeled humility for us while conversing with the philosophers of Athens. Despite his grief over their idolatry (see Acts 17:16), he did not say, "Your faith was spawned by the devil and has no truth in it!" Rather than disrespect their beliefs, he made known to them that their "unknown God" (verse 23) was really Jesus, our Lord and Savior.

Incidentally, when Paul wrote to Titus about the people of Crete, he referred to "a prophet of their own" who had said, "Cretans are always liars, evil beasts, lazy gluttons." Then he added, "This testimony is true" (Titus 1:12–13). Paul was commending a non-Hebrew, non-Christian, first as a prophet, then as having given a true word from God!

How much has unnecessary arrogance, elitism and exclusivism shut doors against Christian witness? How much repentance will it require to reopen those doors, that we may preach the Word of God as we should (see Colossians 4:3)? How fervently must we repent before God is free to hear our prayers for the healing of the nations? I don't know. But we must begin.

This is the first call of this book, then, to the Lord's intercessors. We need an army of those who will repent before the Lord for all the harm that our judgmentalism has done in disrespecting the thoughts and differences of faith, belief and culture in those to whom we would minister.

Distinguishing between Christ and Culture

Another issue needs to be addressed with penitence: the difference between the claims of Christ and the patterns of particular cultures. Our disrespect of the songs, dances, worship and societal practices of other cultures is one of the most painful and unresolved areas of Christian missionary history throughout the world.

I love missions. Paula and I were appointed as missionaries to Angola before riots there caused our mission board to cancel the appointments of all missionaries with young families. Thereafter I served seventeen years on the missions board of my denomination, and I know firsthand that missionaries have done great sacrificial work for the Lord.

But our ignorance of culture and our condemnatory pride have too often hindered or even blocked the loving work of the Lord. Too often Christian missionaries transplanted into other cultures have been unaware of the difference between the culture in which they were raised and the content of the Gospel. We have been proud, as though our own culture were altogether Christian and the only acceptable way of life in the sight of God. For widespread examples we need look no farther than the United States.

My mother was Osage allottee #2229. My ancestors were devout, prayerful people, worshiping God as Wahkontah, the

41

great spirit of mystery. Most were monotheists who served God devoutly as they knew Him, praying to the great spirit. How grievous it has been for me, therefore, to hear Christian teachers declare that all Indian worship is satanic! How ignorant such remarks are, and how offensive! Some Indians fell into occult practices, but not all, just as is true among Christian churches. (Shall we say, therefore, that all Christians are occult?) Some Indians believed in and tried to relate to multiple pantheistic types of spirits in animals and plants, but not all.

Unfortunately, however, some Christians have broad-brushed all Indians with unfounded guilt by association. Respect should demand proper research and scholarship before pronouncements of judgment. How offensive and wounding it would be to us if such charges were leveled at our local churches or denominations because of the actions of a few! And how foolish and arrogant for us to treat others that way.

Lessons from the Past

A chief among the Coeur D'Alene tribe saw a vision of Jesus on the cross and was told in this vision that whites would come and that those wearing black robes would know the truth about God. The tribe, hungry to know about God, waited for more than a century for the black robes to appear. In 1841 Father Pierre Jean DeSmet, a Jesuit, founded St. Mary's Mission among the Flatheads of Montana. When the Coeur D'Alene Indians heard of it, a delegation was sent to plead with him to come to them, which he did in 1843. This was typical of the hunger among many tribes for the truth about God.

The Jesuits did a good and honorable work among the Northwest tribes. But other missionaries, filled with spiritual pride and supercilious rejection of native culture, caused hungry Indians to turn away in disgust.

The Puritan missionaries of the Congregational Church, for example, sponsored by the American Board of Commissioners for Foreign Missions in the nineteenth century, opposed Roman Catholic rituals, sacraments, robes and statues. But in eastern Kansas in 1817 they encountered the Osage tribe, whose lives were wrapped around ritual, symbol and sacrament. Osages had developed spiritual thoughts and elaborate prayer rituals to consecrate every item and to govern every area of life. The Osages were a devoutly sacramental and ritualistic people.

Given their opposition to Roman Catholicism, the Congregational missionaries had no respect for Osage religious practices and, worse, thought of these Stone Age people as nothing but pagans and devil worshipers whose minds were filled with the darkness of superstition. They would enlighten the Indians, they decided, with the benefits of civilization (note: with civilization rather than solely with Christ). But because most of the missionaries remained ignorant of the vast difference between their faith in Jesus Christ and their Anglo-European culture, what they had to say to the Osages fell on deaf ears.

White man has done great damage among Indians in many ways, perhaps none more hurtfully than through our disregard for all the knowledge and wisdom the Indians had gained from the Spirit of God. Wahkontah had taught the Osage that all creatures were their little brothers, to be cared for with respect. (Doesn't that sound a little like St. Francis, or even the Garden of Eden?) By contrast, when white men wearing the cross came, they slaugh-tered animals for sport, killing far more than they needed to eat, and wasted the life and materials of what the Osages considered *Mo'n To'n* ("the sacred earth"). They concluded, therefore, that the God of the white man is an angry, vengeful, killing deity.

All four missions of the American Board of Commissioners for Foreign Missions among the Osage failed.

Andrew Maracle, a Christian of Huron descent, reports that after five hundred years of missionary work among American Indians, fewer than seven percent have accepted Jesus Christ as their Lord and Savior.

Countless loving Christians have laid down their lives in service, and many have been martyred for the sake of Christ, with souls saved for eternity. But even some of these self-sacrificial servants have displayed such disrespect for the truths of God sculpted out of the rock of others' experiences that untold doors have been closed to the ministry of our Lord.

Mistakes in the Present

The false identification of culture with Christianity has been made not only throughout North America but around the world.

Most native songs and dances today are still regarded as occult or demonic. Most native beliefs about nature are denounced as animistic, spiritistic or pantheistic. And when their life and culture are denigrated, native peoples are made to feel that nothing in their heritage can be redeemed and used to the glory of God. The only way to be Christian, they conclude, is for them to reject their roots and culture—including everything their forefathers taught them, and the songs and dances that help them define who they are—and, in effect, to become white Christians or "red apples" (in America, the derogatory term put on them by other Indians, meaning red on the outside, white on the inside).

This destroys their identity.

Cutting Free from Culture

It is true that, having once received Jesus, we must obey Luke 14:26 by renouncing all that formed us so we can be formed anew in Jesus. We are to cut free from the culture that molded us and from all previous allegiances—to mother, father, brothers, sisters, spouse, children, race, nationality, culture—so that only the Holy Spirit can rule our lives. (See chapter 18, "Renunciation, or Cutting Free," in Paula's and my book *Restoring the Christian Family*.)

But when we have laid all our old allegiances and knowledge on the altar, the Lord gives them right back. He only wants us to release everything to Him—so that, for example, duty to mother and father will not overrule our first duty to our Lord.

The same is true for everything we inherit from our forefathers through our race, nationality and culture.

Renounce, Then Receive Back

A black brother I love was a great storytelling preacher, but every once in a while a bit of bitterness would creep into his sermons. Then he heard as I taught, in a church-based conference, on the necessity to cut free from our heritage. He asked the Lord for forgiveness and renounced his blackness. The next day the worship leaders asked him to lead, and he turned our predominantly white congregation gloriously black! We sang and worshiped as never before. Being black could no longer rule him; and now the Holy Spirit could reach into the riches of his African-American heritage and glorify the Lord through it.

Before I cut free from my Indian heritage, sometimes my inherited Osage mysticism would rise up in me and I could do many mystical things—without the aid of the Holy Spirit. I did not know the difference between what I could do naturally and what the Holy Spirit could do through me. After I asked the Holy Spirit to put my Osage nature to death on the cross, it could no longer rise up and control me. But now the Lord could reach into those inherited skills and operate the clean gifts of the Holy Spirit more fully in and through me.

This is how the Lord cherishes, redeems and longs to use whatever we have received through our forefathers. Germans can lay on the altar their logical, mechanical ways, and the Lord gives these right back, tempered and filled by the love of the Lord. The English can lay down their stiff, principled ways, and the Lord can use these as stubborn strengths to serve Him righteously. Italians can lay down their emotional, demonstrative natures, and the Lord can have a ball using them (as He does so beautifully in brother Francis Frangipane!).

We are not deprived of what God has built uniquely into the understanding and character of our culture. But native people all over the world have been deprived.

Culture Is Transformed, Not Rejected

Hear it another way. When Jesus died and was resurrected, He did not return to a different body. He was resurrected within the old body, now made new and glorified. That is the way of the Lord—to make us new creatures within the very stuff that formed us.

Individuals who have known hatred and loneliness are better able to minister to those who hate and are lonely. Our Lord enters into the structures of hate and loneliness that have been built into us, dies with them on the cross, and then transforms them into love and ability to live in fellowship with others. Thus our individual histories are cherished and redeemed into blessing for ourselves and others.

What is true for aspects of personal character is also true for aspects of culture and all that formed us. God transforms what we have received through our heritage into blessing for ourselves and others around us.

The Search to Rediscover Old Ways

But Native Americans, convinced that nothing can be redeemed of their culture and heritage, are left with nothing of their own nature into which to be resurrected and transformed as Christians. If they are unable to pick up in a redeemed way what they laid down from their youth and heritage, they are robbed of the truth that they have something worthwhile and beautiful to contribute to others. As a result, in many cases, they are turning away from Christianity to rediscover the old ways.

Such wounded Indians are actually seeking who they are. Many had wanted to find themselves within Christianity. But when immature or bigoted Christians have told them that all that formed them is occult or devilish, and that it cannot be—and ought not to be—redeemed and cherished, the choice is either to become a rootless "white" Christian who does not know who he is, or else to reject Christianity and try to rediscover those denigrated roots in their culture, history, dance and songs.

We white Christians are responsible for this. Many of us have blamed and even persecuted Indians who are attempting to rediscover the old ways, not recognizing that our own supercilious rejection drove them to it!

We must learn to see their search for what it really is—the quest of native peoples to rediscover who they are. The fact is, they can find their roots without having to turn from the Lord Jesus Christ. If more of us had exercised the spiritual humility to follow Paul's approach to the Athenians and had ceased judging what we do not understood as occult or demonic (see

46

Jude 10), we could have had a great ministry among native peoples all over the world—and still can.

The mistakes of Christian missionaries among American Indians are only a type of what has happened across the globe. The same phenomenon, with variations, has taken place in Africa, Asia, South America, the South Pacific, India, Australia, New Zealand—even among the Saami tribes of Norway and Sweden, who were forbidden to speak their native language, deprived of their songs and dances, and forced to become like the Christians who came among them with the Gospel.

The Lord will guide His children, in time, to perceive what is occult or demonic, what can and should be redeemed and what cannot. We can help in this process—but only if we die to our pride and arrogance.

Here is another important place where the healing must begin: *first before God on our knees, then in humble dialogue with the lost children of God the world over.*

Building and Dying to Self-Image

I trust that, mentally, you have grasped this concept quickly. But I know from sad experience how blind we all are and that we need to hear this message several ways before our hearts become truly open to understand and repent. Let me try to convey this message, then, in one final way.

Paula and I have learned from counseling Christians that none of us needs a self-image. A self-image is something we all build as we grow from childhood to maturity. It is composed of powerful memories as well as emotionally laden images that either give confidence or destroy it: "I'm a good runner but I'm not good at football." "I'm good at reading, but math's a mystery to me." "I'm O.K. with people, but around authority figures I'm all thumbs."

Psychologists want to boost our self-image so as to restore confidence. But building and maintaining a good self-image is hard work. We have to identify it, live up to it, make sure others validate it, and forgive ourselves endlessly when we keep failing to live up to our pictures of what we think we ought to be.

This is one reason Jesus said, "Come to Me, all who are weary and heavy-laden, and I will give you rest" (Matthew 11:28). When we receive Jesus as Lord and Savior, one of the most important elements that dies with us is our self-image. No longer do we have to strive to make it work. Now we have a Christian identity.

Your Christian identity is a gift. You neither earned it nor built it. You are a child of God who can do anything by His Holy Spirit. Strength through self-image, by contrast, is confidence in your flesh. As a Christian you are to "put no confidence in the flesh" (Philippians 3:3). Your reliance is on the Lord, through whom you "can do all things" (Philippians 4:13).

So die to your self-image! Stop trying to live up to it, and come to rest in Jesus, so He can express through you what you need to be, by the Holy Spirit.

Being Denied the Process

Any believer still living to establish his self-image is filled with unnecessary striving. Christians who have died to trying to make their self-images work rest in the knowledge that it is our Lord who lives in us and expresses His nature through us.

But a person must first build a self-image before he or she can die to it. When you die to your self-image, Jesus resurrects you with the very skills you had built without Him. He redeems both the bad and the good aspects of your self-image and transforms them into glory. The new self is resurrected within the old, just as Jesus was resurrected within the physical body He had on earth, and just as your new body in heaven will be resurrected within the mold of the old.

Native people the world over have been denied this process. They have not been allowed to build a self-image, but have been told (as we have seen) that there is nothing in their heritage and youth, nothing in their old self-images, to be resurrected and transformed. To live as Christians they must take leave of who they have been and become copies of another culture not their own. This has resulted, even among saved Christians, in lostness.

Since Indians were placed by the U.S. government on reservations, everything that defined them to themselves has been destroyed. Hunting, for example, and all the "medicine" and stages of manhood connected with it, are gone. Almost all the aspects of native culture by which they defined and built their self-images is gone, too. Consequently they have not been able to build a viable self-image that can be laid down and picked up again. The result: confusion, depression, desolation and consequent flight into alcohol and drugs.

A Ministry of Repentance Comes First

If we believers are ever to evangelize and heal the lost natives of the world, we must first recognize our sins of arrogance and bigotry that have resulted in the destruction of the very loved ones to whom we are sent. Fullness of repentance must be allowed to reopen long-closed doors.

Repentance, then, is the vital first step in the healing of the nations. "First take the log out of your own eye," Jesus said, "and then you will see clearly to take the speck out of your brother's eye" (Matthew 7:5).

People can read your spirit and mine. They sense when our hearts are filled with judgment and arrogance, vainglory and self-vaunting ambition masked as good works. My Osage Indian ancestors used to say, "If you see a white man coming toward you with a gleam in his eyes to help you, run like hell the other way!"

Our prayers are hampered so long as we think ourselves above everyone else. Our witness will never bear fruit so long as the nations read arrogance in our spirits. Unless we repent of pride, we shall have nothing to say to Indians—or to any other native peoples around the world. Is this not where we must focus our first efforts to heal the nations?

Let's take the logs out of our own eyes; then we shall see clearly to take the specks out of the eyes of the nations.

FOUR

WHO ARE THE NATIONS?

You are A CHOSEN RACE, A ROYAL PRIESTHOOD, *A HOLY NATION*, A PEOPLE FOR GOD'S OWN POSSESSION, that you may proclaim the excellencies of Him who has called you out of darkness into His marvelous light.

1 Peter 2:9, emphasis added

I looked, and behold, a great multitude, which no one could count, *from every nation* and all tribes and peoples and tongues, standing before the throne and before the Lamb, clothed in white robes, and palm branches were in their hands; and they cried out with a loud voice, saying, "Salvation to our God who sits on the throne, and to the Lamb."

Revelation 7:9–10, emphasis added

The Bible uses the words *nation* and *nations* in many different, sometimes confusing ways. In 1 Peter 2:9 the Church is called "a holy nation," though nations today are usually thought of as secular entities. In biblical times nations were most often allegiances of ethnic groups, like the twelve tribes of Jacob's descendants, or the political, territorial spheres of great city-states like

50

Babylon, or the fiefdoms of rulers, like the kingdom of Og, king of Bashan, whom the Israelites defeated with "all his cities" (Deuteronomy 3:4). In biblical days one tribe or a collection of tribes that shared the same language, customs and beliefs about their gods usually composed a nation. Nationalism, and nations as we know them today, did not arise until the latter half of the nineteenth century.

Revelation 7 speaks prophetically of all nations standing before the throne in the end time—though few people today could be said to fit solely into either a political or an ethnic description. Most are miscegenations (mixed bloods) from the melting pots of nations containing hundreds of tribal and ethnic ancestries.

What, therefore, or who, is a nation? Is a nation a collection of ethnic tribes? a political entity? a people who share the same language? a people who live in a geographical area and are in some definable way gathered into a distinctive body?

It does not seem possible to define the word *nation* biblically and confine it to say, "This, and only this, is what God's Word means when it refers to *nation*." We should ask, therefore, "What does the Bible mean when it says we are to go to all the nations, and that people from every nation will stand before His throne?"

Imagine if God's angelic herald came at this moment and announced, "It's all over. Meet before the throne in fifteen minutes for the great celebration of Revelation 7:9. Pick the nation with whom you will stand." With whom would *you* choose to stand?

If nations and territorial bodies are political entities, then are people of merely one nationality?

A fine young man interned a few years ago at Elijah House, the international Christian teaching and counseling center Paula and I founded. Simon Pollit is English and his wife, Dagmar, is Austrian. Their baby was born while they were staying with Paula and me. Having been born in America, she is an American citizen, if she so chooses, and she can also hold British and Austrian citizenship. If, at the end, we stand with our own nation among all the nations before the throne, with whom will Simon and Dagmar's daughter stand?

Thank God, the Word says merely that we will be *among* that "great multitude . . . from every nation." We will not have to choose because we belong to the one and only great "holy nation," which counts in God's eyes! From whatever political, national, ethnic or racial heritage we have come—however diverse, however warring their histories—we will be as one family, one nation before God, by the grace of our Lord Jesus Christ.

The New American Standard Bible mentions the word *nation* 59 times and *nations* 484. We tend to think individually, celebrating our own salvation, but Jesus preached the Kingdom. Our Father in heaven planned the salvation of all the nations. In His Word He placed huge emphasis prophetically on nations. Of the first ten times *nation* appears, nine are prophetic. In Isaiah, solely from chapters 60 to 66, *nation* and *nations* are spoken of nineteen times—all nineteen prophetic of what shall happen among the nations. More than half of all references to a nation or nations in the Bible are prophecies, and most of those are eschatological. To God, apparently, nations—whomever that may mean— are extremely important, especially for the end times.

Consider the many eschatological references to the nations. Isaiah 4:5 foretells that, in the end time, the *shekinah* glory shall return to Zion, the "holy nation" of 1 Peter 2:9. Isaiah 2:2 predicts that "all the nations will stream to" the Lord. Isaiah 42:4: "The coastlands will wait expectantly for His law." Isaiah 43:9: "All the nations have gathered together." Isaiah 52:10–11: "The LORD has bared His holy arm in the sight of all the nations, that all the ends of the earth may see the salvation of our God." Daniel 12:1 foretells a time of distress at the end "such as never occurred since there was a nation." Micah 4:3: "Nation will not lift up sword against nation, and never again will they train for war."

We could recall dozens more Old Testament passages, but the New Testament speaks even more dramatically. Matthew 24:7, Mark 13:8 and Luke 21:10 all say that nation will rise against nation until the end. Matthew 24:9: "You will be hated by all nations because of My name." Matthew 28:19: We are sent to "make disciples of all the nations." Romans 16:26: The faith "has been made known to all the nations." Revelation 2:26: "To [him] who overcomes, . . . I WILL GIVE AUTHORITY OVER

THE NATIONS." Revelation 15:4: "ALL THE NATIONS WILL COME AND WORSHIP BEFORE YOU." Revelation 22:2 climaxes all eschatology—and history—with the wonderful promise of the tree of life, whose leaves are "for the healing of the nations."

We cannot miss that nations are central to the plan of God, that all of history moves toward that time when all nations will bow before Him, and that the leaves of the tree of life (who we are) shall heal the wounds of all history among all the nations. But when Isaiah 52:10 says that "the LORD has bared His holy arm in the sight of all the nations," and Matthew 28:19 that we are to "make disciples of all the nations," what is the Bible talking about? To whom are we sent? *Who are these nations?*

The Nature of *Nations* Is Threefold

Let's jar our minds out of what we have always thought nations to be. It is not enough to fulfill God's purposes if we confine our definition to the modern concept of political, territorial entities such as those belonging to the United Nations. I believe we will likewise miss God's intent if our definition is only ethnic or racial, such as Indian or Arab or black or Asian. These are surely nationalities, but *nations* means far more than such groupings. Nor are mere religious definitions adequate. Truly we as Christians are a holy nation, but could not Muslims, Buddhists, Shintoists and Taoists also be spoken of as nations?

I believe all of these—*political entities, ethnic groupings* and *religious communities*—are the nations the Bible speaks about, and more, if we count combinations of the three.

I know that many Christians today popularly define the word *nations* as "ethnic groups." But perhaps that is too confining a definition. Let's look at the evidence of Scripture—first, one of the verses with which we began this chapter:

> You are A CHOSEN RACE, A ROYAL PRIESTHOOD, *A HOLY NATION*, A PEOPLE FOR GOD'S OWN POSSESSION. . . .
>
> 1 Peter 2:9, emphasis added

53

Christians are indeed a nation but certainly not an ethnic grouping; the Church comprises every race and tribe on earth. Nor are we primarily political, or ever to be so. So what did God mean when He promised Abraham, a homeless, landless wanderer at the time, that he would become "a great nation" (Genesis 12:2) and "the father of a multitude of nations" (17:5)? And of Isaac, "I will make him a great nation" (17:20)?

The promise was first *ethnic*, when Abraham fathered a special race for God; and then *political* and *religious*, when Israel became a great nation under David and Solomon, an attempt to become a theocracy. After the destruction of the Northern Kingdom in 722 B.C. and the Southern Kingdom in 586 B.C. and Jerusalem in A.D. 70, did Israel cease to be a nation? Politically, yes, for 24 centuries (until A.D. 1948), but she did not cease to be an ethnic and religious nation. Hear Deuteronomy 26:18–19:

> "The LORD has today declared you to be His people, a treasured possession, as He promised you, and that you should keep all His commandments; and that He shall set you high above all nations which He has made, for praise, fame, and honor; and that you shall be a consecrated people to the LORD your God, as He has spoken."

Great as Solomon's reign was, Israel has never yet become the prophesied political entity "high above all nations." But Jesus said Scripture cannot be broken, so the prophecy that God's people will become "high above all nations" will be fulfilled. Religiously the prophecy has become true, at least in part, in that she was raised far above every other nation, because from her sprang "a shoot . . . from the stem of Jesse" (Isaiah 11:1), who is our Lord Jesus Christ, the Son of God.

A basic principle when interpreting prophetic Scriptures is that if events have totally fulfilled a prophecy, they are its meaning and there is no more. But when that is not the case, look for more to come. I am sure there is far more to come before the prophecy of Deuteronomy is exhausted. It may mean, among other things, the same as 1 Peter 2:9—that Israel will also become "a holy nation."

Do we need to track out the various Scriptures that refer to political and ethnic nations? Even a cursory reading reveals numerous references to the nations of the Philistines, Hittites, Assyrians, Egyptians, Babylonians, Greeks and Romans. Many texts refer to ethnic or political groups. *The Bible speaks of all three—ethnic, political and religious—as nations.* Let's not confine our definition to any one of the three, lest we miss the fullness of what God is saying to us—and what our calling is.

Distinctive Characteristics of Nations

If nations can be political, ethnic or religious, how are we to delineate what is a nation and what is not? Nations are defined by at least nine characteristics:

1. A nation is a body of people who define themselves by a name—American, English, Canadian, German, Sioux, Christian, Muslim, even the hate-filled Aryan Nation, which meets two miles north of my home in Hayden Lake, Idaho.

2. A nation commands allegiance. "I pledge allegiance to the flag of the United States of America, and to the republic for which it stands, one nation under God. . . ." Allegiance to whatever nation we belong to should call us into regular intercession. More than that, we give ourselves every day in unswerving allegiance to our Lord Jesus Christ—one holy nation under Him.

3. Every nation has enrollment lists. Most nations take a regular census and keep records of all their citizens. Ethnically and politically, according to the 1953 Osage census, I am listed as #4601, son of Osage allottee #2229. What a hallelujah it is that our names are written in the Lamb's Book of Life!

4. There are duties, rights and regulations pertinent to every nation. Service may be required—jury duty; induction into the armed forces; committee memberships in churches; voting in city, county, state and national elections.

5. Each nation has its own laws, protecting rights and demanding obedience. Had I gotten into legal trouble before adult status, the Osage Nation would have taken care of all my expenses as a ward of the tribe! All Americans are protected by the Constitution and Bill of Rights. Christians are required to live by God's laws, and we enjoy the innumerable benefits—and duties—of being children of God in His Kingdom.

6. Dues or taxes must be paid by the members of any nation— in the United States, to the Internal Revenue Service, as well as to state and local entities. In the nation of the Church, similarly:

> "Will a man rob God? Yet you are robbing Me! But you say, 'How have we robbed You?' In tithes and offerings. You are cursed with a curse, for you are robbing Me, *the whole nation of you!*"
>
> Malachi 3:8–9, emphasis added

7. Political nations punish citizens who break their laws. Some ethnic groups and churches excommunicate or otherwise punish those who betray. Ananias and Sapphira were punished by death for lying to the Holy Spirit (see Acts 5). Paul instructed the church at Corinth in disciplining an immoral man, and then disciplined him himself by handing him over "to Satan for the destruction of his flesh" (1 Corinthians 5:5).

8. Nations are established by some form of covenant. The U.S. Constitution and Bill of Rights are covenants by which Americans bind themselves to their declarations, allowing these covenantal provisions to govern and test their behavior as a community. Political nations can change their laws—to allow abortion, for example—but Christians are covenanted before God to one another and to prescribed standards that never change, resting as they do on the revealed Word of God.

9. Nations define to their citizens who they are. A political nation is a living organism whose self-identity undergoes change constantly, affecting both national consciousness and conscience. Hitler's depraved definition of German identity, through inflammatory speeches and his book, *Mein Kampf,* warped the minds and identities of those who ruled Germany, casting the nation into war and genocide. In the United States, relativism has eroded the foundations of national beliefs and conscience, hurling countless children, for example, into being "sexually active" (sexually sinful—I hate our lying euphemisms!). Only a few years ago the collective conscience of the nation did not tolerate such behavior. (Here we see how the loss of standards of righteousness within a religious nation affects the political.)

Crucifying the Nations in Us

Americans carry a mixed identity—known on the plus side for largeness of heart, generosity, inventiveness and leadership in good causes; and on the minus side for loudness, arrogance, insularism, lack of courtesy, pride and disrespecting the ways and thoughts of others. Australians project a "down-under" mentality—they are honest, straightforward, even brash—but they expect to get the dirty, man-killing jobs in war. Scots bear the reputation of frugality. Sicilians have to fight being identified as Mafia. And so on.

You and I do not have to think or practice to become our national identity. It comes with the package. We express naturally the mentality in which we have been reared. In fact, we have to think and apply the cross in prayer *not* to express both positive and negative aspects of our political, ethnic and religious identity. I heard an evangelist say he is half-German, half-Italian. Joking ruefully about his need for redemption, he said, "If someone insults me, my emotional Italian nature wants to kill him—and my German side calculates coldly how to do it!"

Christians are caught up by the Spirit into striving to live their identities as children of God in the new Kingdom (the holy nation) of God. Our entire lives are to become expressions of the nature and life of the Lord Jesus Christ, our King. *Nothing is more important than our manifesting the nature of Jesus if we are to heal and transform the nations.*

This means that from the moment of your new birth into Christ, you are engaged in a necessary and continual struggle to crucify all the "nationalities" that live within you, so that your walk in Christ might not be overcome. It is for this reason, before all others, that you need to know who the "nations" are—whether political, ethnic or religious. All those varieties and combinations live within you, built into your character by living in your nation. Everything in you must become transformed, so that evil may be purged (see Isaiah 4:4; Malachi 3:3), and changed into glory for Him (see Isaiah 51:3; Romans 12:2).

If we think *nations* refers only to political entities, how shall we face and subdue the characteristics we have inherited ethnically? Or if *nations* to us are only ethnic groupings, how shall we not miss God's call to transform every kind of nation, including the political that surrounds us? And, finally, if we limit our definition of *nation* to our own religious nation, how shall we not become irrelevant to the world, and thus to our calling to all the nations?

It was Christian ignorance of the differences between our national, cultural identity and our identity as believers, as we saw in chapter 3, plus our lack of appreciation for the good aspects in other cultures, that has destroyed some of our witness around the world.

Our call is to make disciples of all nations and to become the leaves of healing in the tree of life for all nations. Let us study, then, to make ourselves servants who rightly divide not only God's Word but whatever nationality needs our witness and healing.

Understanding the Threefold Nature of *Nations*

We could continue to catalogue other aspects of what it means to be a nation, but it may be more important to confine our definition to more manageable terms, such as what are *not* nations.

Kansas is not the United States of America. New South Wales is not Australia. Hesse is not Germany. Tribes among the Navajo are not the Navajo Nation. The tribe of Levi is neither ethnically nor politically the state of Israel. No local church or any one denomination constitutes the whole Body of Christ. Why not? Because *nation* expresses the totality of any particular grouping.

The political state of Germany, for example, gathers territorially resident Germans into one collective, functioning unit. The government attempts to express the joint will of the people who live within its borders or under its jurisdiction. The name *German*, however, expresses the ethnic identity of all who are descended from that heritage—in whatever degree, full or attenuated, wherever they may live.

When the Declaration of Independence states that "all men are created equal; that they are endowed by their creator with certain unalienable rights," it defines the mentality of all who come to live within the borders of the United States. Nations set the boundaries of identity and accountability for all within their lists and lands.

A *nation, therefore, is any political, ethnic or religious group that bears the above characteristics for all within their classification.* The Aryan Nation marks itself as a distinctly un-American, rebellious people because its belief that blacks, Asians and Jews are not equal to whites contradicts the fundamental, uniting principle of what it means to be American—but its name gathers as a distinct nation all who believe that lie. The fifty states of the United States of America are independent entities but submitted to the fundamental principles and laws of the union. North American Indian nations are distinct entities but submitted to the founding covenants of the United States and Canada— thus, nations within nations.

Christians are sent to all three kinds of nations—political, ethnic and religious. We go, for example, to the political nation of India, to ethnic tribes descended from Caucasians who migrated into India centuries ago, and to the "nations" of the Hindus, Buddhists, Muslims, Sikhs and others.

Each kind of nation—political, ethnic and religious—contains its own history, consequent mentalities, practices and generational descendancies—blessings and sins and sinful nature. Each nation, even the religious, was formed in the world, in some instances far from Christian influence, in others an admixture. Some nations are admirable, by our standards; others detestable and, by biblical standards, quite sinful.

It is important that we understand the threefold nature of nations, for each nation must be approached sensitively and appropriately from within its own frame of reference. Once again St. Paul is our model:

> Though I am free from all men, I have made myself a slave to all, so that I may win more. To the Jews I became as a Jew, so that I might win Jews; to those who are under the Law, as

under the Law though not being myself under the Law, so that I might win those who are under the Law; to those who are without law, as without law, though not being without the law of God but under the law of Christ, so that I might win those who are without law. To the weak I became weak, that I might win the weak; I have become all things to all men, so that I may by all means save some.

1 Corinthians 9:19–22

The hallmark of the Kingdom of God is courtesy—the art of respecting the feelings and thoughts and rights of others. But how do we do this and maintain our Christian distinctives?

Some American Christians have never distinguished their political and cultural temperaments from their faith. If I do not understand the difference between my politically derived temperament and the temperament that belongs to my Christian identity, I may do more harm than good in the nation where I am sent. I must bring to death on the cross my Americanisms (or other politically, ethnically or religiously derived temperaments) and meet my brothers and sisters of whatever nationality on their own terms.

At a conference for three thousand Roman Catholic charismatics in Sacramento, California, Paula and I were asked a question about pronouncing forgiveness for those who confess sins. Though as Protestants we believe that James 5:16 and John 20:23 give all of us ample authority to pronounce forgiveness for sins, I answered that in personal relationships, when someone has sinned against us and apologizes, of course we should declare our forgiveness, but that in matters of sin against God and mankind, we should obey the rules of our own denomination, which for Catholics and some other liturgical churches means going to the priest to make confession.

How arrogant, unnecessary and divisive it would have been for Paula and me to insist on our own doctrinal beliefs at that moment! "I have become all things to all men, so that I may by all means save some." There is time enough later, if He considers it important, for the Lord to lead others to what we might consider a better understanding (see Philippians 3:15).

Why major in minors, to the detriment of His cause? *Arrogance closes doors.*

It is not merely a matter of respect and courtesy, but the need to be appropriate to where people are:

1. In their political, national temperaments;
2. In their ethnic heritage and consequent loyalties and prides; and
3. In the "nations" of their belief systems.

Inescapable Problems in Evangelism

Throughout missionary history a great debate has raged between accommodation, on the one hand, and demand for instant change on the other.

St. Francis Xavier typified the latter. This sixteenth-century Jesuit, who introduced Christianity to Japan (and died trying to make his way into China), converted children in India, then led them to destroy all their parents' idols, calling for all to leave the old, accustomed ways and adopt Christian ways immediately. He regarded this as necessary and the only way to deliver a nation from its sinful habits.

Matteo Ricci, on the other hand, another Jesuit who was born the year Xavier died, preached a doctrine of accommodation. To all intents and purposes, except for his saving knowledge of Jesus Christ, this pioneer missionary entered into Confucianism. Arriving in China in 1582, he became expert in Chinese and the Confucian classics, and did not see honoring ancestors as conflicting with the Gospel. If Chinese could just be won to the Lord Jesus Christ by his becoming "all things to all men, that I might win some," he believed that teachers and religious orders would follow who could slowly purify and transform.

It is on the basis of accommodation that missionary strategy, mainly among Catholics but also among some Protestants, has aimed to convert the leaders of a nation, and by their authority declare the entire nation Christian, hoping to convert and disciple the people afterward.

Before Ricci's death in 1610, he saw several important persons, including a Chinese imperial prince, convert to the Christian faith. Historically, however, accommodation has not worked very well. It has given rise to syncretism and opened doors to many false doctrines and practices, especially occultism.

St. Francis Xavier, for his part, baptized whole villages and was responsible for the conversion of many of the Paravas people of southeast India, who remain strong in Roman Catholicism today. But Xavier's way has wounded many and shut hundreds of doors to evangelism around the world.

If the world is to be healed in any degree before the Lord returns, sensitive evangelism must find a way of healing and transformation based in the love of Jesus.

How Do We Handle Old Customs?

One of the built-in problems in evangelizing and healing people of other faiths, as we observed earlier, is the biblical "arrogance" of saying that only through our Lord Jesus Christ can a person truly come to God. Some areas of Christian doctrine and lifestyle inevitably conflict with the beliefs and practiced ways of other religions and cultures.

Hugh White, the father of one of my dear friends, was a Presbyterian missionary in China at the turn of the century. He converted many Chinese and trained some who were then raised up as elders (acting as pastors) in local churches throughout his area.

One day, while discussing problems in a church, one of these elders asked casually, "And what is to become of the second Mrs. Wu?"

This elder, as it turned out, had not one but two wives, and had seen the biblical texts stating that overseers and deacons in the local church must have only one wife (see 1 Timothy 3:2, 12).

The problem was not simple. Centuries of practice and established protocol, in a nation that values courtesy above all else, had been built around polygamy. What was Pastor White to do?

He felt he could not declare imperiously, "You'll have to put that second wife away, or you cannot be an elder." The elder could not simply put away the second wife. Close family members and countless relatives, from within long-practiced propriety and protocol, would have been "justifiably" offended, and most likely would have rejected their newfound faith as unjust and insensitive. In the people's eyes the elder would be disgracing himself and his second family—and the name of the Lord—for failing to fulfill his obligations as a husband and father, for which there are ample and equally compelling Scriptures.

On the other hand, if Pastor White were to summarily demote the elder, his parishioners would conclude that their way of life had been insulted and their pastor treated unfairly. Rebellion or spiritual falling away might ensue.

Then Pastor White discovered several other elders with the same problem. He sought the Lord's wisdom. If I remember rightly, he decreed that since these elders could not with grace and righteousness put their second wives away, he would grant them a special dispensation (under a grandfather clause, as it were), but that in the future no Christian could become an elder unless he was the husband of only one wife. The entire Christian community would thus move gradually and graciously toward compliance with the Word of God.

Doubtless some would be offended by that solution, believing he should have taken a tougher stance. But that would have set off instant reaction and rebellion against the "foreign devils trying to upset all our practiced ways."

The point is, grace, sensitivity and wisdom must guide our decision-making as we confront other national cultures with the Word of God. Unfortunately that has not been the case in many instances around the world, *which is part of what we as intercessors must undertake to overcome by our prayers of repentance and humility if we would open the doors that our "righteous" demands have shut.*

The greatest revival the world has ever seen is under way. The most massive problems will be those that arise as the way of our Lord Jesus Christ confronts old, cultural ways in the political, ethnic and religious nations. Missionaries, newborn Christians and their leadership have to wrestle with the tangled issues of what to do about political and ethnic belongings, loyalties and idolatries, and the beliefs and customs of other religions.

Using Wisdom, Grace and Prayer

Recently our daughter Ami and her husband, Tony, spent a week teaching our Elijah House lessons to a group of Hopi and Navajo women. In their religious culture, centuries old, it is the sacred duty of a godmother—chosen and consecrated as such at a child's birth—to instruct her godchild carefully in the ways of their people. That includes how to relate to the *kachinas*, or guiding spirits, who are in reality demons.

A godmother who is a devout Christian came to Tony and Ami to ask what she should do. If she teaches what is expected, she will violate her Christian conscience, rightfully feeling traitorous to her Lord and Savior. If she does not fulfill her duty, she will have demonstrated that Christianity promotes lack of responsibility and disrespects the "holy" traditions of the elders. And if she teaches that the Holy Spirit is the only true Guide, her tribe will consider her judgmental, ungodly and denying all that is holy in their religion.

There are no easy answers. Is it copping out for this godmother to stand as a Christian and say, "Your way is all wrong"? But wouldn't it be just as wrong for her to continue teaching what is clearly wrong and even harmful? This is why we must be able to answer the question "Who are the nations?" *It requires tact, wisdom, grace and much prayer if the recalcitrant ways of the political nations, ethnic groups and religions are to be transformed into the nature of our Lord Jesus Christ.*

Awareness of our missionary history describes for us the first battles to be won if we are ever to be allowed to move on to the healing of the vast other woundings in the history of the nations. This is why the simple but eloquent words of the apostle John, which we quoted in chapter 3—"The one who loves his brother abides in the Light and there is no cause for stumbling in him" (1 John 2:10)—are so crucial. It is love that overcomes. It is love that finds a way. It is love that builds and maintains the bridges of acceptance and understanding that the simplistic answers of arrogance and "righteous" demands try to tear down.

We must first simply connect people with Jesus wherever we go. Walking out the necessary changes that follow will be determined by whether our human love and humility continue to hold open the doors of dialogue and change.

Thus, again, *repentance is the first call of intercession for the healing of the nations.* We must remind ourselves constantly of Jesus' words that if we would remove the specks from our brothers' and sisters' eyes, we must first remove the telephone poles out of our own! We must be wise as serpents and harmless as doves.

Learning the Hard Way

Confrontation with the practiced ways of political, ethnic and religious nations is a monumental and ongoing task as we enter into dialogue with all the nations and fulfill the Great Commission. It is like what happens in a marriage. Only after the courtship and honeymoon do we begin to encounter the many differences of which we had been unaware, and which now grab us emotionally and threaten to carry us beyond the walls of self-control into anger and abuse.

So far, except for missionaries like Hugh White, most of us remain blissfully insular, confident in our unchallenged arrogance, sure that our beliefs and ways are the only right ones. Now the Holy Spirit calls us beyond our provincial mentalities into discourse with a needy and broken world.

Those who serve on the front lines of encounter—including evangelism, healing, teaching and social programs—usually have to learn the hard way, finding by trial and error what unnecessarily wounds and affronts. *Humility will make possible, as well as undergird, repentance and change.* Meeting and cherishing one another must take precedence over doctrines and dogmas, important as these are. Relationships are more important than our policies and practiced ways of doing things.

The Pharisees put their beliefs and traditions ahead of people, wounding and rejecting the needy. Jesus always put people before doctrines and traditional ways, comforting and healing whoever came to Him.

Schooling Is Needed

Evangelists, healers, teachers and social workers must ferret out of their hearts whatever cultural snobbery could insult others, and would do well to attend missionary schools that teach the cultural ways of the people to whom they are sent, lest arrogance and ignorance close the doors the Holy Spirit has opened. Christian tourists would do well to consult with missionaries on the field before traveling among mission stations, lest they undo what untold labor has accomplished.

These issues are not new. Missionary schools have long prepared their people. What is new is the advent of general exposure. Now the Body of Christ as a whole must mature—and quickly. God is calling the entire Church, as never before, to be His instrument to reach the nations. Never before have we had the tools of modern media, technology, rapid transport and medical science, or so many people filled with God's Holy Spirit traveling around the world.

The stage is set for the last great scenes of the final act of history. It is incumbent on us to learn humility and repentance if we would reach the masses with His grace—both for conversion and for the healing and transformation that need to follow.

Making Decisions Corporately

We must all learn how to become more "corporate"— that is, entering at heart level into the life of the people among whom we minister, so as to discuss and wrestle *together* about the issues of culture and the claims of Christ. Handing down imperious decrees must stop. We need to mature into the ability to "speak the truth to one another in love" so that *newly converted Christians struggling with the contradictions between what was acceptable and what now seems right are invited into the enterprise of decision-making.*

66

Compromise is not always tantamount to temporizing. Wisdom may find ways to move by increments, step by step, out of the unbiblical old into the holiness of the new.

Free to Risk

In culture after culture, nation upon nation, we who minister will be put on the spot. Decisions will have to be made that may frighten us or seem to temporize or compromise our holy faith. May I plead with us all to remember that Jesus always chose grace and mercy and ministry in love to people before the strictness of law?

The work of the healing of the nations is not always clean and safe. We have to take risks. May I also plead with you, my brother or sister, not to flee behind the rule books? It *is* safer that way. But a hurting world looks for grace and for the modeling of a Christianity that chooses to risk itself for others when tough decisions loom.

Jesus was unafraid to be defiled. In the house of Simon the Pharisee, He knew what sort of woman was washing His feet with her tears and drying them with her hair (see Luke 7:38). Jesus knew that those present believed her touch was defiling Him. But He allowed it, for *her* healing.

Our Lord Jesus could have sat uninvolved in heaven, cleansed the earth and "spin-dried" us in the heavenly laundromat. But He chose to come—and, by coming, to be defiled by what we are. In the end He became our sin, "so that we might become the righteousness of God in Him" (2 Corinthians 5:21).

Do you understand that becoming corporate with others means being enmeshed in, and often defiled by, others' problems, and perhaps having to make risky decisions? Do you see that we cannot heal the nations and keep our own hands clean at all times?

Corporateness means risk and demands vulnerability. And the humility of corporateness requires involving others with us in making decisions that may bring healing, but that also risk error. Can you see that, in the end, whether we remain willing to risk being corporate depends on one simple thing: How great and how deep is our trust in our Father's graciousness and mercy?

Are you free to fail, knowing God will pick you up and cleanse and teach you gently and tenderly? Pharisees and scribes, who must be right because they remain afraid, will not be part of our Lord's army to heal the nations. The healers in the Lord's army are those unafraid to make risky decisions and to be touched by sinners.

"Neither do I condemn thee" (John 8:11, KJV) will be one of the leaves in the tree of life for the healing of the nations. God grant us first His loving nature, and then His wisdom—and His mercy.

FIVE

DEFEATING SATAN'S MASTER PLAN

. . . so that no advantage would be taken of us by Satan, for we are not ignorant of his schemes.

2 Corinthians 2:11

God's master plan was simple, and still is. Our loving heavenly Father wants to raise sons and daughters with whom to have fellowship throughout eternity. Love by definition is relational. It needs to express. How could there be love without someone to love?

There were angels, of course. God could, and does, love them. But it seems that, for Him, angels were not enough. The Bible does not say that they, like us, were created in His image. They could not know the depth and range of feelings that might satisfy the longing heart of the Almighty. Nor have angels ever fallen and returned by grace. Apparently the angels who fell with Satan had already done so before Adam and Eve were created, but the Bible speaks nothing of redemptive efforts to return them to the Father's fellowship. The angels who did not fall could know nothing of the joy and gratitude that fill the hearts of believers who understand from what they have been redeemed!

69

Redeemed human beings choose to love God. We do not have to; we want to. God the Father longs for love and fellowship that springs from hearts who know free will, who know damnation and redemption, who love Him because they want to, though they have a choice.

But the fact that we have fallen and been redeemed and choose to love God does not explain why what He had already created was apparently not enough to satisfy His longing heart. Angels also have free will and can sin, else how could one-third of them have chosen to accompany Satan in his rebellion (see Revelation 12:4)? And others chose not to "keep their own domain, but abandoned their proper abode" (Jude 6) to cohabit with the daughters of earth, though that was forbidden (see Genesis 6:2). They also chose wrongly, and sinned.

Isn't it strange that our gracious Father, who spared nothing to restore us, even to the ghastly death of His own Son, has seemingly done nothing for those who married the daughters of earth, except to hold them "in eternal bonds under darkness for the judgment of the great day" (Jude 6)? Where was grace and redemption for them? No salvation is spoken of for these who cohabited—or for the third who fell earlier.

I suggest it was not because they are not "sons of God." They are. Genesis 6:1–2 says that when daughters were born to men, "the sons of God saw that the daughters of men were beautiful." It is clear to me that *the sons of God* refers to angels.

Similarly Job 1:6 refers to the "day when the sons of God came to present themselves before the LORD, and Satan also came among them."

Angels are definitely sons of God—but strangely, as we have said, the fallen angels are not redeemed for fellowship with Him throughout eternity.

The difference may lie in the one word *begotten*. Hebrews 1:5: "To which of the angels did He ever say, 'YOU ARE MY SON, TODAY I HAVE BEGOTTEN YOU?' And again, 'I WILL BE A FATHER TO HIM AND HE SHALL BE A SON TO ME'?" Angels are sons, yes, but of a different order. They have never been begotten, as Jesus was. We also are begotten—first humanly, then by being born anew by the will of God (see John 1:13). Angels, on the other hand, were never incarnated. They will not be raised as creatures with new and perfect bodies.

I confess I do not know why the difference is so vast that God would go to the greatest lengths to redeem us and not angels. But the distinction speaks of a level of fellowship that only humans can give to God—and that is what God wants.

God knew from before creation what Satan's master plan would be. He knew Satan would tempt Adam and Eve and that they would fall. He knew Satan would try to incorporate them into his own kingdom in opposition to God. But the Fall did not coerce God from Plan A to Plan B. Before all time our heavenly Father planned to send His Son to pay the price on the cross for our sin, and to use the consequent suffering of mankind to write lessons onto our hearts for heaven (see Jeremiah 31:33).

Our resultant varieties of character would delight His heart and afford Him opportunity to lavish riches of kindness on us throughout eternity (see Ephesians 2:7). God ordained the cross and all the blessed transformations of our character from before any one of us existed,

> just as He chose us in Him before the foundation of the world, that we would be holy and blameless before Him. In love He predestined us to adoption as sons through Jesus Christ to Himself, according to the kind intention of His will.
>
> Ephesians 1:4–5

But Satan wants the fellowship and worship that belong only to God. His master plan has at least three major prongs.

1. Satan's Plan to Build His Own Kingdom

Just as humans are essential to God's Kingdom, we are also essential to Satan's. And just as it apparently did not fulfill our Father's heart to rule over only His created sons in all their degrees and kinds—including archangels, angels, seraphim and cherubim—so it does not satisfy Satan's cravings to rule only his many levels of principalities, world rulers and demons.

He wants to build mankind into his own devoted, if craven, followers, whose kingdom perpetually exalts him.

Through the Babel Tower

Satan's first kingdom attempt was the tower of Babel. "Come, let us build for ourselves a city, and a tower whose top will reach into heaven, and let us make for ourselves a name" (Genesis 11:4). Satan wanted to make a name for himself higher than the name of God (see Isaiah 14:13–14). In the Babel tower he thought to manipulate mankind to do it for him. But God came down, confused the languages of men and "scattered them abroad from there over the face of the whole earth" (Genesis 11:8).

This was the beginning of the nations. Before this time men and women had become so evil that God sent the flood to destroy all but Noah and his family; but mankind had so far remained united—one people, one language, one nation. *Henceforth God would not allow His rebellious children to unite as one nation, until redemption and transformation could make mankind safe to become united as one.*

Through Nations and Empires

Satan has kept on trying to build his kingdom. Again and again he has found charismatic leaders whose unredeemed zeal could be molded to his purposes. We can trace history through empires built by men with noble ideals to establish a utopia and save mankind from chaos and corruption—only to fall ignobly to the degradations of ambition, power and lust.

To be sure, perhaps most of history's empires were built for no purpose nobler than someone's desire to aggrandize— Genghis Khan, for instance, and the Huns and Vikings and countless other conquerors. Theirs were not so much attempts to build Satan's kingdom as they were Satan trying to tear down what God had established.

But some empires were mistaken attempts to build something noble. Satan managed to convince the Roman city-state that it was building a civilization for whom the *Pax Romana*, the peace of Rome, was to be honored as something just and good so as to necessitate killing whoever threatened it—namely, those god-defying Christians. The Holy Roman Empire that followed proved to be anything but holy, excusing brutal wars and inquisitions.

Each time in history such a "noble" empire has been raised up—including the League of Nations, dissolved after World War II—God Himself has smashed it once its tasks were done. *God will not allow mankind to build unity and cohesions of peoples and nations without His grace and planning.*

Through Ongoing Attempts at Unity

Satan is still trying to gather the nations in rebellion against God, to overcome all God has been building among mankind and to establish his own dominion. But our Father was aware of his plans before Satan ever thought of them, and laughs:

> The kings of the earth take their stand and the rulers take counsel together against the LORD and against His Anointed, saying, "Let us tear their fetters apart and cast away their cords from us!" He who sits in the heavens laughs, the LORD scoffs at them.
>
> Psalm 2:2–4

Our Father allows Satan's machinations in history as part of His own plan to redeem mankind and the nations:

> I saw coming out of the mouth of the dragon and out of the mouth of the beast and out of the mouth of the false prophet, three unclean spirits like frogs; for they are spirits of demons, performing signs, which go out to the kings of the whole world, to *gather them together for the war of the great day of God, the Almighty.*
>
> Revelation 16:13–14, emphasis added

Verses 15 through 21 describe God terrorizing the nations with thunder and an earthquake worse than any before in history, "and the cities of the nations fell" (verse 19), islands fled away and mountains tumbled and hundred-pound hailstones dropped.

The next chapter describes God's judgment on the harlotry that has seduced the kings of the earth. Then Revelation 17:14 says:

"These will wage war against the Lamb, and the Lamb will overcome them, because He is Lord of lords and King of kings, and those who are with Him are the called and chosen and faithful."

Satan will not win. All he does will be used by God to bless His own:

After you have suffered for a little while, the God of all grace, who called you to His eternal glory in Christ, will Himself perfect, confirm, strengthen and establish you.

1 Peter 5:10

Many believers today denounce anything that promises to establish unity, fearful that Satan is deluding Christians and that these deluded Christians are helping establish Satan's kingdom. These believers fail to distinguish between what God is doing and what Satan is doing. They criticize and attack other Christians as though all others lack proper insight into Scripture. They are called (they believe) to denounce or sabotage any attempt to bring about corporateness and unity anywhere in the Body of Christ, or among the nations, as though these were only serving Satan's plans.

Unwittingly these misguided souls uproot the good with the bad and actually do Satan's work. Our Lord Himself prayed "that they may all be one; even as You, Father, are in Me and I in You, that they also may be in Us, so that the world may believe that You sent Me" (John 17:21). Paul urged us to be "diligent to preserve the unity of the Spirit in the bond of peace . . . until we all attain to the unity of the faith" (Ephesians 4:3, 13).

No one yet knows what the unity of the faith is—although we know it is glorious and that it depends on our maintaining the unity of the Spirit—until together we come to "the knowledge of the Son of God, to a mature man" (verse 13). Note, *a mature man*, not a bunch of individual mature Christians. This speaks of coming into a corporateness so complete that we have become as one man, "to the measure of the stature which belongs to the fullness of Christ" (verse 13).

God wants us to grow up, not merely as individuals, but into a unity of faith that alone can allow Him to mature us all into His Son's likeness.

A Call for Prayer and Discernment

Lack of trust amid the maelstrom of current events produces reactions that serve Satan's purposes. This calls for wisdom—and faith. In the very moments when we see satanic forces uniting nations (perhaps all three kinds of nations—political, ethnic and religious), we need to walk so purely in God's Holy Spirit that we can discern and cherish God's actions as He unites political and ethnic nations and the religious nation of Christianity.

This sovereign work of the Holy Spirit summons us to petitions that we ourselves may not be deluded, and to miles and piles of intercessions that the will of our loving heavenly Father be done on earth as it is in heaven. *Perhaps there can be no greater purpose in God's mind for the writing of this book than to call for His own to stand in the gap and to pray.*

You may recall from chapter 2 that I said obviously not all will ever desire our Lord's return, and that 2 Chronicles 7:14 may not be calling for *all* of any kind of nation to repent and pray, but specifically for those who are "the called." Listen again, then, to Revelation 17:14:

> "The Lamb will overcome them, because He is Lord of lords and King of kings, and those who are with Him *are the called and chosen and faithful.*"
>
> emphasis added

> "Many are called, but few are chosen."
>
> Matthew 22:14

> You are A CHOSEN RACE, A ROYAL PRIESTHOOD, *A HOLY NATION*, A PEOPLE FOR GOD'S OWN POSSESSION, that you may proclaim the excellencies of Him who has called you out of darkness into His marvelous light.
>
> 1 Peter 2:9, emphasis added

Do you think preaching, testifying and teaching exhaust what Peter meant by *proclaim*? Prophetic intercession proclaims powerfully in the heavens and on earth.

Intercession occurs whenever God's servants hear clearly what our Lord wants and pray for that to happen. All intercessory prayer ought to follow that course; we should offer prayers only after God has made clear His directives. But prophetic intercession is unique in that it happens when one or more of the Lord's established prophets reveal His will as they have heard it, and other prophets have weighed and confirmed it. God's speaking through prophets who are called, trained and raised up for that purpose carries an authority and consequent expectation of fulfillment far beyond what others not of that office hear and obey and pray.

God is restoring the office of the prophets in these days for many reasons—perhaps none more cogent than His desire to call men and women into prayer for the healing of the nations. He wants to direct His armies. Prophets might be described as God's messengers bringing His orders to His generals of prayer on the field of battle. This entire book is designed as precisely that—giving not specific instructions for concrete instances of warfare, but providing direction for a general plan for warfare—or, to change the metaphor, a blueprint for builders. God will raise specific prophets for particular details during the battles of the war.

I am not, as I have suggested, encouraging a proud elitism, exalting ourselves—or prophets—above everyone else. I am addressing a chastised and humble few who know what God is doing and stand as "the called." Who knows how many that will require? God knows. He will find those who will respond. The question for us is, *Is that me?*

A People for Unity

God wants a people determined never to tear the fabric of unity He is weaving and to lend no support to Satan. This calls for discernment. God wants a people resolved to keep the unity of the Spirit at whatever cost, who will cherish what others are doing to bring us all into a mature man—into one Christian nation.

Our Father is calling for a band of intercessors who will lay down their lives in burden-bearing and prayer, that His kind of loving unity—which alone testifies that the Father has sent the Son—may be made manifest among all mankind, until all nations, of whatever kind, know who Jesus is.

The Key to Discerning Rightly

Earlier we looked at the first four verses of Psalm 2, in which God laughs at those who conspire against Him. Now let's look at the rest of that psalm:

> Then he will speak to them in His anger and terrify them in His fury, saying, "But as for Me, I have installed My King upon Zion, My holy mountain. I will surely tell of the decree of the LORD: He said to Me, 'You are My Son, today I have begotten You. Ask of Me, and I will surely give the nations as Your inheritance, and the very ends of the earth as Your possession. You shall break them with a rod of iron, You shall shatter them like earthenware.'" *Now therefore, O kings, show discernment; take warning, O judges of the earth. Worship the LORD with reverence.*
>
> emphasis added

We may not be those kings and judges who have risen against Jesus Christ, but we can surely take home a *rhema* word, enlivened to our hearts by the Holy Spirit, to show discernment (as the psalmist writes) and take warning.

The key to discerning rightly and to responding as those on God's side may be nothing more profound than practicing the art of worshiping Him "with reverence" (Psalm 2:11). Perhaps those who have been caught up in the current revival of worship and adoration are capable of walking close enough to Him to possess the requisite nearness in His presence that alone makes possible true discernment.

Discernment arises not out of logical sharpness or sound doctrine or knowing the Bible cover to cover, although these are prerequisites. I think all of us have met people whose knowledge of theology and Scripture makes us feel like kindergartners but who nevertheless lack true discernment of what God is doing! Godly perception comes from familiarity with Him, knowing His nature, understanding His ways, sensing what He loves and what He is doing through walking close by His side. (I suggest, in this regard, Tommy Tenney's powerful book *The God Chasers* and Dutch Sheets' delightful *The River of God*.)

Such nearness comes not merely from disciplined habits of private devotion, though that helps, but from corporate worship that fills our hearts with the fullness of who God is. *We need to be wrapped in such corporate glory of Him that it elevates our minds and hearts beyond carnal feelings and thoughts into feeling and thinking with Him and in Him for what He wants.*

God wants a people given to Him *with* one another. Such a people will tear down what Satan builds and build what God wants. These are "the called" whose intercession counts in the healing of the nations.

2. Satan's Plan to Kill the Heir

Jesus spoke of the second prong of Satan's master plan in the parable of the landowner, recounted in three of the four gospels:

> "When the vine-growers saw the son, they said among themselves, 'This is the heir; come, let us kill him and seize his inheritance.' They took him, and threw him out of the vineyard and killed him."

> Matthew 21:38–39

Jesus was prophesying His own death—how He would be "thrown out" by being crucified outside the walls of Jerusalem. The inheritance Satan wanted to seize was and still is the nations: "Ask of Me, and I will surely give the nations as Your inheritance, and the very ends of the earth as Your possession" (Psalm 2:8). The devil thought that if only he could make the Son of God accursed, he could claim the nations for himself.

But it was the most Pyrrhic victory in the history of the world, redounding to the defeat of the victor! Jesus' death has made possible the blessed deliverance of all who call on His name. It has become mankind's victory over the snares of death and the ultimate defeat of everything Satan desires.

Jesus was not murdered, as Satan thought. He *accomplished* the cross, having planned it from before He came to earth. On the Mount of Transfiguration He consulted with Moses and Elijah about what "He was about to accomplish at Jerusalem" (Luke 9:31).

Satan has realized his error and knows he cannot kill the Son of God. But he still wants to steal His inheritance (see John 10:10) and the attention and worship of the nations—and kill Jesus' seed.

Martyrs, Murders and Deaths

More people are being martyred today than ever in the history of the world. Muslims in the Sudan are practicing systematic genocide against all Christians. Communism in the former Soviet Union and China is responsible for the martyrdom of countless thousands of Christians. As Satan's master plan unfolds, opposition to Christians and consequent persecution and martyrdom are increasing all over the world.

At the same time God is sending His own into the world, as Jesus told His disciples when He explained the parable of the weeds in the field: "The one who sows the good seed is the Son of Man, and the field is the world; and as for the good seed, these are the sons of the kingdom. . ." (Matthew 13:37–38).

As history draws to its climax, our Lord is sending His own into the world in especially great numbers. They come, like everyone else, infected with Adamic sin and in need of salvation; but they also arrive equipped with gifts to serve the Lord in power. Satan comprehends this, and knows by his intelligence network whenever any of God's children is about to be born, and sets out to kill that one.

We saw this when Moses was born and had to be hidden in the bulrushes. After Jesus was born, Satan induced Herod to kill all the male infants in Bethlehem two years old and younger, trying to murder the supposed heir to Herod's throne—and the real heir to all the nations.

Today, when many are being sent by God to bring about the unity and devotion that will heal the nations and begin to establish His Kingdom before Christ returns, Satan is redoubling his efforts to kill them. Paula and I have counseled literally hundreds of parents who know their children are special for God and who have told horror stories of near-death experiences, in their own lives and in those of their children. Only the Holy Spirit's vigilance and many miracles have preserved them alive.

I suggest you mark when prophecy has foretold the birth of one of God's own. Death will stalk that one—*in utero,* at birth and throughout childhood.

Paula and I have experienced this with every one of our six children—and our family is not unique. We have heard countless stories of accidents, diseases, errors and other ways Satan tried to kill before his own head is crushed (see Genesis 3:15).

Abortion

By far Satan's greatest weapon to try to destroy God's sons and daughters is abortion. Millions upon millions have been murdered. Satan delights in murder: "The thief comes only to steal and kill and destroy" (John 10:10). By instigating mass murder through abortion, the devil hopes to forestall the Father's plan to heal the nations and establish His Son's Kingdom.

God has not left Himself in any age without witness. Tragic as abortion is—and perhaps some of God's designated servants have been killed by it—the Father will have known about it beforehand and provided others to complete His good intentions. Satan will not win, or even postpone God's timetable.

But faith in God's providence must not be allowed to lessen our determination to fight to save His own. *Those who would enlist in God's end-time army for the healing of the nations and the establishing of His Kingdom must consider it a high priority to defend God's own, that they may ascend to their tasks undeterred, the better for their struggles.*

We need to pray and work on this major battle front, to stop abortion on demand. We may not win, but at least we can pray to preserve the lives of His saints.

3. Satan's Plan to Raise a Leader of Lawlessness

Satan wants to raise up his own kind of messiah—and the Holy Spirit has predicted he will do just that:

> Let no one in any way deceive you, for [the day of the Lord] will not come *unless the apostasy comes first, and the man of lawlessness is revealed*, the son of destruction, who opposes and exalts himself above every so-called god or object of worship, so that he takes his seat in the temple of God, displaying himself as being God.
>
> 2 Thessalonians 2:3–4, emphasis added

Since Satan copies all things, he wants to elevate someone who will do for him what our Lord Jesus Christ has done for Father God: command the allegiance of the multitudes, put down every other expression of faith and worship, and, ultimately, rule over all and return all to the Father. But Satan's messiah is to rule until only the beast (who is Satan) is idolized.

Some Christians think the Antichrist has already been born and is being prepared to step onto the stage of history. Muslims are looking for the coming of the *Mahdi*, their version of a messiah. The Mahdi, they believe, will unite all the divisive factions of Islam, teach, prepare and hurl all Muslims into a mighty *jihad*, a holy war, that will forcibly convert all the world into belief in Allah as the one true god, with Muhammad as his prophet. Other prophets expect a great leader to arise who will unite Chinese Communism and Islam in a great third world war to conquer and control the world.

It is not the purpose of this book to speculate as to who, how and when the predicted man of lawlessness will arise. It *is* my purpose to encourage faith and to enlist an army of knowledgeable intercessors to stand as that time approaches.

Revelation 12 says that Satan tried to kill our Savior when He was about to be born, but when Jesus "was caught up to God and to His throne" (verse 5), Satan poured water out of his mouth like a flood, causing "her [the Church] to be swept away with the flood" (verse 15).

It is to understand at least part of what that flood is, and to call us to stand for healing, that I write. Psalm 32:6 says:

> Let everyone who is godly pray to You in a time when You may be found; surely in a flood of great waters they will not reach him.

Neither Satan's predicted man of lawlessness, nor his "one-world" government, nor invisible marks on hands that will allow citizens to buy and sell, can touch our souls. We have nothing to fear; we belong to God. Our names are written in the Lamb's Book of Life with indelible ink—the blood of Jesus. "The name of the Lord is a strong tower; the righteous runs into it and is safe" (Proverbs 18:10). Satan's world will last but a flick of a moment, while we will reign with Jesus Christ throughout eternity.

We cannot prevent, forestall or ameliorate the effects of these events. They are predicted by holy Scripture. My concern, however, is for us to see Satan's master plan for creating the climate into which his man of lawlessness can come. We *can* do something about that—not as though to prevent his coming altogether, but to heal the nations before and after he arrives. *We must direct our thoughts and prayers into the work of changing the climate that prepares for the coming of the man of lawlessness and the effect of his coming.* This is a major part of the healing of the nations.

I confess I do not know how much of the healing of the nations is to be accomplished before our Lord returns, or after. But our Lord told us to be serving without let up *until* He comes:

> "Be dressed in readiness, and keep your lamps lit. Be like men who are waiting for their master when he returns from the wedding feast, so that they may immediately open the door to him when he comes and knocks. Blessed are those slaves whom the master will find on the alert when he comes; truly I say to you, that he will gird himself to serve, and have them recline at the table, and will come up and wait on them. . . . You too, be ready; for the Son of Man is coming at an hour that you do not expect."
>
> Luke 12:35–37, 40

I do not think Jesus is calling us to read the latest, most scholarly book on eschatology (though that might not hurt!). Nor do I believe He is calling us to study Scripture so as to hazard a good guess as to when He may return. If we read Luke 12 objectively, for what it actually says, and without fear, we will see that our Lord was exhorting us to be serving at all times, no matter what time He may return.

Rather than try to figure out how much of whatever task is to be done before, during or after His return, we must be found doing whatever the Lord has called us to do *when* He returns. The nations need to be healed. *Let's be at it and let the Lord determine how much He wants us to do before He returns, and how much He will heal after His return.*

The Beginning of Lawlessness

Satan wants to do more than to raise up the man of lawlessness; he wants to prepare the ground for him, in the same way God prepared the ground for the coming of His Son.

God had delivered a broken, enslaved people; given them commandments, leaders, rituals of worship and cleanliness. He had marched them across a barren desert, tried and tested them, found them wanting and sent them back into the desert for forty years. Then He brought them into the Promised Land of milk and honey. He gave them a king, priests and prophets; taught, rescued and restored them again and again—all to write into their minds and hearts enough understanding of His nature to prepare them to receive Jesus, in the fullness of time, as the Savior of all mankind.

They did not understand His plan and eventually, rebelliously, killed their promised Messiah. But the ground had been prepared for Jesus' coming. It was there in the Scriptures for all to see, once the blinders were taken off, as Jesus did for Cleopas and the other disciple on the road to Emmaus (see Luke 24:13–31).

The Jewish people could, at least in a rudimentary way, receive Jesus' teachings. Faith had been established sufficiently that, in many places, Jesus could work miracles (unlike Nazareth; see Matthew 13:53–58). The common people had come to see the laws of God as absolute, on which foundation Jesus could construct His Sermon on the Mount and His parables. Law was understood—though carried too far, opposed as such by the Lord and used against Him for crucifixion. Scripture was acknowledged as holy and true—a guideline not only for the people but for Jesus and His ability to withstand Satan's temptations.

Thus the ground was prepared for our Lord Jesus Christ.

Satan needed to nurture a very different kind of soil for the man of lawlessness. It would not be enough merely to appeal to people's hidden fleshly desires and seduce them into sin. Too many could resist temptation and hold in check their fleshly urges. Belief in God's laws, the fear of God and the fear of consequences were still too prevalent, even among unbelievers, for lawlessness to rule. Something had to be done.

Ever since the Garden of Eden, Satan has been working at the destruction of law. After the Dark Ages, when hunger for truth grew, came the Renaissance—the revival of classical art, architecture, literature and learning starting in the fourteenth century. Everywhere men and women began to question long-established notions of reality. In the sixteenth century Copernicus burst out of the ancient bounds of astronomy to declare the "heresy" that the earth revolves around the sun. Universities sprang up all over the known world. The search for truth blossomed beyond theology, which had been called the "queen of the sciences," into exploring the natural world. Some nobles actually carried cadavers in their carriages so they could cut and explore the human body.

It was good that mankind was exploding past the boundaries of ignorance. But Satan managed to portray the Church as repressive and ignorant, blocking the sunlight of knowledge and the rebirth of mankind. In the seventeenth century, for example, the Inquisition persecuted truth-seekers like Galileo for his outspoken support of Copernicus' theory, so that Satan's job was made easy.

Science and Rationalism

Two hundred years later came the onslaught of scientific technology. Now mankind would find out what makes things tick, and rationalism would banish the bugaboos of superstition and fear. For many that meant religion would be banished as well. Progress became the watchword, rationalism the new Babel tower to reach to heaven. Science would finally lead us out of darkness into the utopia for which many hoped. Though Satan was behind this deception, many thought the real enemy was the ignorance and superstition of religion.

The horrors of two world wars, the cold war, fear of atomic warfare and the constant carnage of regional conflicts throughout the earth have smashed such foolish idealism. But while the heyday of rationalism lasted, Satan turned man's pride in science and in his own logical ability against the Bible and the tenets of faith. So-called higher criticism and other scholastic endeavors began to tear Scripture apart, declaring the Ten Commandments only men's ideas, denying that God had spoken once for all, elevating human thoughts above the divine inspiration of the Bible and destroying reverence for the holy.

Next came the ascent of relativism in the twentieth century, which mandated the examination of everything within its cultural and historical context. Nothing was to be regarded as absolute. To acknowledge absolute truth was to assume an arrogance and elitism that belonged only to the immature or foolishly deluded.

When I was studying in a liberal seminary, I longed for an event so miraculous and undeniable that I could be sure my faith was built on more than my own fabrications. But God does not jump to our tune; we jump to His. To Mary, who believed, He gave confirming signs, but only a rebuke to disbelieving Zacharias (see Luke 1:18–20; 34–38). So neither I nor anyone in my seminary witnessed any miracles to disabuse us of our confusion.

Our thinking about God had become semantically confused with God Himself. Paul Tillich's religious philosophizing about "the God above God" had become all the rage. No longer did we know if indeed there *was* a God beyond our thoughts about Him. Intellectual humility and honesty demanded that one be forever on a search for deity. No one was supposed to find—or be found. After I graduated and was ordained, the Holy Spirit radically changed my thinking. I was led by the Holy Spirit to believe the Bible from cover to cover, no matter what my professors had taught.

Then I began to testify to my former classmates—and ran into almost total rejection. No longer a pilgrim on the way, I had abandoned the honesty of the search and forsaken intellectual humility: "The very idea, to say you've found God!" Never mind that I had testified that God had found me—for them that was not only impossible but prideful, as though God would pay special attention to any one human being! "Who do you think you are? You're deluded and, worse yet, filled with pride. Do you think the God of the whole wide universe would take time to act just for you? What about the rest of us? Doesn't He love us just as much as you? How prideful and deluded you are! You're going to wind up in an insane asylum."

No matter that I had tried to tell them God loved them and wants to speak to all His children. Obviously if they were not hearing Him, it was not possible.

Satan's plan was to seduce theologians and scholars of the Bible, who would then train pastors, through seminaries, in unbelief. That plan worked—in institutions of most of the old-line Protestant churches and even some of the Catholic.

The Bible has withstood the challenge. It always will. Archeology and other sciences are now proving, to the surprise of many modernists and liberals, the veracity and accuracy of Scripture. Millions of evangelicals and charismatics who believe the Bible and who know God can and does speak far outnumber the remaining unbelievers in the old-line and other churches.

But Satan's primary purpose has succeeded. He wanted to remove from the minds and hearts of the general populace the belief that God's laws are true for all time and eternity. He knew that if he could do that, he would destroy the boundaries in men and women that corral the evil desires of the flesh. Once the fear of law and the holy fear of God were obliterated, conscience would be destroyed. Since holy fear of God and reverence for His eternal laws are the basis of conscience, lawlessness would be free to run rampant throughout mankind. The stage would be set for the rising of his intended man of lawlessness.

Rejecting God's Laws

Part of Satan's scheme is to use whatever hurts we have suffered in relation to parental and other authorities to delude us into thinking that all laws are meant only to deprive and control, to keep us from enjoying life.

As I sat by a window one afternoon watching young people skate on a nearby pond, the Lord taught me a vital lesson about His commandments.

He led me along this line of thinking: Suppose a father were to give to his son a pair of ice skates, and with them some rules about skating: "Don't skate near thin ice. Don't skate on rivers where currents can undercut and you could fall through. Don't skate fast in a crowd of people, or do fancy figures and leaps too near others, lest your skates cut someone." The Holy Spirit then caused me to realize that most of those ten commandments of skating are *thou-shalt-nots*. So doesn't the father want his son to enjoy skating? Or is he giving him those commands so that his son can safely enjoy skating to the full?

God impressed me, as I watched the young people skate on the pond, that all His commandments are for our happiness— not to keep us from enjoying life, but to enable us to enjoy it fully, safely. Jesus came, after all, to give us not misery but life in abundance (see John 10:10). It is the same for every statute and ordinance in His Word. God's laws are His gifts of love to us, to be cherished with all our hearts. Just as the ancient mariners of Greek mythology needed to navigate carefully between Scylla, the sea monster, on the one side, and Charybdis, the whirlpool that devoured ships, on the opposite side, so we need to let God's laws guide us through the perils of life. Only when we are prisoners of God's laws are we free indeed.

I am not calling us to fall back under the law, as though obedience would earn us the salvation that has already been given freely! But whoever knows Jesus loves Him, and everyone else, and the laws of God tell us how to do that safely and with joy. His commands are expressions of His love for us—guidelines to living in love and joy.

Once God's law is written into our hearts, temptation is easier to withstand, since nothing worthwhile can be gained outside His law. But Satan has persuaded many that God's guidelines are repressive and ugly.

Dr. James Wilder, in his new book *The Red Dragon Cast Down* (Chosen, 1999), explores Satan's strategy to convince Christians and non-Christians alike that the laws of God deprive people of power, fun and becoming who they were meant to be. One begins to comprehend Psalm 2:3 more fully as it quotes kings rebelling against God and against His anointed ruler: "Let us tear their fetters apart and cast away their cords from us!" Deluded people want to cast away control and be "free," not comprehending that rejecting God's laws leads only to licentiousness and captivity to sin (see 2 Peter 2:19).

But greater than that deception that God's laws prohibit fun is Satan's plan to take God's laws out of people's hearts altogether, by the twin delusions of relativism and unbelief. This strategy is working.

Where Lawlessness Has Led Us

In my youth many of us hormone-driven teenage boys would get into the back seat of a car with a girl and soon want to go too far. Even back then some did not have the parental training that writes the laws of God onto the heart. But most were like myself. When I was a young man and in the back seat of a car with a girl, the Word of God would rise up like a fire extinguisher, and the Holy Spirit would use it to fog down the flames of lust—just as for the psalmist:

> How can a young man keep his way pure? By keeping it according to Your word. . . . Your word I have treasured in my heart, *that I may not sin against You.*
>
> Psalm 119:9, 11, emphasis added

Today's generation of young people has no such protection. Many do not even know God's laws. Those who have heard them may no longer hold them reverentially in their hearts. God's commands no longer seem eternal, absolute and compelling. They may even seem irrelevant. In my generation it was rare for a bride or groom to arrive at marriage not as virgins. Today it is more rare if either or both have not long since lost their virginity! Years ago, if it became known that a girl was "loose," reputable boys would not date her. She became a target for lust. Young people today are taunted by their peers if they have not already lost their virginity.

The result: alarming rises in sexually transmittable diseases, teen pregnancies and all manner of social disruptions—exactly the lawlessness Satan has worked for.

"Senseless" murders (as though any murder could make sense!) are reported daily on TV. Who would have thought a few decades back that hurling a bomb into a crowd of innocent people could benefit the organization that proudly claimed responsibility for such carnage? Teenagers are massacring fellow students and teachers. Conscience is evaporating more and more as novels, movies and television trumpet "free" sex and violence—with few apparent destructive effects.

It used to be that even people who did not believe in God *did* believe in the law of sowing and reaping (see Galatians 6:7)—rewards for good deeds and dire results for evil deeds. But this generation of instant-on TV, microwaves and fast food no longer comprehends gestation periods before reaping results. Dire consequences for sin, which wait for fullness before being reaped, do not seem to happen.

The truth is, absolutely every sin sets into motion forces that *must* be reaped. There is no escaping the law of sowing and reaping, except by the grace of God. (More about this in chapter 7.) But often reaping comes only so long after sowing that many see no connection; they only get disappointed and maybe even mad at God, who has let this awful thing happen. The time lapse has made it easy for Satan to convince people that God's laws mean nothing: "See, nothing bad happened. He just didn't want you to have fun!"

God's Word, by contrast, says, "The soul who sins will die" (Ezekiel 18:4). But for those who do not realize that yet, the mystery of lawlessness continues to run amok.

The other night a television news commentator reported that in 1998, six million couples lived together in America without benefit of marriage. Never before in history have unmarried couples cohabited so openly, even in secular society, and certainly never among Christians blithely attending church, as some of these doubtless do, as though they were good Christians. Most are not hypocrites; they simply do not believe God's laws are absolute or relevant.

Homosexuality and lesbianism, both forbidden in Scripture (see Leviticus 18:22; 20:13; Romans 1:27), are lauded as an acceptable alternate lifestyle. In fact, certain legislation currently under consideration would not only guarantee equal treatment for gays, but term as a "hate crime" any declarations that homosexuality is a sin, even if part of a sermon at church! This would have been impossible only thirty or forty years ago. But in that time the mystery of lawlessness has been powerfully at work.

In politics one does what is expedient—whatever accomplishes a purpose or promotes an image. Only a fool sticks his neck out for what is actually right. A few years ago a candidate's run for the Presidency foundered instantly when a sexual affair was discovered. Since then God's law has been so eroded out of the mentality of American citizenry that President Clinton's sexual sins were excused as irrelevant. The Senate's acquittal of the President for perjury and obstruction of justice has released even more of Satan's plan of lawlessness into modern society. Their actions have said it no longer matters what political figures do in their moral lives, so long as that does not affect their day-to-day decision-making. But just a generation ago no one would have made such an asinine statement!

In 2 Samuel 24 David sinned against God by taking a census of Israel and Judah, and as a result a pestilence struck down seventy thousand sons of Israel and Judah! What every leader does (whether political, ethnic or religious) sends blessings or afflictions to all under his or her domain. Listen to Proverbs 11:11: "By the blessing of the upright a city is exalted, but by the mouth of the wicked it is torn down." But because Satan has cut our minds loose from the safe moorings of God's Word, we think one man's idea is as good as the next man's, although the one brings heaven and the other hell. Ignorance is not bliss; it is the door to hell.

Grieved about this, I asked God, the best Father who ever was, why we do not see Him disciplining His children. He reminded me of Hebrews 12:7–8:

> It is for discipline that you endure; God deals with you as with sons; for what son is there whom his father does not discipline? But if you are without discipline, of which all have become partakers, then are you illegitimate children and not sons.

That gave me even more grief. What a terrible loss—that unbelievers and Christians are walking so far apart from Father God that He cannot treat them as sons. Because of that separation and lack of immediate Fatherly discipline, Satan can even more easily persuade men and women that there are no consequences, and lawlessness takes a stronger grip on the hearts of believers and unbelievers alike.

The stage is now set for chaos.

The Man of Lawlessness

The man of lawlessness may be an individual who embodies the nature of lawlessness. *But lawlessness is first what we are ourselves*. All of us at heart, in the baseness of our flesh, are the man of lawlessness. Satan's plan has been to so destroy the rule of law in our hearts that the worst of evils in us can, and will, find expression.

2 Thessalonians 2:1–4 says that the man of lawlessness will surely come before the Lord returns. Paul goes on to write:

> You know what restrains him now, so that in his time he will be revealed. For the mystery of lawlessness is already at work; only he who now restrains will do so until he is taken out of the way.
>
> verses 6–7

This has led some Christians to the conclusion that someday God will remove His Holy Spirit, which will release lawlessness. But Scripture says clearly that the Holy Spirit will remain forever: "I will ask the Father, and He will give you another Helper, *that He may be with you forever*" (John 14:16, emphasis added). It will not do to say that the Spirit will remain with Christians but be taken from the rest of the world. He has never been that much in control of the rest of the world so as to have much effect by being removed! I confess that in the 2 Thessalonians passage quoted above, I do not know who Paul meant by "he who now restrains," but it is important that all of us know *what* restrains the sinful nature of mankind.

It is abundantly clear to me that what has been restraining the sinful nature of mankind is the holy fear of the laws of God. We have seen how much evil has already been released, as the bonds of law have been loosened in the hearts and minds of men and women. How grateful we ought to be that God still keeps His laws firmly grounded in the hearts and minds of true believers!

Satan's plan is to so increase insane foolishness as to throw nation after nation into such carnage-ridden chaos that the world will cry out for a strong leader to return the world to some semblance of stability and safety. Even an evil ruler will seem preferable to chaos.

The call on those of us who would heal the nations is to repent on behalf of the world and pray fervently for the world to rediscover the absoluteness and loving nature of God's holy laws and statutes. This will become an enlistment in terrific spiritual warfare (as we will see in chapter 9) against corporate mental strongholds of deception. There must come a return to sanity; a revival of balance and common sense; a return to the gentle, sure wisdom of God in His holy Word.

Enough belief and sacrificial prayer must be found among enough sufficient numbers of praying Christians to put a stop to lawlessness.

The Defeat of Satan's Master Plan

The stoppage of evil must be accompanied by the healing of generational national wounds. This will require vast armies of individuals willing to carry the burdens of healing in their hearts and in their prayers.

It can and will be done. Our Lord will lead the charge. The question is, *Will we respond as we ought, or must He find a later generation more willing to do His bidding?* "Your people will volunteer freely in the day of Your power" (Psalm 110:3).

God the Father will have His army. The nations will be healed. Whoever joins the forces of intercession and warfare will eventually become recognized and sought out for help. Confused, hurting masses will hunger for those who can make sense of increasing chaos and provide a feeling of security in a frightening, collapsing world:

> "In those days ten men from all the nations will grasp the garment of a Jew, saying, 'Let us go with you, for we have heard that God is with you.'"
>
> Zechariah 8:23

> It will come about that in the last days the mountain of the house of the LORD will be established as the chief of the mountains, and will be raised above the hills; *and all the nations will stream to it.* And many peoples will come and say, "Come, let us go up to the mountain of the LORD, to the house of the God of Jacob; that He may teach us concerning His ways and that we may walk in His paths." For the law will go forth from Zion and the word of the LORD from Jerusalem. And He will judge between the nations, and will render decisions for many peoples; and they will hammer their swords into plowshares and their spears into pruning hooks. *Nation will not lift up sword against nation, and never again will they learn war.*
>
> Isaiah 2:2–4, emphasis added

The law *will* go forth from Zion. Nations *will* never again learn war. Satan's kingdom *will* be brought down, his murder of God's children *will* stop and his master plan *will* be defeated— but not before the man of lawlessness comes to power. Nevertheless victory will come, as surely as God's Word is true and our Lord of Hosts is victor.

Will all this happen before the Lord Jesus returns? Will it happen in the process of His coming? Or will it be a joyous mop-up afterwards?

Who knows? The call on us is to do His work of prayer and healing until, during and after His return.

SIX

WHOSE JOB IS IT TO HEAL THE NATIONS?

The Lord says to my Lord: "Sit at My right hand until I make Your enemies a footstool for Your feet."

Psalm 110:1

This extraordinary instruction is interpreted in the New Testament as God the Father addressing His Son, Jesus Christ (see Acts 2:34–36). When the Messiah is told to "sit at My right hand," *sit* means to rule restfully. In biblical symbolism the right hand is the hand of honor. It is also through the right hand that action in the world is taken.

How long is the Messiah instructed to sit? Until all His relationships with people (nations) have been healed, or made into a "footstool" for Him. Footstools are for the comfort of weary feet. The nations are to become the place where Jesus can let down and relax—a joy to His mind, a home for His heart.

When the Father says, "Until *I* make Your enemies a footstool for Your feet," we can make a vital inference: *It is the*

Father's job to heal the nations! He declares that fact Himself. Why? Because the nations are our Father's gift to His Son.

We have already seen the nations referred to as a gift in another messianic psalm:

> "I will surely tell of the decree of the LORD: He said to Me, 'You are My Son, today I have begotten You. Ask of Me, and I will surely give the nations as Your inheritance, and the very ends of the earth as Your possession.'"
>
> Psalm 2:7–8

Jesus Christ is testifying that the Father has given the nations to Him as His inheritance. This means the Father is the General on the battlefield for the nations. He has planned all of history to climax in the coronation of His Son when all believers, like the 24 elders, cast our crowns before Him and cry out with them,

> "Worthy are You, our Lord and our God, to receive glory and honor and power; for You created all things, and because of Your will they existed, and were created."
>
> Revelation 4:11

How should comprehending that it is our Father's job to heal the nations alter our actions and attitudes? In at least three ways.

It means, first of all, that *those of us who would answer God's summons to enlist in His end-time army for the healing of the nations must develop a deep relationship with Father God.* Second, *we must give ourselves to burden-bearing intercession for the nations.* And third, *we must be available to be summoned into extraordinary heavenly councils as the nations hang in the balance.*

In this chapter and the next two, we will look at each of these three requirements.

Resting in the Father

We must have a deep and ongoing daily relationship with Father God. To be effective in the healing of the nations, we

95

must have not only the corporate experience of worship mentioned in the last chapter, which enables us to feel and think within God's nature, but *we must learn to think and feel as our Father thinks and feels.*

How is that different, especially since the Father and the Son are one? We must learn to think from a father's perspective.

Children look forward to what their dads will give them. Fathers wait, from a position of authority, until with joy and pride they can bestow on their children what they always wanted to give. Those with "fathering faith" will impart God's good gifts to others, even as Moses gathered seventy elders on whom the Lord placed His anointing (see Numbers 11:24–25).

People young in faith tend to petition God, wondering if He will really hear and answer. Often human zeal—and sometimes anxiety—colors their prayers. More experienced Christians hear more accurately what God wants, possessing in their spirits a confidence that turns prayer from petition into the fulfilling of God's purposes.

I know from experience with our own six children how gratified I felt when my children sensed my heart and knew when to continue asking about something and when to stop. It brought me both rest and pride that my sons and daughters trusted my heart and knew I meant the best for them.

In the coming struggle to heal the nations, God is looking to rest His heart and purposes in those who know Him and can work alongside Him restfully.

"Fathers and Mothers in Christ"

Abraham could challenge God about Sodom and Gomorrah because God wanted him to (see Genesis 18:16–33). Those who really know the heart of God can identify with both God and Abraham in that conversation. They can sense that the Lord was signaling Abraham to keep on asking—whether fifty, or forty-five, then forty, thirty, twenty and finally ten righteous people would be enough for God to spare Sodom and Gomorrah—until at ten there would have come an unmistakable unspoken message: *That's enough. That's as far as I will go.* And then, "The LORD departed" (verse 33).

Many times in the coming days, intercessors will be in a similar position with God. He wants that kind of relationship with us so that when crises come, He can talk things over with us and work out solutions. (More about this in chapter 8, "The Councils of God.") As history draws to its climax, those I like to call "fathers and mothers in Christ," who know how to rest and trust in the Lord will be found standing in place, provided by our Father's planning for those days. These Christians are entering into God's rest—or are already there:

> There remains a Sabbath rest for the people of God. For the one who has entered His rest *has himself also rested from his works, as God did from His.*
>
> Hebrews 4:9–10, emphasis added

Dead works are actions *not* prompted by the Holy Spirit. Live works are those accomplished by the Spirit through us, at His direction. Youthful Christians often charge into action, moved by fleshly zeal. At best they are motivated by human compassion and kindliness; at worst, by pride and ego. But those at rest in our Father's love are moved not by human compassion or kindliness or any lesser motive. These feelings prompt them to turn to God to ask what He wants done in any given moment. At rest in Him, they have died to their own works—hidden agendas, needs, wishes, compulsions, pride, fleshly desires.

At the end of history God will have a sizable corps of sons and daughters who are no longer children doing their own thing but a disciplined army, dead to self-seeking striving, a company with whom He can sit back and relax and know that His will is what will be done—neither more nor less.

Some Christians deliver messages from God in a way that stirs fear and dread, and the result is threat, guilt and condemnation. Others present direst warnings in a way that reinforces peace and security and results in faith to stand. Good fathers radiate a security in which their children can rest. Father God is raising up a group of fathers and mothers in

Christ who will project such security that multitudes will be prevented from stampeding into foolish actions.

Isaiah prophesied the rising of such "princes" of faith along with the revelation of the King, Jesus Christ:

> Behold, a king will reign righteously and princes will rule justly. Each will be like a refuge from the wind and a shelter from the storm, like streams of water in a dry country, like the shade of a huge rock in a parched land.
>
> Isaiah 32:1–2

This company of princes—men and women of faith—will be like safe, comfortable rocks against which the seas of people's emotions can crash, and stop.

Knowing the Secret of Power

In one weekend conference I drank in more from brother Winston Nunes of Canada—at that time more than forty years in the Spirit—than from many others over many years! I would trot out a favorite theory and try it out on Winston. He would answer with such grace and wisdom that it was as though my thoughts smashed against a wall and came tumbling down to dust—but comfortably. Then I would try out another idea on him. He would come back with an "innocuous" question that impaled error like a dart pinning a target for all to see—and it felt freeing!

In the coming age of chaos, God will establish more and more of His long-planned rocks of refuge, like Winston, in a sea of storms.

Fathers and mothers who know the Lord intimately comprehend not only mentally but deep in their hearts that Father God has already won the battle in our Lord Jesus Christ. Knowing "Him who has been from the beginning" (1 John 2:13), they do not have to strive and petition to make things happen. They are no longer servants but friends of God, "for the slave does not know what his master is doing; but I have called you friends, for all things that I have heard from My Father I have made known to you" (John 15:15). Even in crises they sense what the Father is doing. When they do not know God's immediate will, they simply wait, trusting His Fatherly goodness and providence. Whatever His will is through them will happen, so they can restfully declare and wait confidently.

Those who know Father God know the secret of power: "The words that I say to you I do not speak on My own initiative, but *the Father abiding in Me does His works*" (John 14:10, emphasis added). Those experiencing a less full relationship with God cry out in the stress of battle for the Holy Spirit to come, hoping anxiously that He will act. Those who have learned to rest in the Father do not have to call for the Holy Spirit to come; they know He is there already and that God is already acting on their behalf. "The work of righteousness will be peace, and the service of righteousness, quietness and confidence forever" (Isaiah 32:17).

The Lord knows better than any what is coming. He is preparing His older children to stand for others as that time approaches: "There will be a shelter to give shade from the heat by day, and refuge and protection from the storm and the rain" (Isaiah 4:6). Our Father wants to secure His children, much as younger sons and daughters find safety in the strength and wisdom of older siblings. "Then my people will live in a peaceful habitation, and in secure dwellings and in undisturbed resting places" (Isaiah 32:18).

Not Taking Criticism Personally

As His mature ones stand, waves of chaos will batter against them—and be stopped, like an ocean against a headland. Slanderous attacks and persecution will increase while fathers and mothers in Christ remain at peace, unruffled. They will not take even unfair reproach and derision personally. They remember what our Lord was saying to Saul on the road to Damascus.

The Pharisee had been persecuting Christians viciously and was traveling to Damascus with letters from the high priest in Jerusalem, authorizing him to haul Christians there for trial.

Jesus said, "Saul, Saul, why are you persecuting Me?" (Acts 9:4).

It was people of the newborn faith Saul was persecuting—but Jesus asked why he was persecuting *Him*!

In the same way mature Christians know that attacks are leveled not against them but against their Lord.

Years ago I was arguing with the Lord about this, with regard to a church I had pastored.

Reflecting on Matthew 5:11 I said, "Lord, I could rejoice when people say all manner of evil against me, if I could just be sure it was always 'falsely' and 'on account of You.' It seems to me it's most often on account of my mistakes."

John, the Lord answered, *did I know what mistakes you would make, and how many, when I sent you to that church?*

"Yes, Sir."

Did you preach and teach about Me?

"Yes."

If they had really wanted Me, do you think your mistakes could have turned them away from Me?

"I guess not. But I still feel guilty and responsible."

It's really Me they are persecuting and rejecting, John. You just aren't that important!

Absorbed in Eternal Purposes

In the coming days of increasing conflict, warfare and confusion, our Father God wants a people who do not lose focus on what He is doing and become entangled in their own pursuits. Fathers and mothers in Christ must have so died to self that they have abandoned hidden personal agendas; they are no longer trying to establish their own reputations or ministries; they know they have no righteousness worth anything more than filthy rags, or any reputation better than the offscouring of sheep (see 1 Corinthians 4:13).

The New American Standard Bible dresses that text more politely, saying we are "the scum of the world." But the verse actually says we are "offscouring." *Offscouring* is "refuse; something that is scoured off." In New Zealand Paula and I learned that offscouring is the feces that collect on the rear ends of sheep that have to be cut off!

Fathers and mothers live for their Father's reputation and purposes. In a *rhema* way, as the Holy Spirit quickens God's Word to their immediate situations, they expand the part of 2 Timothy 2:4 that says, "No soldier in active service entangles himself in the affairs of everyday life." To fathers and mothers in Christ, this also means: "No soldier . . . entangles himself in struggling to maintain his own reputation or ministry." Fathers and mothers will not allow themselves to become distracted from what God is doing.

Our Father God wants a people on whom He can depend in the thick of the coming warfare, who will not lose focus, who will not become lost in their own personal pursuits.

How Do We Recognize Those He Has Called?

Many today are looking for the raising up of apostles in our midst. I am, too. This is certainly that time in which the Lord is giving His gifts back to the Church—"some as apostles, and some as prophets, and some as evangelists, and some as pastors and teachers" (Ephesians 4:11). As we approach end-time warfare, apostles and prophets are foundational to the life of the Church (see Ephesians 2:20).

Some of us recognize Dr. C. Peter Wagner as one of God's modern-day apostles—and some recognize many others. But I think the Lord will also raise up many humble, unrecognized saints who hold no recognized office whatever. 1 Corinthians 1:26–31 tells us that God exalts those who are neither wise nor mighty nor noble—even "the foolish things of the world," the weak, the base, the despised—in order to bring down the things, and the people, who are high and mighty.

How shall we recognize such Christians if they hold no scripturally listed office?

Genuine apostles bear the stamp of everything I described in the last section. Look for those who walk close to God the Father. Look for those who are corporate—humble enough to

101

check with others what they sense in the Spirit. And look for those who (as we will see in the next chapter) are given to Him in intercession and burden-bearing.

We have already discussed the kind of behavior that characterizes mature, "called" Christians. What personality and character will they manifest?

Fathers and mothers in Christ are not puffed up. They are not always heavy and serious; they remain childlike and can laugh and enjoy life even in the most threatening circumstances.

If you feel tense and on the spot in the presence of an older Christian, it may be due to your own immaturity or unhealed relationships with authority figures. But a true father or mother in Christ overcomes that after a while, until you feel safe and secure in his or her presence. You do not have to put on airs or act out a role that is not really you. Relax and be yourself. If you goof and make a fool of yourself, that will not lock you into a permanent status. Change is somehow made more comfortable, even if it takes many failings and trials before the new "you" emerges.

You are not always a "little one" in this person's presence, and never belittled. You can challenge what this older one says or does, and he or she will hear it without taking offense, and thank you for it. True fathers and mothers can receive rebuke even from newly born Christians and profit from it: "Reprove a wise man and he will love you. Give instruction to a wise man and he will be still wiser, Teach a righteous man and he will increase his learning" (Proverbs 9:8–9). God's own know this, and live it.

What especially attracts us to such people is that they are real. They are the same offstage as on. They are vulnerable within the limits of wisdom. They can hear challenges from the Spirit calling for changes in their plans or in themselves, and they change quickly and easily—and can stand like immovable rocks when called by God to do so.

They don't always have to be "spiritual"; they can serve in the heights of spirituality one moment and play a game or laugh with friends the next.

As the ship was docking that had borne St. Francis Xavier to India, the Jesuit priest is said to have been playing a game of dice with sailors on deck. An onlooker scoffed and said, "That's no saint of God!" But a few moments later, St. Francis was on his knees on the shore, praying fervently for the great subcontinent. The same sailor fell on his own knees in repentance, exclaiming, "He *is* a saint! Forgive me, Lord."

When you are with such "saints," something inside clicks in recognition and says, "That's what I want to be." When we find models of what Christians ought to look like, we want to spend more time in their company—and we find it difficult to be offended if they set boundaries to preserve time and privacy for themselves.

Such a person may be a devout mother of children whose only degree is from the school of hard knocks, or a church member who may not even be an elder. You will recognize such saints by what happens in you when you are nearby. An old proverb says, "If you find a man of wisdom, let your foot wear out his threshold."

I worked my way through seminary in Chicago by driving a taxi at night. One night a call came from a fancy address in Hyde Park, an island community of houses owned by wealthy whites but surrounded increasingly by waves of black migration. An old black woman walked out of the servants' quarters behind the mansion. As she stepped into the taxi, I felt myself enfolded in love. Dignity, poise and the gentle presence of God emanated from her until it filled the cab.

She directed me to the parking lot behind Providence Hospital, where a young black woman emerged from a waiting taxi and climbed into the back seat beside her grandmother. The young woman had gotten into a fight and her beautiful face had been slashed from ear to ear under the chin. She would carry the scar, I knew, for the rest of her life. It was probably a miracle of her grandmother's prayers that her throat and jugular had not been cut.

I will never forget how that lovely woman listened to her granddaughter's story. Compassion radiated from her. Without saying, "I told you so," the message could not be missed—but it was couched in kindliness and commiseration. There was no harsh scolding, no condemnation, only mercy and compassion. I could feel the girl drinking in comfort as she laid her head on her grandmother's shoulder, and the old woman pulled her close and held her. Her love filled me until I was fighting tears, glancing into the rearview mirror, as I drove them to the girl's apartment.

The old woman needed assistance to mount the three flights of stairs. I felt honored to escort her, a hand under her arm to support her, but not so much as to make her feel helpless or dependent. I wished I could have stayed to listen as she counseled her granddaughter. Refusing the tip she offered, I went back down the stairs uplifted in spirit, wanting to go and see her again just to visit and talk. Her presence and loveliness stayed with me for days.

That grandmother had probably never held a position higher in the world's eyes than a servant, but she will judge the saints and even angels in the age to come (see 1 Corinthians 6:2–3). She will sit high on one of God's thrones in heaven and counsel men and women who have spent years in academic learning.

Immersed in the Love of the Father

It used to be that Paula and I would come into a city or church and, by the gifts God has given us, sense the oppression of principalities, demons and human energies. Ministry in those places, we acknowledged to one another, would be tough. And because that was where our faith was, it *was* tough.

Then the Lord reminded us that we carry His atmosphere with us, that He is stronger than any force in the world and that His presence will overcome. Psalm 84:5–7 is a testimony of those who have learned to walk in the Father's presence. It was what emanated so powerfully from that grandmother in the taxi:

> How blessed is the man whose strength is in You, in whose heart are the highways to Zion! Passing through the valley of Baca they make it a spring; the early rain also covers it with blessings. They go from strength to strength, every one of them appears before God in Zion.

I am not saying that fathers and mothers in Christ do not make mistakes. But within them lies a restful acceptance of their frailty. Secure in Him, they do not expect more of themselves than prideful children do at times. They know that as they walk, doing whatever God commands, He will be moving to accomplish His will. It is not up to them; they merely stand and see, knowing that our Lord Jesus Christ will turn whatever jar of water they can produce into the best wine for the feast (see John 2:10).

Whereas children, and fools, rush in where angels fear to tread, mature Christians do not have to prove anything. They can enter into warfare content to do less than their flesh demands. They have discovered what Paul testifies: "I have learned to be content in whatever circumstances I am" (Philippians 4:11).

Since children ask for favors and gifts from fathers, who then give them, those who enlist in the army of the heavenly Father approach spiritual warfare (as well as all other kinds of prayer) from a differently developed character. Youths get excited, filled with zeal and striving (and, perhaps, fear). The emotions of fathers and mothers are heightened, too, but differently—not from striving but from the knowledge that fulfillment is coming.

Fathers and mothers in Christ have a confidence (as I said before) that others lack, which may be crucial in extended and dangerous places of warfare.

> I am writing to you, little children, because your sins have been forgiven you for His name's sake. [This is entry-level faith.] I am writing to you, fathers, because you know Him who has been from the beginning. I am writing to you, young men, because you have overcome the evil one. I have written to you, children, because you know the Father. I have written to you, fathers, because you know Him who has been from the beginning. I have written to you, young men, because you are strong, and the word of God abides in you, and you have overcome the evil one.
>
> 1 John 2:12–14

What children do can also be done by young men and fathers, and what young men do can also be done by fathers. But children cannot do what young men can, and young men cannot do what fathers can. Fathers, therefore, are forgiven and strong; they have overcome the evil one; they have God's

105

Word abiding in them; and they know Him who has been from the beginning.

The healing of the nations will require maturity. Spiritual warfare against principalities is not for children in the faith. But more important, *the healing of the nations requires men and women whose hearts are so immersed in the love of the Father that His ways are evident in all they think and do.* A hungry world waits to see that kind of lifestyle.

It is our Father who will heal the nations and present them to His Son to rule as His Kingdom. The "children" of our heavenly Father will be His instruments. Those who would enter this work must allow their hearts to be enraptured, captured and held by our Father's love.

SEVEN

TRANSFORMING PRAYER FOR THE NATIONS

It is the job of God the Father (as we saw in the last chapter) to heal the nations, which alters our actions and attitudes in three ways. Anyone answering God's summons to enlist in His end-time army must:

1. Develop a deep relationship with our Father God;
2. Engage in burden-bearing intercession for the nations;
3. Be available for extraordinary heavenly councils as the nations hang in the balance.

We looked in chapter 6 at the first requirement—that we learn to think and feel as God does, walking out His will, immersed in His love. In this chapter we will look at the second requirement: that we give ourselves to intercession, and in particular a most effective form of intercession, for all three kinds of nations—political entities, ethnic groupings and religious communities.

107

We see such intercession exemplified in the lives of Moses, Ezra, Ezekiel and Daniel. Each repented of the sins of his forefathers and interceded for the nation of Israel. Daniel continued praying even though, by the king's decree, it meant his own death.

Intercession is distinct from other kinds of prayer, those that begin within human beings. We want something, so we petition God. Grateful, we praise Him. Hurting, we cry out for deliverance or seek His face for healing. These prayers begin with us—at best with our spirits, at worst with our fleshly desires.

Intercession is unique. It always begins in the heart of God. Intercession is God's Holy Spirit brooding over His creation, as at the beginning—finding what has become void and moving to fill it. Intercession is God the Father loving His children, taking the initiative to look after their welfare. It is our Creator still creating—or re-creating—whenever need arises. Intercession is our protective Shepherd calling out from heaven to rouse His own. Intercession is acting to save His sheep from trouble. It is the one true Prophet seeing what is coming and searching for someone to tap on the shoulder, saying, "Stand in the gap, and call others. I don't want this tragedy to happen."

The Price of Free Will

Intercession is necessary because of our own free will. God the Father, wanting sons and daughters with whom to have fellowship (as we saw in chapter 5), knew He could not just snap His fingers and receive love and fellowship from His created beings. Robots can give back only what they have been programmed to give. No, God decided to grant us free will, knowing we would use it wrongly and become lost. From the beginning blueprint, before anything was, God planned that at the right moment in history He would send His own Son to pay the price on the cross for all the damage our free will would cause.

Even today our Father must pay the price for our sin. He sees, long before every catastrophe, when and where it will occur. "He waits on high to have compassion on [us]" (Isaiah 30:18)—before any illness hits, any death approaches, any accident looms. These events are never His first plan, though sometimes He sends famine, drought, scorching wind, mildew, insects, plagues, war or death to get His children to return to Him (see Amos 4:6–11). Our heavenly Father, so much better a Father than any earthly father could ever be, wants to keep us close to Himself.

But He has given the earth and our lives into *our* care. He is careful not to do too much, lest He rob us of the enterprise of our lives. He restrains His loving desire when everything in Him yearns to help. Just as we older parents occasionally step in to help our children's families (less often than we want to!), so God can and does act sovereignly once in a while. But His wisdom holds Him in check.

It is as simple as when we have neighbors next door whom we love. Through the open windows we can hear they are having a terrible argument. Because we love them, we are pulling for them and want to help. But it is their argument and their house. We do not feel we have a right to interfere. But if they pick up the telephone and say, "Hey, neighbor, you love us and we know you want to help; would you come over here?" then we feel free to enter into their problems with them. Restrained by tact and by the Holy Spirit's gracious ways, we can still mediate, counsel, lead in prayer or whatever the Holy Spirit prompts, because our neighbors have invited us in.

It is the same with God. He is far more loving and considerate than we will ever be. He wants to help but restrains Himself because it is our house. But if we pick up the telephone of prayer, He is set free to act.

Intercession is not human beings prevailing on God, persuading Him to do something He does not want to do. It is exactly the other way around! Intercessory prayer is God finding someone on earth who will invite Him, in prayer, to do what He wants to do. He gives believers the joy and privilege of shaping the prayer in our own thoughts and words; but the more we practice prayer, the more artfully He will shape our thoughts until they are His, more and more cleanly.

Intercession interposes the cross between someone's sin and what he or she is due to reap. Galatians 6:7 says there must be a reaping for every sinful action. Forgiveness and the blood of

Jesus wipe away our guilt. But that still leaves whatever evils we have committed whistling like boomerangs through time, waiting to swing back and hit us. There is no escape from the inevitability of reaping. Willing it away has no effect. Ignoring it only allows it to accrue increasing dividends. Father God's loving desire to protect us waits on our repentance and prayer to give Him opportunity to place His Son's cross in position to bear, in place of us, whatever we are due to reap.

The Normal Life-Breath of Every Christian

We saw in chapter 5 that, all over the world, lawlessness is rising to a crescendo of murder and violence. Sin is daily sowing evils that will require greater and more destructive reaping. People in the world, and even some in the Church, are seeking help from the occult and thus sowing yet more harm to be reaped. More and more families are being fractured. Resultant sins flow in where, in previous centuries, evil would never have been allowed. *All this is creating a flood of demand for intercession and intercessors far ahead of supply!*

Intercession is not, therefore, a once-in-a-lifetime event, nor even an occasional activity, when we might happen to feel like it. Hebrews 7:25 says that Jesus "always lives to make intercession" for us. I think that if He were to stop, the earth, like the tape in *Mission Impossible*, would self-destruct in five seconds! The reaping our sins so richly deserve would bring down doom and destruction on us almost instantly. It is the ever-increasing burden and pain of intercession our Lord bears for us that keep us from devastation. We live, moment by moment, by grace, on borrowed time.

Since Jesus is always interceding for us and He lives within us by His Holy Spirit, then the normal life-breath of every Christian is intercession. If you are born again but not given to intercession, you may have the Lord in your life but you are not letting Him live His life fully in you. He is languishing in your heart through inactivity, longing to work in your heart for others in prayer.

To be sure, there are those in the Body of Christ who have been designated from before birth to be His special prayer warriors. But every Christian, especially as the storms of end-time tribulation darken the horizon, is called into the Lord's army of intercession.

What Is Burden-Bearing?

Often intercession is objective and detached. God calls us to pray about something and we do. We may forget about the prayer, but God never does, and acts to bring about His will on earth.

The Holy Spirit told me one day that a small airplane had gone down in the Gulf of California. The family had gotten out safely and into a raft, but the searchers were looking in the wrong place, two hundred miles away. The family had run out of water and would die if not found soon. Would I pray for them? I did. And the next day, as I learned later on a news report, a search plane flew off-course by accident, directly over the family. They were rescued just in time.

I never learned even their names. I was merely a listening ear and a prayerful voice, inviting God to help.

Sometimes, however, we are not detached and uninvolved but caught up in bearing someone else's burden through prayer. Burden-bearing is spoken of in Galatians 6:2: "Bear one another's burdens, and thereby fulfill the law of Christ."

Note first that burden-bearing is a supreme act of love; it fulfills the law of Christ. (We will discuss that later in this chapter.) Observe, too, that it is not an option, something you can do if you feel like it. Burden-bearing is a command. We are ordered by Holy Scripture to bear one another's burdens.

What *is* burden-bearing? It is one of the most effective forms of intercessory prayer. It is not, like other forms of intercession, objective and detached. Nor is it the opposite, asking God to give us someone else's pain or sickness, so that we can bear it for him or her. That is the heresy of substitution—as though we could substitute ourselves in place of God in Jesus! Only Jesus is the burden-bearer:

111

He was pierced through for our transgressions, He was crushed for our iniquities; the chastening for our well-being fell upon Him, and by His scourging we are healed.

Isaiah 53:5

God sees when any of His children become overwhelmed in heart. Sometimes so many woes, cares, disappointments, persecutions and afflictions hit us that we have neither time nor energy to process them. We become mired down emotionally. We cannot pray the load off. We may even lose the ability to pray altogether. Troubles so enmesh our hearts that our subconscious minds travail, while conscious concentration is broken frequently. In the middle of a sentence we may forget what we were saying. We may go to another room to get something and forget what we came for. We cannot think as rationally and clearly as we used to.

Have you ever felt like that?

When that happens, God may send one of His prayer warriors. The Lord Jesus lives in that servant, whether standing physically in front of us or across space in the Spirit, and He reaches through him or her (or many servants) to identify with our hurting hearts. The Lord does this by empathy. He becomes one with us and draws some, or much, of the hurts of our heart to Himself on His cross. This form of intercession acts like a poultice, drawing out whatever poisons us. This is a major way Jesus Christ "always lives to make intercession" for us.

The Lord will not take away all our burdens at one time. Galatians 6:5 says (only a few verses after the admonition for us to "bear one another's burdens") that each of us "will bear his own load." God does not want to rob us of the enterprise of learning. He wants mature children who have grown into wisdom through what we have suffered. Our strength, as we wrestle with the problems of life, is "made perfect in weakness." He takes away only enough, therefore, to restore our ability to pray and think clearly again.

And Jesus gives His burden-bearing servants the joy and privilege of sharing that ministry with Him. They bear the burden of it as it goes through them to our Lord's cross. That is what burden-bearing is. *It is not as though in actuality we are bear-*

ing anything. Our Lord bears every burden. We only minister to Him as His intercession operates through us.

What Does Burden-Bearing Accomplish?

Jesus often said, "He who has ears to hear, let him hear" (Matthew 11:15; Mark 4:9; Luke 8:8—just three examples among many). The frequency of repetition speaks of the importance of Jesus' statement. People do *not* have ears to hear when subliminal activity robs the conscious mind. For a heart too full of trouble or the inner mind too busy, even good news is sometimes difficult or impossible to hear.

Any housewife can testify to hours of frustration because her overburdened husband did not hear or remember what she had been trying to tell him. Pastors and counselors are amazed at how many times they have told someone (or an entire congregation) something, only to have that person say, "Why didn't you tell me that before?" They simply did not have ears to hear.

When that is the case, many things can help, but burden-bearing prayer clears away the static most effectively and tunes our "radios" to receive what God and others are broadcasting.

"Faith comes from hearing, and hearing by the word of Christ" (Romans 10:17). But hearing, and thus faith, can happen only when men and women have ears to hear. This is why every great revival has always been preceded by a great outpouring of intercessory, burden-bearing prayer, which prepares the ground of people's hearts to receive the seed (the Word) of God.

Burden-bearing also clues those in ministry. A counselor can identify with a counselee and feel by burden-bearing what is troubling his or her heart. This tells the counselor what to ask in interview sessions, and informs prayers with uncanny accuracy.

Burden-bearing is a primary way God wants to call us to intercession. He sometimes allows us to sense some of the grief, fear, hurt, anger or whatever has been weighing a brother or sister down.

Paula and I have given ourselves to the Lord for burden-bearing intercession, putting ourselves at His disposal any time of the day or night. It is only one of the many ways God informs us for prayer. But we find it the most immediate and accurate.

Paula may say to me, "Have you been feeling sad for the last half hour?" Or I may ask Paula if she has been feeling angry or lonely, embarrassed or awkward. The Lord almost always gives us the same burden at the same time, since we pray and serve as a team. Then one of us says, "The Lord is laying someone's trouble on our hearts. Let's pray." Sometimes the Lord shows us who it is, sometimes not. We pray accordingly, whatever the Holy Spirit prompts.

Sometimes the burden lifts the moment we pray. Sometimes He asks us to share it with Him for a while, or else we ourselves are unable to release it. When the burden is for cities or nations, it may weigh heavily on our hearts for days or weeks.

Burden-bearing is a sign of healing or rescue or resurrection. In other words, it is a sign that God is acting. The Holy Spirit is taking the initiative, moving on someone's behalf and calling His own into partnership with Him as He acts. Burden-bearing is, therefore, a sign of our Father's love for us: "For God so loved the world, that He *gave* His only begotten Son" (John 3:16, emphasis added). He is still sending His Son wherever need arises, and we have the joy of being part of it. That is why Ecclesiastes 7:2–4 says:

> It is better to go to a house of mourning than to go to a house of feasting, because that is the end of every man, and the living takes it to heart. Sorrow is better than laughter, for when a face is sad a heart may be happy. The mind of the wise is in the house of mourning, while the mind of fools is in the house of pleasure.

At times it becomes so sorrowful for me to bear burdens with our Lord that it feels as though my chest cavity is filled with whatever the burden is and I can hardly breathe. Lest I sound like a masochist, however, let me testify that in that same moment of heaviness in burden-bearing, I "rejoice with joy inexpressible" (1 Peter 1:8), because Paula and I are sharing our Lord's victory as He moves to set something or someone straight.

Burden-bearing reaches beyond denominational lines, and even beyond Christendom itself. God loves all His children everywhere, and calls His own to share His suffering for whatever segment of humanity needs help. Nor is burden-bearing limited to the needs of mankind alone. God may call us into His working for animals or nature—whatever aspect of His creation needs His attention.

Where Is It in Scripture?

In Jesus' time burden-bearing was so much a normal part of life and of biblical understanding that the Bible speaks little about it. It is as though the Holy Spirit expects everyone to know and understand without laying it out in so many words. But the few references about it are clear and revealing.

The first has already been noted: "Bear one another's burdens, and thereby fulfill the law of Christ" (Galatians 6:2). Few commands are as incisive and unequivocal as this. It is simple, direct and unmistakable. And shortly we will see that the statement that burden-bearing "[fulfills] the law of Christ" is filled with almost inexhaustible meaning.

Paul speaks again of burden-bearing in 2 Corinthians 4:10–12—that we are

> always carrying about in the body the dying of Jesus, so that the life of Jesus also may be manifested in our body. For we who live are constantly being delivered over to death for Jesus' sake, so that the life of Jesus also may be manifested in our mortal flesh. So death works in us, but life in you.

We carry the dying of Jesus through burden-bearing, as He takes death in people onto Himself. In the mystery of time, although Jesus is not on the cross today, what He did there affects us in every moment. If this were not the case, we would still be in our sins, because the cross would have been of no effect for the last two thousand years. Our Lord draws what we are presently due to reap, and the pain of our hearts—all of which is death—back to His cross, and pays the price of death for us constantly, day after day.

That is why Paul said we "are constantly being delivered over to death." He is not speaking of being martyred, as some people think. You cannot be martyred more than once! But you can lay down your life in burden-bearing again and again. Burden-bearers have given themselves to the Lord, to minister to Him, as He takes death inside people to Himself. Thus are we given over to death constantly.

"So death works in us, but life in you." It is the normal life-work of every Christian to be "on call" so that death can be drawn from people, and the Lord's life can be poured back into them. Whenever you pray for a person in this way, you are consciously allowing the Lord to do that—to siphon out hurt and death and to pour life in.

A Lack of Understanding

If we have presented ourselves to the Lord as "a living and holy sacrifice" (Romans 12:1), He takes the opportunity to touch His broken and shattered world through us. When He reaches into people, the community, the state or the nation, "vacuuming" hurt and sorrow into Himself, we feel that sorrow. But it may be that no one has ever helped us understand this process. This chapter, I hope, will begin to awaken and call forth many more than have already responded, and help many who have endured such seasons and not fully understood them. The battle to heal the nations will require ever-greater armies of those who know what they are doing as consummate artists in prayer, especially burden-bearing.

God says, "My people are destroyed for lack of knowledge" (Hosea 4:6). The Body of Christ has understood little of burden-bearing, although it is one of the most important aspects of our Christian lives. Much confusion has resulted.

Some people bear burdens just because they are naturally empathetic. But since they know little about it, they may think the fear or hurt they feel is their own, when it is not. Then they worry about themselves unnecessarily, and fail to respond to the call to intercession that burden-bearing sounds, because they have no idea what their feelings mean.

One problem with burden-bearing is that those specially called to it are gifted with it from birth. Their spirits leap out to take on the burdens of others even before they know the Lord. Then, after they are born again, but before anyone has instructed them in the proper employment of their gifts, they get into trouble with them.

Burden-bearing is far too heavy when we do it without the Lord. But when the Lord does it through us, it is different: "My yoke is easy and My burden is light" (Matthew 11:30). Jesus carries the load; we share only a small portion. But many called to become adept burden-bearing prayer warriors have no training, or else they act in their own flesh, without the Holy Spirit, and so become lost in wounding.

They feel someone's fear, think it is their own and suffer panic attacks or worry that something bad is about to happen to them. Or the Lord lays someone else's grief and sadness on their hearts. If they think it is their own, and if this happens a number of times, they can slide into depression. Or, worse, the Lord allows them to share as He draws someone's anger, and they look for a reason for it and let fly with hurtful remarks at innocent people around them. See Paula's and my chapter on burden-bearing in *Healing the Wounded Spirit*, or order the video *Healing the Wounded Burden-Bearer* from Elijah House.

One of the most common troublesome delusions from burden-bearing happens through empathetic defilement.

Peter Horrobin of Ellel Grange in England had delivered a number of women in the area from witchcraft and its attendant demons. One young woman came to worship while Paula and I were there, and suddenly found her heart and mind filled with lustful feelings and images.

Oh, no, she thought. *Demons have got me.*

But Peter discerned no demons in or around her, and sent her to Paula and me. A few minutes' questioning revealed that she had sat down in the service next to a young man filled with lust. Being a burden-bearer, she had picked up his lust and thought it was her own.

A pediatrician heard Paula and me teach about how burden-bearing can become defiling when we are not sufficiently trained.

"Now I understand what's been happening in my office," he told us. "I'm a competent doctor, but every once in a while a mother comes in with her child and I find myself confused, thinking, *I don't know what to do for this child.* That lack of confidence has been very troubling to me."

Now he understood that, as a good doctor, he was being sensitive to his clients' moods. Those strange emotions were not his, but the young mothers' own feelings of insecurity, and his confusion resulted from a lack of understanding about burden-bearing.

A choir director told us a similar story. A well-trained musician, the graduate of an honored school, she directs choirs in which many do not know how to read music, but sing by ear and watch the position of the notes on the page. Sometimes, while conducting, she would find herself thinking, *I don't know what I'm doing! I can't read this music. I don't even know how to keep time.*

That used to bother her terribly, she told Paula and me, but now she sees that those thoughts were what several in her choir had been feeling, and she had absorbed them through burden-bearing. To be a good director, she needed to tune in to the choir members sensitively, but since no one had taught her, she felt confused and frightened.

The Church needs to learn much in this area because as the warfare of intercession and healing mounts in the struggle for the nations, *many Christians will become needlessly confused and maybe even overwhelmed by fear for themselves.* Here again we must walk close to Father God so that His anointing and presence can inform and protect us.

Father God and the Act of Burden-Bearing

We have discussed what burden-bearing is, what it accomplishes, some of the scriptural bases for it, and what may happen if we remain ignorant about it. Now let's address the two central issues of this chapter: how burden-bearing affects our relationship with Father God, and how it can affect the healing of the nations.

Paula and I were puzzling one day as to why some people get well and stay whole, while others always seem to have one problem after another.

The people who get well and stay well, the Lord told us, are those who have learned the secret of life: "Whoever wishes to save his life will lose it, but whoever loses his life for My sake, he is the one who will save it" (Luke 9:24). The Lord went on to say that Christians who want to get well, so that they can be better servants and lay down their lives for Him, remain healthy. Those who want to be healed just so they can enjoy the good life are self-centered and will always have another problem.

Then the Lord said, *Look up Romans 8:1–4.*

For clarity's sake I will quote just verses 2 and 4:

> For the law of the Spirit of life in Christ Jesus has set you free from the law of sin and of death . . . so that the requirement of the Law might be fulfilled in us, who do not walk according to the flesh but according to the Spirit.

John, He said, *verse four says that the requirement of what law might be fulfilled?*

"I suppose it must be the law of love," I replied.

Yes, Jesus responded, *but there's more.*

He went on to teach that if believers are walking in the Spirit, He can call us into intercession to interpose His cross between a man's sin and his need to reap evil from it. Thus the law of sowing and reaping is fulfilled on the cross by those who walk according to the Spirit and not by the flesh. Burden-bearing intercessory praying is Jesus' supreme act of love—and ours with Him.

Then the Lord addressed verse 2.

John, He said, *what is the law of the Spirit of life?*

"I suppose it's the law of love," I replied.

Yes, but how does it set you free from death?

119

"I'm born anew by Jesus' love, and therefore I'm free from sin and death."

Yes, Paul does say that in other places. That's not what he's talking about here. Read it again.

So I read it again, and saw *the Spirit of life*.

"I have the Holy Spirit," I said, "so I'm free from sin and death." And I thought of 2 Corinthians 3:17: "Where the Spirit of the Lord is, there is liberty."

Yes, Paul did say that in 2 Corinthians, but that's not what he's talking about here. Read it again.

Then Lord laid hold of the text and stamped it onto my mind, as I indicate here by italics:

> For the *law* of the Spirit of life in Christ Jesus has set you free from the *law* of sin and of death.

Oh, I thought, *He's talking about Law.*

So I asked, "Lord, what is the law of sin and of death?"

Read Romans 7:22 and following.

Paul had studied under Gamaliel. He knew how to use the word *law* rightly. But here he used it figuratively—note how many ways as I quote the text and six times italicize the word *law:*

> I joyfully concur with the *law* of God in the inner man, but I see a different *law* in the members of my body, waging war against the *law* of my mind and making me a prisoner of the *law* of sin which is in my members. Wretched man that I am! Who will set me free from the body of this death? Thanks be to God through Jesus Christ our Lord! So then, on the one hand I myself with my mind am serving the *law* of God, but on the other, with my flesh the *law* of sin.

The Lord helped me to understand. Our practiced habits in our old nature (see Colossians 3:9–10) act as a law unto themselves. When we receive Jesus as Lord and Savior, they receive a death blow. But they will not stay dead! They keep coming back to life. (For this reason Paula and I teach inner healing, which is actually nothing other than bringing to death and transformation those practices in our old nature that already died when we received Jesus.)

But it is not enough merely to bring old ways to death. New ways have to be built in, else we will fall back into acting out the familiar ways we have always known. Paul is saying that when we build into ourselves new, practiced, unselfish habits of laying down our lives in the Spirit for others, our old, selfish ways are finally defeated, and we are free from the old ways of sin and death.

If I just lay down my sins and sinfulness and serve others, I thought, *that's laying down my life.*

But the Lord said, *You didn't understand that, either. Your sinfulness is not your life; that's your death. I didn't say to lay down your death for others. I said to lay down your life.*

"If I just lay down my time and energies, that's laying my life down."

Your time and energies are not yet your life. I said to lay down your life.

Exasperated with my apparent inability to understand, I exclaimed, "Lord, what *is* my life?"

John, what was My *life?*

Then Jesus began to teach me that when He left heaven, He did not leave His Father. His very life was His purity of relationship with His Father. When tired, He went to the mountains to visit with His Father. He always pleased His Father:

> "Truly, truly, I say to you, the Son can do nothing of Himself, unless it is something He sees the Father doing; for whatever the Father does, these things the Son also does in like manner. For the Father loves the Son, and shows Him all things that He Himself is doing. . . ."
>
> John 5:19–20

Jesus said to Philip:

> "Have I been so long with you, and yet you have not come to know Me, Philip? He who has seen Me has seen the Father."
>
> John 14:9

121

And to all the disciples:

> "I came forth from the Father and have come into the world;
> I am leaving the world again and going to the Father."

John 16:28

The blessedness of Jesus' relationship to His Father, which to Him was life itself, was what He laid down in the Garden of Gethsemane. There the Father asked Him to drink the cup of wrath that, in Jeremiah 25:15–16, He gave all the nations to drink, "and go mad." Jesus was to become identified with the sin of the entire world. "[God] made Him who knew no sin to be sin on our behalf, so that we might become the righteousness of God in Him" (2 Corinthians 5:21).

Because Jesus was fully God and fully man, He had power to do it, and in prayer in Gethsemane He expressed willingness to drink into Himself the wrath of the life of every person who had ever lived, who was alive then or who would ever live. Jesus made Himself to become one with us in all our sin and degradation. The next day He went to the cross to die for us.

Legally He could not reap on the cross the evil we were due to reap unless He fully identified with us and our sin. I see the prayers of the Garden of Gethsemane, then, not as a moment of panic, which Jesus overcame by prayer, but His willingness to *become* us—all our hatred, jealousy, fear, cowardice, unbelief, idolatry, vengeance-taking, murder and every evil thing that resides in our hearts. He could and did legally reap our evil by dying for us, *as* us, on the cross.

When Jesus prayed, "My Father, if it is possible, let this cup pass from Me; yet not as I will, but as You will" (Matthew 26:39), it was not physical death He feared. That would have meant Jesus could go home to His Father. But to take all mankind's evil into Himself would mean that He could no longer come into His beloved Father's presence. "Who may ascend into the hill of the LORD? And who may stand in His holy place? He who has clean hands and a pure heart . . ." (Psalm 24:3–4). Jesus' hands and heart, filled with our evil, would no longer be clean and pure.

Not that our Father would cease to love Him. The loving heart of Father God is too great for that! But their fellowship would be broken. Such evil as we are cannot ascend into the purity of heaven. The flaming sword of the Garden of Eden stood not only between man and the Garden, but between him and heaven as well. Jesus would be separated from His Father, and to Him that was the worst of all possible deaths.

In obedience, however, the Son of God did it, fulfilling in Himself the law of love, laying down His life in the greatest act of burden-bearing the world will ever know. His suffering in the Garden of Gethsemane was so intense that His capillaries ruptured and He sweat blood, which meant, suggests medical evidence cited in Jim Bishop's classic work *The Day Christ Died*, that He was near physical death, and God had to send an angel to strengthen Him (see Luke 22:43–44). And entering into the death of all mankind on the cross, Jesus felt the excruciating separation with His Father until He cried out, "MY GOD, MY GOD, WHY HAVE YOU FORSAKEN ME?'" (Matthew 27:46).

That was, and still is, the heart's cry of every human being when sin separates us from God.

What, Then, Is Our Life?

When we are born anew, we are restored to fellowship with God. We, too, can ascend the hill of the Lord and stand in His holy presence. It is inexpressibly sweet to dwell in our Father's presence—and to know the satisfaction of being at rest in one another's hearts and presence. When worship washes us clean in spirit, we can "read" one another's hearts and enjoy a depth of fellowship that no one else in the world can comprehend, much less enjoy! Is this the life God asks us to lay down?

Sometime soon someone will sidle up to you and begin to gossip. When that happens you have a choice. If you say, "Thank You, Lord, that I'm not like that person," you are hugging righteousness to yourself and dying spiritually by becoming like the Dead Sea, which takes everything in and gives nothing out. Or you can join in and gossip along with that person. That is death as well. Or you can say, "Lord, that person wouldn't be gossiping if he weren't hurting. I'll open my heart and let You take some of the hurt to Yourself through me."

All three choices bring death, but only the last one results in life.

Another example. When someone insults you, you can either snap back with a perfect squelch, or you can take it to the Lord in burden-bearing prayer: "Lord, let Your heart become her heart. I forgive her. Draw her pain to Yourself. I open my heart so You can do that."

Again, both responses bring death, but burden-bearing intercession is the right kind of death.

How is burden-bearing death to us? Multiply incidents like these by hundreds in any normal week. Often the "gunk" comes in faster than we can shovel it up. Unable to release the burdens completely or quickly enough, we become soggy with them. We may become so burdened and distracted that we cannot hear what people are saying; or else we become so loaded down that we cannot pray effectively. Especially we find it difficult to abide in the presence of our loving Father. And in that way we have lost our lives.

When this happens we need to get into corporate worship and let the sweetness of His presence wash over us, and let all our burdens go to Him. Or we can ask someone else to pray over us, lifting off the burdens we have been unable to release. Or there may be no more effective release for us than to receive the body and blood of the Lord in Communion.

The Holy Spirit wants the Church to become a heavenly vacuum cleaner, sucking up the hurts of the world all week and returning to the house of God to dump it all out on our Lord—only to run back out into the world to do it all over again.

Seven Rewards from Burden-Bearing

Whoever presents his body, holy and acceptable, as a living sacrifice to the Lord, which is our "spiritual service of worship" (Romans 12:1), receives at least seven immediate rewards.

1. *You Die Faster!*

If we have died to ourselves in a given area, and then the Lord lays someone else's similar trouble on our heart, we are "transparent," and the burden goes easily and quickly through to Him. But if we have not faced our own sinfulness in a particular aspect of living, and the Lord identifies us with that sinfulness in another, the gunk may not let go cleanly to the Lord. It gets stuck in us. That forces us to pray, "Reveal to me my similar sinfulness, Lord."

He happily does so—and we die faster, the more we bear burdens and cannot let them go.

2. *You Come to Hate Sin*

When you live with the Lord in the results of sin each day, you realize how much sin costs our gentle Lord in pain and suffering. Hebrews 6:6 says that when Christians sin knowingly, "they again crucify to themselves the Son of God and put Him to open shame."

Even though Jesus is not still on the cross, in the mystery of time (as we saw earlier) He takes the legal weight of every present sin back to the cross and pays for it in pain in His own body. Once you understand this, and suffer it with Him, you cannot stand to drive another nail into His hands or pierce His side one more time. You come to hate sin with a passion.

3. *You Fall in Love with Jesus*

When you are living and experiencing Jesus' life and death with Him every day, you experience firsthand the daily cost to Him for mankind simply to continue to exist without self-destructing. Gratitude to Jesus suffuses your heart. He becomes so wonderful to you that there is no way you can describe it to others who do not know the pain and joy of bearing burdens with Him. You will develop such love for Jesus that you can hardly stand it! He is not merely a historical figure who did a wonderful thing for you two thousand years ago; He becomes real to you moment by moment.

4. The Bible Comes Alive

Constantly identifying with the hearts of modern-day people trains into you an ability to sense what biblical people felt. People in various eras differ only in circumstance, not in character. You are living within the Bible, as it were, learning what the disciples' fears and joys were—from inside their experiences with Jesus. You can identify with every thought and feeling that Paul, Peter, John and James experienced as they wrote their letters. It is a joy to find yourself exclaiming, "Oh, I understand that!"

5. You Experience Repentance and Death

Forgiveness, repentance and death on the cross come alive not only in your understanding but in your heart as well. You know all the way through your being what happens when people refuse any of the three. You know not only the suffering they will endure needlessly, but what their recalcitrance will cost the Lord day after day until they repent. You learn to cry out to God, "Lord, give me a humble mind and a penitent heart, so that I don't cost You any more pain than I have to!" You become instantly grateful for every true rebuke, because it means you will not have to continue hurting the Lord. You cannot stand to hurt Him.

6. You Receive a Quickened Conscience

Knowing what every thoughtless action costs our Lord, you learn to let the Holy Spirit check you *before* you utter a careless word or commit some thoughtless action. If you do slip, repentance is instant. You do not have to make yourself feel remorseful; you cannot escape it! The fact that you are hurting our loving Lord gnaws at you until you act to set things right. A quick and active conscience is not an enemy that keeps you from having fun; it is your trusted friend.

7. You Become Intimate with God

The highest and best result of burden-bearing is that it brings you into daily, intimate relationship with Father God.

126

Filled with All God's Fullness

Late one night I was driving home from Spokane to Coeur D'Alene, alone on the freeway. There came a tap on my shoulder.

Jesus said, *John?*

I said, "Yes, Lord?"

I want you to meet My Father.

In the next second, pouring over me was the most gracious, wonderfully loving, secure Presence I had ever experienced. All I could do was hang onto the wheel and cry out, "O Father!"

You know how you can understand a world of things all in one second? I knew in that instant that Father God was not at all as I thought He was from reading the Old Testament. He was not harsh and demanding. There was not a bone of blame in Him. I knew with the apostle John that "God is Light, and in Him there is no darkness at all" (1 John 1:5). James' words sang in my heart: "Every good thing given and every perfect gift is from above, coming down from the Father of lights, with whom there is no variation or shifting shadow" (James 1:17).

The perfect love of the Father was so overwhelming that I thought I might expire from the sheer pleasure of it—and yet wanted more and more. But I had experienced many spiritual highs that turned out to be blind alleys, so I said, "Lord, this is wonderful, but I'm not going to have it unless You can show it to me in Scripture."

He responded instantly. *Look up John 14:21.*

Knowing it was dark, however, and that I was occupied in driving, He just quoted it to me. (Isn't it neat that the Lord knows the Scriptures?)

> "He who has My commandments and keeps them is the one who loves Me; and he who loves Me will be loved by My Father, and I will love him and will disclose Myself to him."

My mind exploded with understanding. Jesus' commandment is for us to lay down our lives for one another. I had just been learning that this is done first and foremost by burden-bearing. *He will be loved by My Father.* This is what was happening to me. *And I will disclose Myself to him.* By keeping the commandment to bear burdens, thus laying my life down, I was coming to know Jesus as never before. Truly He and His Father were becoming manifest to me.

But I said, "Lord, that's not enough."

He said, *Look up John 14:23,* and then spoke it:

> "If anyone loves Me, he will keep My word; and My Father will love him, *and We will come to him and make Our abode with him.*"

> emphasis added

Again, this is what was happening to me right at that moment, and I knew it.

"Lord," I said, "that's not enough."

He replied, *Read Ephesians 3:14 and following.*

> For this reason I bow my knees before the Father, from whom every family in heaven and on earth derives its name, that He would grant you, according to the riches of His glory, to be strengthened with power through His Spirit in the inner man, so that Christ may dwell in your hearts through faith; and that you, being rooted and grounded in love, may be able to comprehend with all the saints what is the breadth and length and height and depth, and to know the love of Christ which surpasses knowledge, *that you may be filled up to all the fullness of God.*

> emphasis added

Again I recognized the concept. I was being "filled up to all the fullness of God!"

Then the Lord showed me that when I first received Him as Lord and Savior, I received the second Person of the Trinity, but that Jesus did not come in without the Father and the Holy Spirit. In reality I had all three members, but consciously I experienced only Jesus. A little later I learned that I could experience the baptism of the Holy Spirit. He did not come in then, since I already "had" Him; I only learned to experience His presence explicitly.

Jesus showed me that He and the Holy Spirit came precisely to prepare me for life with the Father. (I remembered from John 14:6 that "no one comes to the Father but through Me.") To receive Jesus I did not have to qualify; I just needed to acknowledge that I was a sinner and He is the Savior. Nor did I have to qualify to receive the Holy Spirit: "If you then, being evil, know how to give good gifts to your children, how much more will your heavenly Father give the Holy Spirit to those who ask Him?" (Luke 11:13). All I needed to do was ask. But to receive explicit life with the Father, I *did* have to qualify, and the qualifications were right there in those Scriptures.

I remembered the phrases from John 14: *He who has My commandments and keeps them* and *He will keep My word.* Jesus had been teaching me that His commandments and His word meant not merely the Ten Commandments, or even the great commandment in Mark 12:30 to love God with all our heart and soul and mind and strength; it also meant the command to lay down our lives for others: "Bear one another's burdens, *and thereby fulfill the law of Christ*" (Galatians 6:2, emphasis added).

I staggered around in a daze of love for two weeks. Still today I bask in our Father's love every day. To me, life with Him is the great "prize of the upward call of God in Christ Jesus" (Philippians 3:14). Life with Father God is the great treasure hidden in a field, for which a man "goes and sells all that he has" (Matthew 13:44).

When I talk about the secret of power—"The Father abiding in Me does His works" (John 14:10)—I do not mean merely power to live life, or even to work miracles, but resurrection power in our lives. Paul testified about this in Philippians 3:10–11, another of those Scriptures for which it takes faith and experience to see that it is teaching about burden-bearing:

> That I may know Him and the power of His resurrection and the fellowship of His sufferings, being conformed to His death; in order that I may attain to the resurrection from the dead.

Paul was not speaking of being resurrected to life in heaven. He, more than all the other apostles, made it clear that we do not "attain" heaven. Heaven is Christ's gift to us. There is a question, however, as to whether we can come into resurrection power and life here on earth. Paul was teaching us how to come into that resurrection life and power.

When we are conformed daily to Jesus' death, sharing "the fellowship of His sufferings" through laying down our lives in burden-bearing, resurrection life flows from our Lord through us to others—but also *into us*. As Paul testified in 2 Corinthians 4:10–11, death pours through us to the Lord, but resurrection life flows into us and through us to others, "so that the life of Jesus also may be manifested in our mortal flesh."

I believe that those who lay down their lives in burden-bearing actually begin to look and feel younger! If gunk gets stuck in us and brings us to death faster, so also do resurrection life and power become stuck in us, and we enter into resurrection power and life faster. What a blessing it is to know the secret of life—that he who would lose his life in burden-bearing will find it, in resurrection life and power here and now!

I dwell in peace because our Father God is the quintessential giver of peace. I am at rest because I know that Father God has me and will not let me go. If I stumble, He will pick me up. I do not have to wait to die to know the Father. I already know Him and am coming to know Him better every day. I do not have to strive to love any person; God is our Father, and His love burns through my soul for others. I cannot help loving! Not that I express it very well, but I cannot turn down or turn off Father God's love for all His children. It is a given, flowing not from me but through me.

Being Used to Heal the Nations

What has all this to do with the healing of the nations? Remember, it is our Father's task to heal the nations. How will He do it?

First, by raising up mature sons and daughters against whom the raging seas of mankind's emotions can bash and stop. Next, by maturing enough of His sons and daughters that through them He can act without worrying that they will get lost in their own problems and lose focus in the days ahead. Not that they are to become an elitist club, but they will be as bellwethers to a troubled and lost world—signposts along the way, examples of how to live as the Body of Christ.

Those who are at rest in our Father's love can be used by Him to work untold wonders of healing among the nations through one of the most effective forms of prayer: burden-bearing intercession. Imagine what could happen in every region and country if the Lord were to raise up a corps of adept, burden-bearing, intercessory prayer warriors! How much misery could be eased or stopped altogether? What changes would take place among religious, political and ethnic groups? How much healing of the nations might result?

The Lord has told Paula and me that He can do more through us than we can do for Him. By way of analogy, think about the change that takes place when a strong but gentle new boss or foreman comes on the scene at work. Chaos and confusion dissipate, and everyone feels rest and peace settling over the workplace.

Think about the kind of order that could settle into a region or nation if enough of God's own children were active! I believe that, as the burden-bearing intercession of those who know the love of the Father begins to have greater effect, Satan's schemes of lawlessness will be stopped cold and transformed into times of blessing.

I cannot say whether enough burden-bearing intercession will arise before, during or after our Lord's return. Regardless, burden-bearing intercession is a major part of God's master plan for the end times.

The representatives of our loving heavenly Father will give themselves freely and our prayers *will* have effect. It remains only for enough of us to arise out of self-centered seeking, to grow into the love of Father God and to learn the ways of intercessory burden-bearing.

EIGHT

The Councils of God

Our heavenly Father does things by council. We see this as early as Genesis 3. After Adam and Eve fell, God asked them questions, to which they lied and passed the buck—in the presence of what can be seen as a council of the sons of God. Then God looked over the heads of Adam and Eve and spoke to the council:

> "Behold, the man has become like one of Us, knowing good and evil; and now, he might stretch out his hand, and take also from the tree of life, and eat, and live forever"—therefore the Lord God sent him out from the garden of Eden.
>
> Genesis 3:22–23

Adam and Eve had not become like God, as the serpent had promised. We do not become better by sinning. They were now fleeing, buck-passing and lying. These are not the ways of God, but of the devil. The one in whose likeness they had become was Satan. They had to be put out of the Garden, separated especially from the tree of life, lest their likeness become eternal.

This introduces a third and final requirement for those who would cooperate with the Lord in His work of healing the nations. Not only are we to develop a deep relationship with our Father God, as we saw in chapter 6, and engage in burden-bearing intercession for the nations, as we saw in chapter 7, but *we are to make ourselves available should we be summoned into heavenly councils, as nations hang in the balance.*

It is possible that the creation of mankind was the result of God acting in council: "Then God said, 'Let *Us* make man in *Our* image" (Genesis 1:26, emphasis added). There is no way to be sure, of course, but it sounds as if the Trinity of Persons in the Godhead were consulting among themselves and acting accordingly.

Another example is found in Job: "There was a day when the sons of God came to present themselves before the LORD, and Satan also came among them" (Job 1:6). To me this is a council of God, held in order to make decisions. Here the decision was made to allow Satan to test Job (verse 12).

The prophet Micaiah, advising the kings of Israel and Judah, refers to another council experience (since these kings did not want to hear godly advice, it is not clear in context whether Micaiah was using sarcasm or describing an actual event):

> "Therefore, hear the word of the LORD. I saw the LORD sitting on His throne, and all the host of heaven standing by Him on His right and on His left. The LORD said, 'Who will entice Ahab to go up and fall at Ramoth-gilead?' And one said this while another said that. Then a spirit came forward and stood before the LORD and said, 'I will entice him.' The LORD said to him, 'How?' And he said, 'I will go out and be a deceiving spirit in the mouth of all his prophets.' Then He said, 'You are to entice him and also prevail. Go and do so.'"
>
> 1 Kings 22:19–22

Psalm 89:6–7 speaks of the councils of God:

> Who in the skies is comparable to the LORD? Who among the sons of the mighty is like the LORD, *a God greatly feared in the*

council of the holy ones, and awesome above all those who are around Him?

emphasis added

Psalm 82 may report one such "council of the holy ones," in which "God takes His stand in His own congregation; He judges in the midst of the rulers" (verse 1). In verses 2–7 He scolds the leaders as "sons of the Most High" (verse 6) who will die if they do not begin to "vindicate the weak and fatherless; do justice to the afflicted and destitute" (verse 3).

The vision of Isaiah 6 is another example of a heavenly council, into which the prophet was transported. His vision was followed by a challenge from the Almighty, and his own response:

> I saw the LORD sitting on a throne, lofty and exalted, with the train of His robe filling the temple. Seraphim stood above Him, each having six wings: with two he covered his face, and with two he covered his feet, and with two he flew. . . . Then I heard the voice of the LORD, saying, "Whom shall I send, and who will go for Us?" Then I said, "Here am I. Send me!" He said, "Go. . . ."

Isaiah 6:1–2, 8–9

When Men and Women Participate

We looked briefly in chapter 6 at when Abraham challenged the Lord about Sodom and Gomorrah. God had heard of the iniquity of Sodom and Gomorrah and was deciding what to do about it.

> The LORD said, "Shall I hide from Abraham what I am about to do, since Abraham will surely become a great and mighty nation, and in him all the nations of the earth will be blessed? For I have chosen him, so that he may command his children and his household after him to keep the way of the Lord by doing righteousness and justice, so that the LORD may bring upon Abraham what He has spoken about him."

Genesis 18:17–19

134

After asking Himself whether to involve Abraham in this decision, the Lord proceeded to invite Abraham into the decision-making process.

This is the first instance biblically—and perhaps the first in all of history—in which God invited a human being to become a decision-making part of one of His councils. (Adam and Eve were in His council but had no part in deciding what was to be done about them.)

From this Genesis passage we can derive at least four qualifications established by God for men or women to participate in decisions in His councils:

1. They are fathers (or mothers) of religious movements or of ethnic or political nations.
2. They are people through whom God blesses others.
3. They are people God can trust to teach others—their own children and their spiritual sons and daughters.
4. They can be trusted to walk in the ways of righteousness and justice.

Where else in Scripture do we see human participation in heavenly councils?

Jeremiah spoke forcefully about councils of God that should have been attended by men.

> "Who has stood in the council of the LORD, that he should see and hear His word? Who has given heed to His word and listened? . . . If they had stood in My council, then they would have announced My words to My people, and would have turned them back from their evil way and from the evil of their deeds."
>
> Jeremiah 23:18, 22

Jeremiah was not speaking merely of listening to God. Had that been the case, he would have said simply, "Who has heard God clearly?" In other verses in this chapter, Jeremiah scolded the prophets for hearing lying words and seeing lying visions. Here he referred specifically to standing in the council of God—

and showing forth the power of that council to turn mankind from evil.

On the Mount of Transfiguration our Lord Jesus Christ held a council with Moses and Elijah—certainly two who met the qualifications of Genesis 18. Together they spoke about Jesus' "departure which He was about to accomplish at Jerusalem" (Luke 9:31).

One might ask, since Jesus' death was foretold from the beginning of time, why a council was necessary. The problem was to get to the cross. Jesus could and should have been stoned to death—the prescribed penalty for blasphemy, which the religious elite thought He had committed. I believe Jesus was strategizing with Moses and Elijah how to so infuriate the priesthood and disillusion the masses that simple death would not be enough. Jesus had to make them want desperately to crucify Him, both for the vengeance of it and because, being hanged on a tree, He would lose all favor in the people's sight and become accursed, "[redeeming us] from the curse of the Law" (Galatians 3:13).

Although many events are predestined—for example, God "chose us in Him before the foundation of the world . . . [and] predestined us to adoption as sons" (Ephesians 1:4–5)—there are always decisions to be made in the process of history. Nothing in God's Kingdom is fatalistic or deterministic. If God knows the end of all things, He also knows how to manage the process that results in whatever was predicted, all the while respecting our free will. Councils are part of His process and providence.

In seeking to corroborate his own ministry to the Corinthians, Paul described a vision widely considered to be his own, but from which he did not feel permitted to share what he had heard:

> I know a man in Christ who fourteen years ago—whether in the body I do not know, or out of the body I do not know, God knows—such a man was caught up to the third heaven. And I know how such a man—whether in the body or apart from the body I do not know, God knows—was caught up into Paradise and heard inexpressible words, which a man is not permitted to speak.
>
> 2 Corinthians 12:2–4

136

A few years later the apostle John wrote from exile on the island of Patmos:

> I was in the Spirit on the Lord's day, and I heard behind me a loud voice like the sound of a trumpet. . . . I saw one like a son of man, clothed in a robe reaching to the feet, and girded across His chest with a golden sash. . . .When I saw Him, I fell at His feet like a dead man. And He placed His right hand on me, saying, "Do not be afraid; I am the first and the last, and the living One; and I was dead, and behold, I am alive forevermore, and I have the keys of death and of Hades. Therefore write the things which you have seen. . . ."
>
> Revelation 1:10, 13, 17–19

Throughout this extended vision John not only saw, but interacted with, heavenly beings and realities.

Standing in the Council of God

Having built a brief scriptural foundation, I would like to describe several of the most extraordinary experiences of my life, which may sound astounding, if not outright unbelievable. I have heard similar accounts from others, although am not free to share them, but I know enough to report only those experiences in which I have been a participant. You may think I have concocted these accounts out of my head—or, worse, that they find their origin in someplace darker. But please read on and ask the Lord for discernment.

It should also be noted that although these visions are of councils and heavenly realities, they are not to be compared or considered on a par with the mighty eschatological visions of the apostle John or the high visions of Paul that could not be repeated among men.

In the early 1960s, during the days of the cold war, another prophet and I were carried by vision into the heavens. There we came to the entrance of what looked like an A-frame building. Several steps led through a wide opening onto a large deck, surrounded by a railing that also appeared to be a bench. Dark glass doors opened into a large room beyond. The ceiling was of convoluted waves of sea blue, ascending into an A-frame arch. The floor was of black-veined marble squares, with golden lines separating the tiles, each about four feet across. A center aisle had high-backed chairs in rows on either side. At the front was a high white curtain, in front of which twelve curved white tables formed a circle. At the head of the circle was a larger white table—straight, not curved—behind which, although we could not see Him clearly, sat the Lord. Behind each table was a correspondingly curved backless white bench. All except the bench and table nearest us on the right were occupied.

Not a word was said, but we knew we were expected to be seated. The council was waiting for us to take our places before beginning.

With no preamble the voice of God said, *Shall we bomb?*

In those days atomic warfare loomed on the horizon of most people's minds. My friend and I knew we were being asked, in the tremendous economy of words in such councils, whether the time had come to take drastic action. Should God let judgment fall, or would He extend mercy and more time?

We thought a moment, then answered, "No, please give the world more time."

Instantly the voice of God thundered, *Do you know the cost of what you are asking?*

Visions of horrors cascaded through our minds. We saw many events that have since taken place and some that have not yet, though they still could: wars all over the earth; massacres as in Rwanda and Yugoslavia; millions of abortions; soaring crime rates; the corruption (and powerful lobby) of homosexuality; sexual immorality; bestiality; drugs and alcohol devouring many; marriages breaking up in divorce; children not raised in solid families crashing into all manner of evils.

All this we saw in a moment. We knew the Lord was telling us that the longer judgment is withheld, the worse mankind will become. The mystery of lawlessness was already at work and increasing its grip on mankind year by year. But we also saw multitudes being saved and a great move of God coming.

We meditated, consulted and finally responded, "No, we don't know the cost of what we are asking. But we still plead for more time for mankind."

A decision was made. We were told to pray in repentance every day for an entire year, and to enlist others. Judgment would be withheld for a while.

Not more than a few weeks later, the world teetered on the brink of nuclear war during the Cuban missile crisis.

Many others, I am sure, were called into prayers of repentance during that time. But I will never forget that dreadful council or the awesome weight of responsibility we felt.

Years later, when Paula and I were invited to speak in Colorado Springs, our hosts took us to see the Air Force Academy. When we came into the chapel, I was dumbfounded. It was almost identical to the A-frame building in the vision many years before! The flooring was a different color, the curtain and curved benches and tables were not there, but everything else was identical.

I understood then that earth is a copy of the heavenly, as Moses was told: "SEE . . . THAT YOU MAKE all things ACCORDING TO THE PATTERN WHICH WAS SHOWN YOU ON THE MOUNTAIN" (Hebrews 8:5). I also grasped that the setting of the vision resembled the Air Force Chapel because the United States Air Force would have delivered the atomic bombs. Its chapel stood for the prayers that could save mankind from destruction.

Receiving the Baton

When I speak of being carried into a council in the heavens, *I am not speaking of astral travel. That is an occult skill that copies what God's Holy Spirit can do with His own.*

Philip was transported to Azotus after the Ethiopian eunuch was baptized (see Acts 8:39–40), and tradition holds that Habakkuk was "carried" to give his meal to Daniel in the lions' den. In the kind of vision or transport that my friend and I experienced, a believer does not leave his or her body. He remains fully sentient and conscious, not in a trance, although in his spirit he is participating fully in what he can see, hear and feel in the heavens.

On January 16, 1997, nine of us were gathered in the home of Dave and Linda Olson in San Diego. Paula was at home, however, suffering from a bronchitis attack. We intended to pray for the series of teachings for the Elijah House conference that would begin the next day. But the Lord had other plans. I began to hear a clarion call to a council.

One does not go to a council because he knows they exist or because he wants to. One attends a council when God calls, and at no other time. I had never heard of nine people attending together. It seemed to be asking a lot for nine to be able to concentrate together and see a group vision. But the Holy Spirit persisted, so I explained what a council is and that I felt God was calling us into one together. They all responded willingly.

Together each of the nine of us saw as the Lord took us to a throne room in heaven. We could all see what was around the throne, but not the throne itself, because the glory of God blinded us. Radiating out from the throne, in a great semicircle, was a beige-and-rose-tinted marbled floor with three steps, each about six feet wide, coming down toward us. The nine of us were in line with many others across that third level. To this day we do not know who the others were or why they were there. Perhaps each in turn had his or her own encounter with the Lord.

An angel came to me from the throne carrying a crown with a white scepter or baton thrust through the ring of it. As he presented it to me, the Lord said, in a strong, imperious voice, *Will you rule?*

I knew I was being raised to some kind of spiritual position of authority, and that the question included, *Will you serve? Will you pray for others? Will you do what I tell you?*

First Vicki Freligh, one of our Elijah House staff counselor-teachers, and then all of us, saw that two others and I were being called forward to the throne. A large, well-muscled black man on our right was moving forward, as was a man on our left who looked to be Middle Eastern, with a sharply trimmed beard and long, flowing robe and turban. Michael Ellis, who often travels with us to do counseling, thought this man looked like a Muslim chieftain; to me the turban made him look like a Sikh. None of us heard what was said to the other two who were also called forward, or why they were there. Near the throne I was so blinded I could not see them—or anything else.

The Lord asked if the nine of us would pray throughout the coming year in repentance for the sins of the world. We responded that we would.

Then He said, *I will give the world more time.* After a pause He added, *The dire prophecies will be withheld for a while.*

Finally I was told that I am to pass the baton to whomever the Lord would point out to me. Then the council ended.

"The Dire Prophecies"

Woeful prognostications have been made by many contemporary prophets—a devastating third world war, nuclear holocaust, natural disasters such as earthquakes of horrendous magnitude, huge hurricanes, tornadoes, famines and diseases that could wipe out millions. So far we have suffered "hundred-year" floods one year apart and the second-severest drought in more than a century, as well as massive hurricanes, tornadoes and other natural disasters. As I write, there are more than 135 wars and rebellions taking place in the world. Truly we have an indescribable need for crescendos of prayers of repentance.

But, terrible as these events are, none of them, and not even all of them together, will be as devastating as any one of the dire prophecies in full magnitude. The Lord was not speaking merely of the dire prophecies of modern prophets. Biblical prophecies are far worse. Though we might look at various passages here, perhaps Isaiah 13:9–10 sums them up more than all the others:

> Behold, the day of the LORD is coming, cruel, with fury and burning anger, to make the land a desolation; and He will exterminate its sinners from it. For the stars of heaven and their constellations will not flash forth their light; the sun will be dark when it rises and the moon will not shed its light.

Remember that Jesus Himself prophesied this very thing in Matthew 24:29 and Mark 13:24–25.

> Thus I will punish the world for its evil and the wicked for their iniquity; I will also put an end to the arrogance of the proud and abase the haughtiness of the ruthless. *I will make mortal man scarcer than pure gold* and mankind than the gold of Ophir. Therefore I will make the heavens tremble, a*nd the earth will be shaken from its place* [or, *The earth will move out of her place*, NKJV] at the fury of the LORD of hosts in the day of His burning anger.
>
> Isaiah 13:11–13, emphasis added

All nine of us called in early 1997 to that council of God, along with many others, persisted in prayer throughout the year.

"Out of the Mouth of Two or Three Witnesses"

Immediately after the teaching series in San Diego, I flew to the Toronto Airport Christian Fellowship to help celebrate the three-year anniversary of the move of God that began there on January 20, 1994. Paula, recovered from her bronchitis, met me there.

On Monday evening, when the congregation and their guests did not assemble for worship and teaching (as on the other six days), an intercessory group met. Paula and I were called forward to be prayed for and given prophetic words. No one had been told anything about the council in San Diego.

The group prayed for Paula to be given strength and courage. She fell to the floor, overcome by the power of the Holy Spirit. Then they began to pray for me with great fervor regarding a baton I had been given, prophesying that I was to pass that baton to worthy Christians all over the earth.

I was dumbfounded.

The next night during the regular service, people were called forward, as usual, onto the stage of the large sanctuary to testify to what God was doing in their lives. A pastor from Indiana, who had brought seventy members of his church, was called forward. He began to try to speak but stumbled over his words. Finally he said, "I'd better stop trying to talk or I'll start prophesying."

Why not? I thought. *What's wrong with that?* But even though powerful prophesying in that congregation is not unusual, everyone laughed, thinking he was so under the power of God that for the moment he was a bit incoherent.

Then Paula and I were called up. After we said a few words, we were directed to the main floor below and to the left of the stage, where a group gathered around us and began to pray.

Then the pastor from Indiana came over, greatly excited. He had never seen Paula or me before. He knew nothing of our Elijah House ministry; he did not know even our names.

"As I arose to go forward," he said, "I saw you, and the Lord began to pour into me such powerful words for you that I could hardly keep my thoughts together! That's why I stammered and sounded confused up there. The reason I said, 'I'd better stop or I'll start prophesying,' is that the word was not for everybody to hear. It was only for you."

Then he began to prophesy about how God had given a baton to me and that I was to pass that baton to worthy Christians all over the world. Sometimes it would happen in dangerous places, and some who received the baton would be martyred. It was possible that I would be, too, but he did not think that would happen.

There was much more to the message, but I was so stunned I could not retain it all.

Twice within a week, from people who knew nothing of what had happened there, the Holy Spirit had confirmed the word given to me in the council.

Since then I have passed the baton to perhaps a dozen individuals, always having to say I do not know what it is or what it means. I know only that receiving the baton represents a call to prayers of warfare and intercession for the nations—all three kinds, ethnic, political and religious—and an elevation to a position of spiritual authority.

I know as I write that the Holy Spirit has prompted me to describe this council and what followed in detail, because some who read this may recognize—from the burning in their hearts or from what the Holy Spirit has already told them—that they, too, are to take up the baton. I cannot travel physically to see enough people to fulfill the mandate, but the pen is mighty and the Holy Spirit can reach whomever He desires.

Do not fear presumption. If the call is truly yours, the Holy Spirit will confirm it "by the testimony of two or three witnesses" (2 Corinthians 13:1). If the call is not yours, there will either be no confirmations or else the Holy Spirit will confirm that you are *not* meant to carry that baton.

In the few years since that council, whenever I am called on to speak of the baton, I have felt embarrassed and awkward. (It is easier to write of it than to talk about it.) I have been unable to hear God in more detail about it—or perhaps He has not spoken—to tell me what it is and what it means. But I cannot deny such powerful confirmations, or the initial nine-person participation in the council of God, so I act in simple obedience and trust.

I know the baton is important and that it has to do with the healing of the nations. I also know that God follows protocol, and that if He raises someone to "sit" (or rule) with Him in spiritual realms, He will especially answer the prayers of those He has called. Perhaps He is enlisting a special cadre of end-time prayer warriors. The purposes of God are far beyond us. Corporals, sergeants or lieutenants often do not know why their commanding officers say to take a hill or retreat to another vantage point. Theirs is simply to obey.

It is the same in the Lord's end-time army.

A Final Request for Mercy

I will speak of only one more council. In January 1998 Paula and I were conducting a teaching and healing mission in Seattle, Washington. With us were Jeff and Sue Guyett, the executive director and office manager of Elijah House, and Michael Ellis, who had been present with us in San Diego the year before.

On January 19 the Lord told Paula and me to speak with Michael and Jeff and Sue, so that the five of us could attend a council with Him the next night.

At that meeting we were lifted by vision into a chapel again, much like the Air Force Academy building. Although on other occasions no non-participating congregation had attended, sitting on the high-backed chairs this time were men and women of all ages and races. They said nothing throughout, only sat with their heads bowed in prayer.

An angel came to each of the five of us, one at a time, bearing a gift that represented an anointing and calling. We all felt, we agreed later, as though our feet were dangling in a delightful stream of healing waters. It reminded me of the river flowing out of the house of God in Ezekiel 47:1:

> Water was flowing from under the threshold of the house [of God] toward the east . . . down from under, from the right side of the house, from south of the altar.

The Lord called us again to prayer, and again asked that fateful question: *Should judgment fall, or should it be postponed in mercy?*

This time it was harder to say, "No, give the world more time." We were keenly aware that the worse mankind becomes and the longer sins remain unrepented of, the more dreadful the reaping will be.

But the Lord told us that not only could He withhold judgment and the dire prophecies, but He could also grant grace so His Son's cross could prevent more drastic accumulation of the need to reap evil for evils sown.

Hearing that, we asked for mercy again and promised to pray petitions of repentance. Again the Lord said He would grant more time. The dire prophecies would be withheld for another season.

A Surprising Summons

Then the Lord surprised us by calling us into a different set of healing prayers.

A rift has occurred in history, He said, between heaven and earth. He reminded us that in biblical times His angels often appeared in power and glory among humans and performed wonders. Part of Satan's master plan to destroy law out of people's minds, God said, was to annihilate belief in anything supernatural, so that we would no longer expect angels to visit in supernatural power among us, or even believe in them.

The five of us understood, as God spoke, that we have trivialized, commercialized and even idolized angels until these heavenly beings no longer feel free to come among us in the fullness of who they are. The Lord said that the mindset of mankind needs to undergo a paradigm shift so that heaven and earth can once again act in concert.

At that moment there was an audible rustle as every head in the room was raised. No one said anything, but we knew the Lord's word had been heard. Then the congregation of observers returned to prayer.

The Lord made us aware that many times He has sent His angels bearing gifts in response to our prayers, but we have stopped praying too soon and the messengers of God could not get through to us. He reminded us that Daniel had prayed fervently for three weeks, and that on the twenty-fourth day an angel of God appeared to him, explaining that

> "the prince of the kingdom of Persia was withstanding me for twenty-one days; then behold, Michael, one of the chief princes, came to help me, for I had been left there with the kings of Persia."
>
> Daniel 10:13

We became aware how offensive the recent movie *Michael* was to heaven, and especially to the archangel Michael himself.

The main import of this council was to call us into prayers of repentance, and to pray for the healing of the rift between heaven and earth. The Lord added that in the coming warfare for the nations, there will be need for angels and mankind to fight alongside one another—they on their plane, we on ours. And He reminded us how His angels fought for Israel, making possible impossible victories.

How many times have the angels of God been frustrated and disappointed because we have failed to persist in prayer, until their access to us has faded away? As we enter these critical days of warfare and healing for the nations, we must come to see that we cannot stand alone, that God wants heaven and earth to join hands in battle together.

Confirmation Again—Quickly

Paula and I flew from Seattle to Colorado Springs for a conference on spiritual warfare. We stayed in the home of our friend Cindy Jacobs, who was to be one of the main speakers at the conference.

I arose one morning to find Cindy excitedly writing out her talk for that evening, fairly bursting with anointing and insights from the Holy Spirit. The Spirit had been giving her the very same message the five of us had received at the council!

He was granting her understanding as to how the prayers of the company of heaven in the book of Revelation are not mere imagination, or entreaties from two thousand years ago, or predictions for sometime in the future, but active and powerful supplications for our lives right now. Part of the message God was giving Cindy was that we must repent of our unbelief and of distancing ourselves from the angels of God. We need them alongside us for these days.

When Cindy spoke that night, the entire assembly at the conference entered into prolonged and powerful repentance, beseeching God to restore relationship between heaven and earth.

Second Thoughts

I have risked sharing these experiences involving the councils of God—although I know some will call me deluded, even insane—because I know there are many others whom the Lord would call to attend His councils.

As the world writhes in tribulation, and every kind of nation hangs in the balance between evil and redemption, the Holy Spirit wants to summon many into councils—for their cities, regions, ethnic, political and religious nationalities. If Christians are to respond, they must be aware and instructed. I have thus intended these testimonies as teachings so that you may answer. You now know as much as I did when I was first called to a council with God. It is enough.

Who is worthy to attend a council of God? None is so fully qualified as Abraham. But all I know who have attended such councils are devout, mature Christians of impeccable moral standards. They have been bondservants and friends of the Lord who habitually lay down their lives in prayer and service to others. Most have been leaders of movements; some have been fathers and mothers in Christ, or founders (thus, also fathers and mothers) of Christian healing or service organizations.

The councils of God are not fun. They plunge us into heavy responsibility. How often I have wished I could dismiss them as vain imaginings! I am sure it was God's wisdom that I was never alone; others saw and shared the experiences with me. And the Lord gave such immediate, undeniable confirmation that I could not escape. One can only obey—or neglect and disobey.

I know to heed Paul's warning not to take my stand on visions I have seen, puffed up and "not holding fast to the head," who is Christ Jesus (Colossians 2:18–19). In fact, I have wished I could relegate the summons to such councils to that kind of deception! But the confirmations that followed make that an unacceptable option.

Most of the major turning points of Bible history were directed by dreams or visions. So it is for us—and it was prophesied that it would be so in the familiar passage of Joel 2:28:

> "I will pour out My Spirit on all mankind; and your sons and daughters will prophesy, your old men will dream dreams, your young men will see visions."

I relate my personal concerns and reservations because whoever is called into councils with God *will* be beset by second thoughts! I understand that; I have wrestled long hours into the night with them myself. But we must not let them dissuade us or turn us from what the Holy Spirit asks of us. If no confirmations come, gladly throw away whatever you thought was a council, along with its responsibilities.

But if confirmations attend, remember that the first grouping of people in Revelation 21:8 found unworthy are "the cowardly and unbelieving." God is a rewarder of the faithful. Just knowing Father God—and loving and being loved by Him—is reward enough for anyone.

Our Calling to Serve

"When the enemy shall come in like a flood, the Spirit of the LORD shall lift up a standard against him" (Isaiah 59:19, KJV). Our loving heavenly Father is enlisting His own in the battle for the healing of the nations. He it is who intends to present the nations to our Lord Jesus Christ as His inheritance.

This means that those of us who would serve Him for the healing of the nations must come to know Father God intimately. We are to be those who will stand as rocks in a sea of chaos, acting at all times within the nature of our Lord Jesus Christ. We are to be a corps on whom our Father can depend. We will not become reabsorbed in our own issues in the coming days of spiritual warfare and the healing of the nations. We will give ourselves as living sacrifices for burden-bearing intercessory prayer for the nations—all three kinds. And among us will be those He can summon into councils of decision, as nations hang in the balance between evil and redemption.

No one knows how much is to be accomplished before our Lord returns. Our calling is simply to serve obediently—until, when and after He returns. What a privilege it is to know and serve our loving heavenly Father! May His Kingdom come soon.

NINE

DEFEATING THE DEVIL'S DEVICES

The worst enemy of our faith is not the devil but our own carnal minds. The battle for the control of human beings, from the very first temptation—eating from the tree of the knowledge of good and evil—has been mental:

> Those who are according to the flesh set their minds on the things of the flesh, but those who are according to the Spirit, the things of the Spirit. For the mind set on the flesh is death, but the mind set on the Spirit is life and peace, *because the mind set on the flesh is hostile toward God;* for it does not subject itself to the law of God, for it is not even able to do so, and those who are in the flesh cannot please God.
>
> Romans 8:5–8, emphasis added

I do not think it a coincidence that Jesus was crucified on Golgotha, which means "the place of the skull." He was killed literally on and by the mind of man.

Notice from the following Scripture that Satan wants to take our minds captive to do his will:

The Lord's bond-servant must not be quarrelsome, but be kind to all, able to teach, patient when wronged, with gentleness correcting those who are in opposition, if perhaps God may grant them repentance leading to the knowledge of the truth, and they may come to their senses and escape from the snare of the devil, *having been held captive by him to do his will.*

2 Timothy 2:24–26, emphasis added

Through their minds, Satan took prisoner those who opposed God. *Able to teach, leading to the knowledge, held captive.* Again the context is mental.

Satan's Most Powerful Device

By far the most powerful devices by which Satan controls the minds of his victims are *individual and corporate mental strongholds.*

Every living thing God creates has a life and free will of its own. So do our minds. Once we have shaped them, they have a will of their own and do not submit willingly to the will of God, or even to our own wills. A *mental stronghold* is a practiced way of thinking that has become ingrained and automatic, with a life and will of its own.

Our minds revert to default patterns we have programmed into them as we grow from infancy to adulthood. This is not all bad. We have been designed this way by the Lord for economy. We do not have to reinvent the wheel every time we want to do something. Once our minds have learned how to manage our tongue, we do not have to learn all over again how to talk each time we want to say something. We do not have to rethink how to walk or eat or do any of the simple things we take for granted. Our minds have been programmed to perform those functions automatically.

The problem is, we do not build ways to do just those things that grant us motion and survival; we also develop practiced habits of relating to God and to other people. Some of these are beneficial; they enhance joy and goodness in our relationships. But some are destructive.

151

Paula's side of the family developed a damaging practice. If one of them felt challenged, or was the butt of a good-humored remark or joke, that family member would shoot back a cutting, hurtful counterattack, just like clockwork.

My family constructed a different way of dealing with attacking words: withdrawal. I knew how to turn a deaf ear to my mother's tirades, showing nothing on my face, until she would blow up like a balloon about to burst. It worked every time.

It takes no genius to see how that crossover dynamic was used by Satan to hurl Paula and me into wounding one another. I would say something, perhaps inadvertent, that wounded Paula. Inevitably I would receive back a cutting squelch, and just as automatically my mind would shut me down in withdrawal—which infuriated her, setting off more sharp remarks followed by more withdrawals. Satan had a field day!

Think about how many practiced patterns of thought lie like hidden pianos in every one of us, waiting for the deft hands of the demonic to play concerts of dissonance! This is why Satan can so easily destroy many marriages and other kinds of relationships. All he has to do is to trigger coping mechanisms that we constructed in response to hurts in our childhood, and we become captive to the old infantile ways that harm and destroy.

There was no way Paula and I could defeat our old habits by willpower. No matter how aware we became of our patterns, determining not to let them get the best of us, the next time temptation came, we were right back in the same old reactions. This is why human beings cannot merely be reprogrammed or taught another way to think. Only repentance and bringing those practiced ways of thinking to death on the cross set Paula and me free.

Strongholds—and every other practice in our old nature (see Colossians 3:9–10)—are brought to death by reckoning them as dead on the cross (see Romans 6:11). We do this by identifying strongholds and practices in our flesh, hating them, repenting of them, confessing them to the Father, and then believing they have died with Jesus. "The Son of God appeared for this purpose, to destroy the works of the devil" (1 John 3:8). Jesus has already become all that we are. *Reckoning* means that we believe

His death has set us free and that we claim its full effect. Reckoning is an application of the cross until it has full effect.

One of the first lessons we learn as born again, Holy Spirit–filled Christians is that there is no renewal without death. The old way has to die before the new can be reborn. Here is another meaning to the familiar verse that "where the Spirit of the Lord is, there is liberty" (2 Corinthians 3:17). Christians empowered by the Holy Spirit can catch those destructive ways and bring them to death on the cross. But people who do not know the Lord have little protection. The devil can play them like a fiddle.

One might say we have practiced ways of un-thought: We do not think, we just react. These strongholds—habitual ways of thinking and reacting—are mental ruts; the thinking that dug them was done long ago.

A mental stronghold has a life of its own. It acts to control us and to preserve its own life. Strongholds block out whatever would upset us or contradict our thinking.

You might be talking with someone who is usually able to grasp concepts quickly. The conversation enters a subject area controlled by a stronghold—for instance, a practiced world of warped thoughts about authority figures, developed in reaction to a domineering parent. You say something about authority so simple and straightforward that a child could understand, and find yourself puzzled when the person says, "I can't see that." Or he switches the subject abruptly. Or he twists what you said into some weird meaning you never intended.

What happened? You came too close to endangering the grasp of the stronghold on that person's mind and heart. Truth threatened to break the hold of deception, and the stronghold fought back. A stronghold uses denial, bluster, flight mechanisms, distractions, humor, threats, loud shouting—anything that might throw off what could threaten its life.

Strongholds create tunnel vision. It is as though the person is wearing blinders so he cannot see anything outside his limited perspective.

Strongholds twist the words of the Bible to make inapplicable or irrelevant any glimmers of truth. The person might say, "Yes, I know, but that doesn't apply to me," or, "I don't think it means that"—when the truth of God's Word is as obvious as the nose on his face.

Strongholds send out smoke screens. They cause a person to obscure and confuse the subject at hand. They make straight lines crooked and clear ideas murky.

Individual mental strongholds may be inhabited by demonic blocking spirits. You may be counseling or witnessing to a person and suddenly be unable to remember what you were going to say. Sometimes you can feel something like a wave of energy smack you in the head and you lose track of your thoughts. Or the demon may block the other person. You can almost see something pass through his eyes, or else he shakes his head and says, "Sorry, what were you saying?" So you repeat it—but he still cannot get it, or else he hears a portion and garbles the remainder.

You are now engaged in spiritual warfare.

Weapons against Strongholds

Paul spoke of wrestling against strongholds in a familiar text on spiritual warfare:

> Though we walk in the flesh, we do not war according to the flesh, for the weapons of our warfare are not of the flesh, but divinely powerful for the destruction of fortresses [*strongholds*, NKJV]. We are destroying speculations and every lofty thing raised up against the knowledge of God, and we are taking every thought captive to the obedience of Christ.
>
> 2 Corinthians 10:3–5

Many Christians have read that Scripture and have run out to chase demons. Although Paul spoke of wrestling demons in Ephesians 6:12, he was not talking about them here. He was teaching warfare against *strongholds, speculations, knowledge* and the necessity of *taking every thought captive.*

Judaizers from Jerusalem had been attacking Paul's ministry. For the sake of those disturbed by the Judaizers, he had to make a defense. The slanderers had been saying, "His letters are weighty but his presence is weak." Paul stuttered and stammered, they said, and his supposed miracles were mere fleshly stuff. In his own defense Paul spoke sarcastically about how he was bold when absent but "meek when face to face with you" (2 Corinthians 10:1). Then he warned that he would come in power and that "the weapons of our warfare" are powerful.

What are those weapons?

The Word of God

The first powerful weapon of warfare is the Word of God.

In biblical days a fortress was built on a *tel*—a mound or hill. A two- or three-gate system was left open until the blowing of the shofar, the ram's horn, warned of the approach of an enemy. The citizens of the valley then picked up their belongings and ran into the stronghold, filling up the gate with boulders. Archers were placed to enfilade sappers; arrows, spears and hot oil would rain down on those who tried to remove the boulders. Ample water and food was stored to withstand a siege.

The enemy army would construct siege machines and catapults, hurl boulders in an attempt to break holes in the wall, and shoot fireballs to ignite roofs so that defenders would have to leave the walls vulnerable to scaling ladders. Paul was saying that, yes, his speech was halting and stumbling (he had already admitted that in 1 Corinthians 2:1–5), but that the Word of God is *not* haltered: "It is the power of God for salvation" (Romans 1:16). Paul intended to lob the boulders and fireballs of the Word until the adversary's walls were broken down and every thought taken captive to obedience to the Lord.

Repentance

This meant Paul would speak the truth of God's Word until repentance took hold. He would not debate or enter into acrimonious quarreling. One almost never defeats a stronghold by arguing logically. For this reason Paul warned us to "avoid foolish controversies and genealogies and strife and disputes about the Law, for they are unprofitable and worthless" (Titus 3:9).

The second powerful weapon, by contrast, is repentance. God's kindness leads to repentance (see Romans 2:4), and repentance removes the legal base of Satan's attack. Individual mental strongholds are broken when truth and the gentle Spirit of God destroy their hold. The basis of their hold is always fear (mental strongholds offer some sense of control and thus a false security), while perfect love casts out fear.

Personal Testimony

Personal testimonies are a third powerful weapon because they reach past the captive left brain into the emotive, feeling right side. Humble testimony enables us to identify with, rather than stand over against. Empathy wins hearts; brains follow. "They overcame him because of the blood of the Lamb and because of the word of their testimony, and they did not love their life even when faced with death" (Revelation 12:11).

The Blood of Jesus

That last phrase in Revelation 12:11 is important because strongholds may cause the one to whom you are ministering to attack and slander you, as the circumcision party did Paul. The blood of Jesus that overcomes, then, is not merely a power you plead in prayer, but the very blood of forgiveness while you forgive and bless. Thus Jesus' blood becomes a weapon of kindness that disarms the weaponry of the stronghold.

Prayer

A fifth weapon is prayer. The other four operate best, and sometimes only, by prayer. It is prayer that applies the blood, cross and resurrection life of Jesus and enables the hearing of the Word. "With all prayer and petition pray at all times in the Spirit" (Ephesians 6:18).

Defeating a Stronghold in Yourself

You can discover more about defeating strongholds in others by reading my book with my son Loren, *The Renewal of the*

Mind, and my book with my son Mark, *A Comprehensive Guide to Deliverance and Inner Healing.*

How can we defeat our own personal strongholds? By the same weapons: God's Word, repentance, hearing the testimonies of others, applying the blood of Jesus, and humble prayer.

But whoever is his own counselor has a fool for a client! We need to come to others so that, "as living stones," we are built up together "as a spiritual house" (1 Peter 2:5). Others can "[speak] the truth in love" to us until we "grow up in all aspects into Him who is the head, even Christ" (Ephesians 4:15). Our carnal minds can fool us into thinking we are dealing with reality, when we may be far from the mark. God wants us to be built by others so we can boast only in the Lord (see 1 Corinthians 1:31).

One important factor needs to enter into any battle against personal strongholds—a rightful and necessary kind of hatred: "Abhor what is evil; cling to what is good" (Romans 12:9). If we do not ripen into hating what we are doing, we will not quit it.

There was a time when I was struggling to stop an offensive habit in relationships. I had prayed about every root cause I could ferret out, repented dozens of times, determined to do differently—and then would commit the fault all over again!

Finally I became angry at the Lord and cried out, "Why aren't You helping me with this?"

He responded, *You aren't disgusted enough yet.*

"What do You mean, Lord? I hate this thing."

No, son, you love it. You love your sin. If you truly hated it, you would quit it.

From this God taught me that there is a reward system behind all our sinning. We derive something from sin that pleases our flesh—pride, perhaps, or the satisfaction of vengeance, or feeling more powerful than the other person. Until we become ripe with disgust at what we are doing, we will not stop it. This hatred has to be born of love for others and will finally grieve us enough, for the sake of those we are wounding, that we become willing to pay the price of dying.

Individual mental strongholds do not lose their grip and die until we reach that point. It is a process. Perseverance brings ripeness.

Corporate Mental Strongholds

Understanding individual mental strongholds is necessary to understanding corporate mental strongholds—necessary because if we war against corporate strongholds, we may expect satanic counterattack, mainly through our own individual strongholds. We must know how to deal with them, therefore, in ourselves and in others.

Corporate mental strongholds—the devil's most cogent and frequently employed device for controlling every kind of nation—are practiced ways of thinking, feeling or acting that we share with a larger group, or with mankind as a whole. Paul warned, "See to it that no one takes you captive *through philosophy and empty deception*, according to the tradition of men, *according to the elementary principles of the world*, rather than according to Christ" (Colossians 2:8, emphasis added).

If philosophy were indeed empty and inert, how could it take us captive? Because words and thoughts grip us with a life of their own. We develop, in the mentality we share with others, corporate, habitual ways that may control us, just as individual habits, refusing to obey our will, may control our responses until we bring them to death.

Corporate mental strongholds have far more power than individual strongholds, just as numbers of people can wield more influence than individuals can. Individual strongholds may be activated and operated by local demons, while it may be that nothing demonic has yet found that available "house." Not so with corporate strongholds. They are *always* wielded not by mere local demons but by principalities of evil:

> Our struggle is not against flesh and blood, but against the rulers, against the powers, against the world forces of this darkness, against the spiritual forces of wickedness in the heavenly places.
>
> Ephesians 6:12

Some of the Devil's Equipment

If one were to ask, "How do the world forces of darkness rule?" the most accurate answer would be, "Through corporate mental strongholds." Corporate strongholds employ all the devices of individual strongholds, and far more.

Added to their arsenal is the stronghold of *ochlocracy* (mob rule), so that, for example, when principalities are manipulating emotions of hatred through the ancient stronghold of *racial prejudice*, the powers can whip a crowd into a lynch mob. Individuals then act in ways they never would apart from the grip of strongholds.

World rulers of darkness take hold of the centuries-old strongholds of *ethnic rivalry* and *hatred* between the Serbs and Albanians, playing on their armies until, like a mob run rampant, they massacre civilians, rape women, destroy homes and villages, starve their own and others' children and drive people into homeless, hungry flight—and do not feel guilty.

Corporate strongholds destroy guilt and most other humane feelings. They reduce a person to an *it* rather than a *thou*. Using the strongholds of *abortion* and *women's rights*, Satan has reduced a child in the womb to an *it* that can be expunged. Because strongholds use euphemistic words or catch phrases to mask evil, children in the womb become merely tissue or "the products of conception." The stronghold blocks from its victims' minds those Scriptures that address pregnancy as being "with child" (Matthew 1:18 as just one example) and obliterate words like *murder*.

Strongholds produce "buzz words." Buzz words are statements that have little or no logical or factual meaning but that are supposed to end all arguments. A woman under the control of the stronghold of abortion may say, "I've got a right to my own body." The stronghold blocks out the fact that the child within her has a right to his or her own body, too.

For a short while our teenage son John came under the ancient and powerful stronghold of drugs. Paula and I would show him scientific documentation of the harmful effects of drugs, and he would retort, "Aw, Dad and Mom, that's scare tactics stuff. I'm O.K. I know how to handle it. You're in the older generation."

The older generation—that was the buzz word. Struggling to talk with John, we got a close, personal look at how strongholds take away ability to reason or hear truth.

After we prayed Johnny out of drugs, my younger brother, who lived across town, phoned. His teenage daughters were experimenting with drugs, too.

"John, my girls can't hear a word I say," he complained. "Would you send Johnny over here? Maybe they'll listen to him. He's their own age, and they say I'm in the older generation."

We sent Johnny.

But about two hours later our son came back, spluttering, "They couldn't hear a word I said. They said I'm in the older generation!"

World rulers of darkness used Hitler to spew strongholds of racial superiority and aggression to establish the supposed utopian Third Reich, plunging the world into a war that demolished cities and killed millions.

The stronghold of *homosexuality* has deceived millions into thinking they are rightfully "gay" and has spawned a well-financed lobby that threatens to undo the moral foundations of our country.

The stronghold of the *rights movement* has captivated many in the legal profession. Lawyers, more than people in most professions, are supposed to remain balanced and logical. But because of the power of the rights stronghold, asinine decisions are sometimes handed down in our law courts.

Opportunism is such a stronghold in politics that hardly anyone could hold office or be respected if he or she stood consistently for what is right rather than for what is politically correct.

The religious strongholds of *fleshly doctrines* and *fleshly concepts* frequently keep denominations inside their own ways and offensive to one another, rather than joined in unity for the Lord's purposes.

Whenever people begin to think in wrong ways, the enemy moves strongholds over their minds, clamps them into place like a helmet and takes them captive to do all manner of evils that none of them in their rightful minds would ever have allowed.

160

The Devil's Modus Operandi

Where do you think some of your thoughts and feelings come from? Do you suppose they always originate with you? Holy Spirit–filled Christians know how often the Holy Spirit influences their minds, giving them wonderful thoughts by His inspiration. Think about it. What is to keep our enemy from copying the same mode of operation?

The Holy Spirit always obeys our Father's rules of courtesy. He will never intervene or control without our consent. But the devil obeys no such rules. He invades, inserts, implants, manipulates and takes captive. To be taken captive by the Lord is to be set free. His nature and laws corral our passions and set us free from unseemly behaviors. The devil's captivation works exactly in reverse, immersing us willy-nilly into horrendous behaviors we would otherwise shun like the plague.

My prayer is that your eyes may be opened to see how the devil controls the masses who do not know the Lord, and even captivates unwary or immature Christians whenever we begin to think and act in ways that are not Christlike. My hope is not for human anger—"The anger of man does not achieve the righteousness of God" (James 1:20)—but for our Lord's righteous anger in us, which can do wonders. "The effective prayer [or *the effective, fervent prayer*, NKJV] of a righteous man can accomplish much" (James 5:16).

Years ago I had one of those spiritual dreams in which the presence of God encompasses and irradiates, and you know He is telling you something important. I rose in the sky and saw circular platforms of various colors. On each was a demonic principality dressed in the same color as the platform, standing in front of a computer with flashing lights. As each principality punched orders into its computer, masses of mankind below were hurled into frantic, senseless activity—wars, massacres, sexual orgies, drunkenness, greedy aggression, murder—while the demons laughed and played on. Enraged, I blasted them all with a machine gun. End of dream.

No one man or woman can do what I did in the dream. But obliterating demonic principalities needs to be done. It is for this purpose that I write. Together we *can* destroy the devil's devices.

How Can We Defeat Strongholds?

Never alone. Individuals fight individuals. Armies fight armies. When warring against a principality and the strongholds it employs, we are battling not only the principality but multitudes of demons as well—hundreds or thousands of them.

No individual believer, nor even an entire army, will be able to eradicate such a stronghold as drugs or homosexuality or ethnic hatred. These are too ancient, too powerful and too entrenched in the minds and hearts of many. Most likely we will not be able to do away with any such stronghold completely until our Lord returns.

What, then, can we do? We can rescue individuals, groups, regions and even nations, "snatching them out of the fire" (Jude 23). We may successfully deliver many from a stronghold, although that stronghold will remain intact until entire masses of people hate it, repent, forgive and ask for forgiveness, and bring it to death on the cross.

It took masses of blacks and whites together, for example, in nonviolent resistance and in multiple group prayer sessions, over many years filled with sufferings and martyrdom, to begin to break the stronghold of racial prejudice and discrimination over America. But prejudice still exists and functions. The war is not over; only a few battles have been won. Still, many individuals have been snatched from the control of this stronghold, and it may never again enjoy the mass support it once held.

Here are a few of the rules of warfare to defeat principalities and the strongholds they make use of:

1. Let the Holy Spirit Guide

First of all we need to get our guidance from the Holy Spirit. One does not rush into war against a principality just because he or she sees it and hates what it does. "Fools rush in where angels fear to tread."

Is the Lord calling? What do you see the Father doing? Is He asking you to snatch an individual from the fire? A group, region or perhaps even a nation? This is not a war for "Lone Rangers"— or, in my case, "Tontos." Who is the army the Lord is calling you to be part of? Is it your prayer group? Your church? Many prayer groups in your city? Is the army aware and fully in unison?

The army of the Lord in Joel 2:7–8 was well trained and disciplined:

> They run like mighty men, they climb the wall like soldiers; and they each march in line, nor do they deviate from their paths. They do not crowd each other; they march everyone in his path.

Climbing the wall like soldiers means they help each other scale the heights; there is no competition or selfish seeking for glory. And note it is *we* who must get *our* guidance clearly.

2. Match the Army to the Endeavor

Normally when God calls His people into such warfare, small groups can battle to free individuals or small numbers of individuals from a stronghold. But *cities, regions and nations require armies that match the size of the endeavor:*

> "What king, when he sets out to meet another king in battle, will not first sit down and consider whether he is strong enough with ten thousand men to encounter the one coming against him with twenty thousand?"
>
> Luke 14:31

One Christian alone can defeat ten thousand, but has the Lord said to do it? Will He empower?

Seldom will any of us be called into battle for such large wars. I hope the day comes, however, when sufficient numbers of Christians have been trained and united to tackle and bring down strongholds and their wielders, and to set entire regions free. Can you imagine an army one hundred thousand strong, or even hundreds of thousands strong, standing in determination to bring down the stronghold of homosexuality over our nation? Or abortion, or racial prejudice, or the rights movement that corrupts our court system, or opportunism in politics, or the sexual revolution? Someday our Lord will orchestrate such victories. For now we are not yet fully cognizant of the need even for boot camp! But the day will come.

The religious strongholds of Pharisaism and legalism are presently being shattered by the Holy Spirit, but we are in only the first stages of the war. Too many Christians are yet unaware, unrepentant, neither joined in battle nor persistent in prayer. To date the principalities of slander and division still win more battles than righteous Christians. But the day is coming. . . .

3. Make Sure the Holy Spirit Is Signing You Up

Is the Holy Spirit enlisting you and others to set free individuals from any strongholds—drugs, alcohol, homosexuality, separation, divorce, whatever? I am not speaking here merely at getting corporate guidance. Was the command of the Lord specifically for your group? Are you personally drafted into battle? Sometimes guidance may be for our church or group, whereas He has other tasks for us personally. There are different tasks within any group. Just because your group or church has been enlisted in a war does not mean *ipso facto* that you are. In an army are soldiers who do the actual fighting, and clerks and cooks who support. Know your own place in the army. Make sure He has called *you* for that particular battle.

4. Seek God's Strategy

It is necessary to strategize. Wars are won by battle plans, not by haphazard actions. Your group needs to meet to seek the Lord's guidance, perhaps many times, before taking any action. He may say, *Search your heart. Remember that if you would see clearly to take a speck out of your brother's eye, you'd better first remove the boulder from your own.* This is wisdom before going into battle. Satan's first counterattack will be to accuse you of the same problem, or to create something similar in your own heart and life.

Inquire into the life history of the person or group under the control of a stronghold. Most often you will need to know why the devil's forces can entrap. What personal histories must be redeemed so as to remove the ground of Satan's attack? Who will repent—in, as and for the person?

Vigils of persistent prayer need to be established. Who will be in prayer, when? A leader and backup leadership should be established who will hold the group to account and on track.

5. Exercise Discernment in Spiritual Warfare

Jesus exhorts us, within the context of casting out demons, to bind and loose:

> "How can anyone enter the strong man's house and carry off his property, unless he first binds the strong man? And then he will plunder his house."
>
> Matthew 12:29

> "I will give you the keys of the kingdom of heaven; and whatever you bind on earth shall have been bound in heaven; and whatever you loose on earth shall have been loosed in heaven."
>
> Matthew 16:19

But remember that if you bind and loose too soon, without sufficient repentance and prayer, the devil will only laugh at you. Worse, even if you succeed temporarily in casting out a demon, you could see seven spirits worse controlling the person (see Luke 11:26). A sergeant who takes a hill without orders exposes his army's flank. Obedience to the wisdom of the Holy Spirit is required throughout such warfare.

But you have been given spiritual authority. When enough prayer is undergirding, you can name the stronghold, bind it, command it to be still, break its hold and cast away the principality behind it. But *do not attempt to cast away the strong-*

hold. Strongholds are flesh. Flesh goes to the cross by repentance. Only demons and principalities are to be cast away.

6. Persist in Prayer

Now especially you must persist in prayer. The devil will try every trick to maintain his hold. The person you are trying to rescue may actually become worse for a while. Don't be misled. The devil is now frantic. He is not winning; he is losing. The Lord will use the worsening of the problem to bring the person or persons to necessary ripeness in repentance and disgust.

You are fighting for a space of time in which the person can be freed—like the Prodigal, under the stronghold of loose living, whose father was praying for him—to "[come] to his senses" (Luke 15:17). You are wrestling to gain liberty for the person to think clearly again, to regain perspective. You are persisting in prayer so he can realize his soul's precarious position, rediscover true feelings for those he loves and has been wounding, and pierce the deception of the stronghold, seeing its lies and grip on him.

There is no guarantee that when he does regain his own mind, he will think any better than when he fell under captivity. His own mind may be an untutored mess! Your team needs to be praying Ephesians 3:14–19 into this person, therefore, that his spirit may be strengthened "to know the love of Christ," and Ephesians 1:17, that his eyes may be opened to receive "a spirit of wisdom and of revelation in the knowledge of Him."

When the person does begin to regain control of his mind, the battle is not over. It is intensified. The devil will try every trick he can to ensnare this person once again—through temptation, flattery, accusation, bad friends who cajole into the old ways, television, movies, inner hungers wrongly identified, wrong solutions for right needs and much more.

7. Do Inner Healing at the Right Time

Inner healing cannot be accomplished while a person is under the control of a stronghold. Every insight will only become enlisted as a weapon in his or her denial system. Your group of believers, apart from the person, *can* offer some prayers like this: "Fill the little boy's [or little girl's] heart with love, Lord." Counsel and prayer in the person's presence should not be attempted, however, until his or her mind shows signs of freedom.

You cannot miss the signs. He will understand things you have long hoped he would. He will be allocating blame and shame where he should, rather than on everyone else. His logic will no longer be twisted; he will begin to think straight again. Wait until his mind is consolidated and his emotions settled. Keep praying. Then you can begin to heal those wounds in his old nature that made him vulnerable to the stronghold in the first place. Inner healing can then seal up the broken places so that nothing can reenter to take control again.

8. Prepare for the Devil's Counterattack

Expecting the devil's counterattack is part of wisdom's protection (see Ecclesiastes 7:12). There are several ways we can prepare.

Practice Spiritual Hygiene

"Your life is hidden with Christ in God" (Colossians 3:3). Normally the devil, being neither omniscient nor omnipresent, cannot see into your life. But when you enter into warfare against his principalities, you are exposed. Now he *can* see how to harm you. Pray every night that the Lord will hide you and obscure all the pathways by which the enemy could gain access to you. As in Wordsworth's "Ode: Intimations of Immortality," you may have come home trailing not "clouds of glory" but clouds of imps!

Take a spiritual shower. Paula and I often say, as we stand under a physical shower, "Lord, as this water cascades over me and washes my body clean, let Your spiritual waters flow through me, washing my spirit clean from all defilement."

Don't Isolate Yourself

Give some friends permission to look into your private life and challenge you when they see something not right in your spirit or thinking or attitudes. Listen to them. "He who hates reproof will die" (Proverbs 15:10).

Maintain Balance in Your Life

Don't always be deadly serious. Keep your Sabbath inviolate as a day of rest—and don't pray great issues of warfare, or even small ones, on those days. The Lord can manage well enough without you for a while! Exercise. Get plenty of sleep. Play with friends, laugh, enjoy life. Remember Ecclesiastes 3: "There is an appointed time for everything [and] a time for every event."

Setting Them Free One by One

Think what could happen if enough prayer warriors began to set individuals free, one by one, from corporate mental strongholds! It may seem slow, but remember that is how the great missionary Frank Laubach taught individuals to read—one by one, following that with the powerful slogan *Each one teach one*. An entire generation on the mission field learned to read!

Freed people, better than all others, know how to set their compatriots free—and they want to. We do not have to stand idly by, grieving, while our friends slide deeper and deeper into destructive captivities. We have the power to set them free.

How long might it take to defeat the stronghold of homosexuality if great numbers of the Church rose up in love and compassion—not in hate and gay-bashing but no longer swallowing Satan's lie that homosexuality is an acceptable "alternative" lifestyle, determined to set those captives free? How long before so many would be snatched from the stronghold of homosexuality, and attrition would so weaken that stronghold, that the Church could largely bring to death its influence in our time?

Bombs in clinics will not stop abortion, but a nation of individual women could be delivered, one by one, if the Lord's people would gain listening ears and march as the Lord's army in their prayer groups and churches, breaking the lies of abortion in prayer.

How about the age-old strongholds of aggression and warfare? Someday "nation will not lift up sword against nation, and never again will they learn war" (Isaiah 2:4). Is that just to happen, or do we have some part in it? Can this very book, along with the writings and treatises of others, be part of the Lord's summons to the Church to arise? A grand hymn implores, "Rise up, O men of God! Have done with lesser things." The hymn goes on to call us in a mighty chorus to bring in the Kingdom of God.

When will great numbers of men arise in prayer, and in righteous fury, bring down the strongholds of war and aggression that kill and maim men and women and children? Someday it will happen. Scriptural prophecy will not be denied. How long will our Lord have to wait patiently while we dilly-dally in our own petty concerns? How I pray that God's men and women will arise and learn the arts of warfare that will heal the nations!

A Testimony for Teaching

Years ago Paula and I had friends who lived in California. Bill and Nancy (not their real names) had built a new house and were proud of it as they showed me through.

When we came into the master bedroom, Bill said, "I don't like this room."

I took one look and knew why.

"Who decorated it?" I asked.

"I did."

"That's the problem. The wife is the nest-builder. Why not give Nancy some money and let her redecorate it?"

He did. She did. And they loved their bedroom.

Later that couple came under the stronghold of male domination of women. A teacher they were listening to told them that the husband should take the wife out to eat, without asking her where she might like to go. He was to look at the menu and order for her, and she should like it, or—here comes the buzz word—she would be "in rebellion." He should also choose and buy her clothing for her. In short, the wife was to become nothing but an extension of the husband.

I tried to warn them, but as usual when people are under the control of a stronghold, they could not hear.

Later I came to California to teach near where they lived. Nancy called me in tears.

"Bill's gone to live with another woman for a week so he can decide whether he wants to live with me or with her. He says if I'm a dutiful wife, I have to let him do it."

That made me furious. I had to fight down my fury in prayer; then I arose in the Lord's anger. Despite what I have said about the importance of praying in spiritual warfare against strongholds and principalities with a group, on this occasion I spoke alone. (Probably many friends had been assaulting heaven on Bill and Nancy's behalf, and he was ripe.)

"Devil," I shouted, "you get off of my friend! You let go of his mind, right now!"

That night Bill came to himself and came home. And the next morning he and Nancy came for counsel and prayer.

I said, "What's the matter, Bill?"

"There's nothing to Nancy. I don't like her anymore."

"Do you remember, Bill, when you decorated your bedroom and you didn't like it? Now you've decorated your wife, and you don't like the result."

Then I turned to her. "Nancy, I want you to unbridle your tongue and tell him off in no uncertain terms. I want you to know that *that's* being a submissive wife. Your life is given into his. He doesn't need a cookie-cutter copy of himself. He needs an adequate counterfoil over against him. And don't you ever let anything shut up your voice again."

Nancy told him off, plenty! Bill regained his respect for her, and they fell in love with each other again.

We *can* win against strongholds, whether individual or corporate. But some say Christians ought not to be involved in warfare at all. I disagree. Why else would Paul have said we wrestle against "rulers, . . . powers, . . . world forces of this darkness, . . . spiritual forces of wickedness in the heavenly places" (Ephesians 6:12)? When the Lord gave us authority over demons, He did not say, "Except over principalities." He placed no boundaries.

Although Psalm 149:5–9 was not addressing warfare against the demonic, I join many in the Body of Christ, in a *rhema*, Spirit-quickened way, in taking it just this way. When the psalmist speaks of *nations, peoples, kings* and *nobles*, see if it doesn't make sense to you to think of these as nations, or hordes of demons, and principalities and rulers of this present darkness:

> Let the godly ones exult in glory; let them sing for joy on their beds. Let the high praises of God be in their mouth, and a two-edged sword in their hand, to execute vengeance on the nations and punishment on the peoples; to bind their kings with chains and their nobles with fetters of iron, to execute on them the judgment written; *this is an honor for all His godly ones*. Praise the LORD!

emphasis added

Can any loving Christian sincerely believe that our Lord would be telling us to wreak vengeance on others, or to bind earthly kings and nobles with chains and fetters of iron? To me this text makes sense in contemporary application only if we understand it as singing about our power and position to defeat the powers of darkness.

Nations await the rising of the Lord's army. Many of us, for many years, have almost despaired that this would ever happen. But the Holy Spirit has been maturing the Father's own at an increasingly rapid rate. We *can* defeat strongholds—individual by individual, then by groups, cities, regions and nations. We must neither quail at the enormity of the task nor rush foolishly in where the Holy Spirit has not led. We must develop more discipline and corporateness than we have ever known. Self-disciplined behavior must replace our personal desires. What the Lord said to Peter is a *rhema* word for all of us:

> "Truly, truly, I say to you, when you were younger, you used to gird yourself and walk wherever you wished; but when you grow old, you will stretch out your hands and someone else will gird you, and bring you where you do not wish to go."

John 21:18

Jesus was prophesying about Peter's death (tradition says he was crucified upside-down). But the deeper meaning ought to be clear to us.

In the early days of the charismatic renewal, we journeyed to wherever we thought the fire was. We girded ourselves with our own thoughts and ideas; we went wherever we wanted. But as the Lord matures His own, those days are passing away. We are learning to listen to others and to gird ourselves with the wisdom God provides through many. Selfish self-seeking is dying. We are learning to submit to others and to let the Holy Spirit take us where we do not want to go—into the fires of war and heavy intercession and burden-bearing, and finally to death, because such warfare calls us more and more to death of self in Him—and possibly even to physical death.

Overcoming Satan's Second-Most Powerful Device

When Satan lures people into occult activity, he wins twice. First, because any occultism, from the least and seemingly innocent involvement to the most adept, is sin and a deadly trap. Second, because all occult involvement creates a descendancy of evil through many succeeding generations:

> "You shall not worship them or serve them; for I, the LORD your God, am a jealous God, visiting the iniquity of the fathers on the children, and on the third and the fourth generations of those who hate Me."
>
> Deuteronomy 5:9

All occultism participates in idolatry; it is turning to other gods, other spirits, sources of power other than God's Holy Spirit. This guarantees descent of harm to the third and fourth generations. The same is said in Exodus 34:7, Numbers 14:18 and often throughout the Old Testament. Though generational sin refers to every kind of sin, it is most virulently active (as we shall see) in occult sin.

The prohibition in Deuteronomy 18:9–11 is unequivocal:

> "When you enter the land which the Lord your God gives you, you shall not learn to imitate the detestable things of those nations. There shall not be found among you anyone who makes

his son or his daughter pass through the fire, one who uses divination, one who practices witchcraft, or one who interprets omens, or a sorcerer, or one who casts a spell, or a medium, or a spiritist, or one who calls up the dead."

Divination occurs whenever someone listens to a psychic reader. That is not innocent fun but a deadly trap of the devil.

Most scholars agree that *one who casts a spell* refers not only to spells and curses from witch doctors and shamans, but also to what we now call hypnotism.

Magic is defined as the operation of principles to obtain a desired end. While the mark of God's Kingdom is always courtesy and invitation, magic attempts coercion by the psychic operation of principles, irrespective of anyone's rights, desires or will. The use of magic disrespects others; it forces consequences on us with no recourse. Magic is Satan's counterpart to God's miracles. Miracles also happen by invisible power, but they are the Lord's gracious love in action.

Many occult snares are just that—hidden in seemingly innocuous activities. A child's Ouija board is nothing other than divination and spiritualism. *Dungeons and Dragons*, and many other video and Internet games, are occult in nature. "Table-Up," a game we children used to play, is also occult.

One of Satan's most effective traps has been, and still is, Freemasonry. Several scholarly books have revealed its satanic base. Paula and I have tracked its devastating generational inheritance in family after family. Those who join the Masonic order are good people, for the most part, who intend well. They believe it is a good organization, even religious or Christian, but that is what makes it such an effective trap: "There is a way which seems right to a man, but its end is the way of death" (Proverbs 14:12).

Occultism copies what God would give at the right time and in the right way by the Holy Spirit's gifts. When faith warrants, God may reveal the future through His prophets. Divination peers without permission and sometimes reveals what God would not yet have us know. When we are fearful and cannot walk in blind trust in God (see Habakkuk 2:4), we want a handle on life, to know what is coming so as to be prepared.

Many national leaders throughout history, including Adolf Hitler, have, for that reason, listened to psychics and astrologers. Kings and rulers in biblical days employed magicians and seers. Moses contended with Pharaoh's magicians. Daniel rose to power when Nebuchadnezzar's seers failed his tests and could not tell him his dreams and their meanings. The kings of Israel and Judah approached the Lord's prophets to prepare for what was coming. God's prophets struggled not to be turned into diviners, communicating God's word purely because God wanted to speak.

It is not my purpose here to catalog the many and various forms of the occult. Readers can find more comprehensive treatment of this subject in my book with Paula, *Healing the Wounded Spirit*, my book with my son Mark, *A Comprehensive Guide to Deliverance and Inner Healing* and many other good Christian books. But it *is* my purpose to say that any who would serve the Lord for the healing of the nations must study this field and be equipped.

Some are afraid to know anything about the occult, as though that would somehow overcome them, or at least taint or defile them. Truly it is not wisdom to become too involved in the study of "the deep, dark things." But those who want to be part of the Lord's army for the healing of the nations will be woefully ill-equipped soldiers if they do not know at least the basics.

Moses was raised in Pharaoh's household, trained in the magic arts. Daniel, Shadrach, Meshach and Abednego, sons of Judah taken into Babylonian captivity, were schooled in the Chaldean magic arts and other sciences. Daniel 1:4 says that they were taught "the literature and language of the Chaldeans." Just as today our public schools are becoming more and more corrupted by teachings Christian parents find objectionable, in those days, history informs us, such schooling would have included all the magic arts of that day.

But they were not overcome. Rather, they overcame the magicians and seers by the power of God's Spirit.

We do not have to be afraid of proper study, only of what ignorance can do to destroy God's people.

You must learn to recognize when a curse has been put on a family, people, city, region or nation. You must contend with witches and warlocks, psychics and seers, spiritists, spiritualists and mediums. (Today's New Age channelers are nothing but spiritualists in modern, euphemistic terms.) Curses have to be broken and evil descendancies stopped, all on the cross of Christ.

Rather than take time and space here to develop such a vast subject, I will deal only with curses and descendancies from occult involvement since these profoundly affect families, groups, cities, regions and nations.

Curses

Curses come in several levels—first, *inherited curses*. Whenever disobedience to God's laws occurs, either by our forefathers or by ourselves, Scripture tells us we inherit curses. (These are listed in Deuteronomy 28:15–68.)

Then there are *pronounced curses*. These can be pronounced by those who do not know or intend what they are doing—as, for example, when fathers exclaim, "You'll never amount to anything!" or when someone disappointed by us declares, "You'll get yours!" Sometimes such pronouncements have no power and effect at all, but at other times such pronouncements, however innocuous, can act as magnets that draw evil upon us.

Then there are curses pronounced by people who are not trained in the occult but who do intend us evil, when they say, for example, "I hope you suffer for what you did to me." Finally there are curses spoken by people in various levels of magic or witchcraft, who know how to craft and pursue a curse.

Curses often bring destruction on families, groups, cities, regions and nations. Those who would heal nations must ferret out the histories behind curses. We need to discover what injuries, misunderstandings, betrayals, woundings, frustrations and disappointments have taken place. Whenever living participants can act out forgiveness and reconciliation, that is best. Second-best is when direct descendants can repent and forgive. Third-best, when uninvolved persons take on the burden and offer the acts and prayers of reconciliation.

Once repentance and forgiveness have cleared the way, we can take up authority and, in Jesus' name, break any curse. It is always best to conclude by praying blessings in detail, speaking the very opposite of the effects of the curse.

Descendancies

Occult involvement causes the descendancy of at least five major evils into succeeding generations:

1. *Unaccountable financial reversal.* Unexpected expenses will be exacted again and again at just about the time the person is about to get a bit ahead. Paula and I suffered this until we repented of high-degree Freemasonry on both sides of our family.
2. *Illnesses that defy diagnosis or, if rightly diagnosed, resist cures that would normally be effective.*
3. *Family feuds and separations*—for example, kinfolk who do not speak to one another for years.
4. *Tendencies that turn true spirituality to the occult.* Frequently descendants do not know the difference. There is a fine line between magic and prayer, between gifts of the Holy Spirit and psychic and occult activity. Generational inheritance from occultism blurs discernment, so that such Christians, until delivered, remain a "mixed bag," impure in their serving.
5. *Blockages.* Credit is not given or well-deserved promotions do not come. Descendants often fail to come into the fullness of their destiny. Life is never fully satisfying somehow.

These inheritances happen not merely in individual families. Paula and I have uncovered them in local church histories and in entire denominations—thus, in the religious nation of the Church. Cities and states harbor deadly inheritances, almost always unaware of their source. Curses hang over America. Occupants of the office of President of the United States have exposed the nation to inheritances of evil, including Abraham Lincoln's wife, who participated in séances in the White House; John F. Kennedy, who pursued multiple sexual affairs in the White House; and much more recent immorality.

After it was discovered that King Saul had broken the covenant made with the Gibeonites, the famine in Israel did not let up until King David made restitution (see 2 Samuel 21:1–9). But not even one of more than eight hundred solemn covenants (treaties) made with Native Americans have been kept! And many of America's founding fathers were Masons. Masonic symbols even adorn dollar bills.

I hope Christian groups will respond to this book, and to other treatises, sermons and statements, until an army arises to break the curses hanging over America—and over other nations as well.

Curses hung over Germany because whoever blesses the seed of Abraham will be blessed and whoever curses him will be cursed (see Genesis 12:3). Paula and I watched as the prayers of many resulted in a jubilee year for Germany fifty years after World War II. Forgiveness descended and the spiritual climate over Germany changed. It was wonderful to behold!

This can happen in nation after nation if God's people, who are called by His name, will repent and pray.

Defeating the Devil's Other Devices

Satan works to divide and conquer. Sin always separates. Some of his primary devices for division are *hubris* (spiritual pride), *slander, invective, rancor, personal vainglory, temptation to seize power* and *hearts of stone.*

Not too long ago most sections of the Church were gripped in the stronghold of hubris. Many were sure they would be the only ones to make it to heaven, or that they would hold pre-eminent places there while others ought to be grateful to be allowed as doorkeepers! The fall of the Holy Spirit on every denomination has done much to break us of that pride. Teaching and sharing now take place across "castes" and denominational lines in a way that would have been unthinkable only a few years ago. But much remains to be done if we are to be part of the Father's answer to His Son's prayer in John 17. We are a long way yet from being one.

177

More and more we are learning the simple fact that Jesus Himself is "the way, and the truth, and the life" (John 14:6). It is dawning on us that nothing of what we think *about* Him, and none of our religious rites or beliefs or doctrines, is so important as to sanction divisiveness. Jesus alone is our life, and that life rests with the entire family of God. It is possible for us to act according to correct doctrine and religious rites while the way, the truth and the life are far from us. Pharisees and scribes consistently chose their own practiced ways of faulty self-righteousness.

Whatever is true is true only according to the nature of our Lord Jesus Christ, who chose people before practiced ways of thinking.

Those whom the Lord calls to stand for Him for the healing of the nations must not only understand this, but be committed wholeheartedly to loving and cherishing what Jesus loves. Our Lord loves unity. So must we. The religious nation of the Church and the nations of the world wait for that kind of loving, self-dying fellowship. Jesus said the world will know that the Father has sent Him when it sees true love manifested among His disciples (see John 17:21).

Satan uses *slander and calumny* to bring divisions and rancor in the Body of Christ—and among every other kind of nation. How can Christians defeat it? By taking abuse without retaliation. By forgiving and blessing. By not repeating in conversation the evils that have been done against us. "He who conceals a transgression seeks love, but he who repeats a matter separates intimate friends" (Proverbs 17:9).

The devil employs *pride and ambition* to cause men and women to trample one another's lives and feelings. The world often celebrates this as the great game of life: "It's a dog-eat-dog world, and may the best dog win." But the Holy Spirit wants to bring to death vainglory and selfish ambition in all of us. We are to be a witness in the world of our Lord's way, in but "not of the world" (John 17:14). Pride and ambition are not mere personal drives, but strongholds built through the centuries. God the Father needs a selfless cadre of Christians who have brought those strongholds to death in themselves, and stand in prayer to deliver others—in the marketplace, in political nations, in ethnic groupings and in religion.

Here is another primary place where the Father wants His own to stand as immovable rocks in a tossing sea, in whom personal drives can come to a halt and where trust in our Father's provision can take hold.

The devil uses *temptation* to bring down promising servants, often sexually, in every field. Jesus defeated temptation by quoting the Word of God. God the Father wants a people whose hearts and minds are so grounded in His Word that they will not sin against Him (see Psalm 119:11). Hear me: *They absolutely will not surrender to whatever is not lawful!* They will manifest the love and righteousness of Jesus to a tattered and weary world, shining as lights to this "crooked and perverse generation" (Philippians 2:15). God wants a company who by their behavior will show forth constantly what is true, unchanging and of eternal value.

We could continue to catalog the devil's many devices, not least of which is *the New Age movement*—an attempt to make mankind into all he is intended to be without death to self in Christ Jesus. That is yet another eating of the tree of the knowledge of good and evil in order to become like God. But all these many devices require the same answer: God and the nations of the world are looking for a people who will stand in the character of our Lord Jesus Christ, no matter what the cost.

I have seen that company arising—often not the recognized and famous leaders of the Church, but those whom God has tempered in the fires of persecution and suffering. More and more the weight of these who are being sanctified in Him will begin to shatter the strongholds that serve as Satan's devices. In the end he will be left holding a bag of useless tricks.

How much of this will happen before our Lord returns? I do not know. The world may need to become worse by far. Scripture prophesies a time (as we saw in chapter 5) when lawlessness will reign. But our Lord will use that time to make mankind disgusted with its ways and ripe to change. Victory *will* come and the age of our Lord's reign on earth *will* arrive.

The only question is, will we be part of His solution or part of the problem?

It is time to set ourselves as never before to do and say nothing our Lord Jesus would not do or say, and—putting it the other way around—to set ourselves to feel, think and act only as He would. He is worth it! And the only way we can do this is by walking so close to Him that His nature shines through ours at all times by the Holy Spirit.

TEN

Healing Generational Sin in the Nations

Generational sin is the evil we inherit from the sins of our forefathers. Satan uses it, more than almost anything else, to afflict individuals, families, groups, churches, cities, regions and nations.

Most of what we receive from our predecessors, thankfully, is not evil. We reap entirely undeservedly our healthy bodies, our intellects, our spirituality and all the practical things of earth we take for granted—good diet, clothing, medicines, houses, cars, radios, TVs. We invented none of those things that bless us every day. We reap the good labors of our ancestors every day of our lives.

We also reap their sins. Whenever unforgiven sins exist in our family lines, the legal necessity to reap remains in force. The Bible speaks of this in many places:

> Then the LORD passed by in front of [Moses] and proclaimed, "The LORD, the LORD God, compassionate and gracious, slow to

anger, and abounding in lovingkindness and truth; who keeps lovingkindness for thousands, who forgives iniquity, transgression and sin; yet He will by no means leave the guilty unpunished, visiting the iniquity of fathers on the children and on the grandchildren to the third and fourth generations."

Exodus 34:6–7

"The LORD is slow to anger and abundant in lovingkindness, forgiving iniquity and transgression; but He will by no means clear the guilty, visiting the iniquity of the fathers on the children to the third and fourth generations."

Numbers 14:18

"You shall not worship [idols] or serve them; for I, the LORD your God, am a jealous God, visiting the iniquity of the fathers on the children, and on the third and the fourth generations of those who hate Me."

Deuteronomy 5:9

Some say, "How can that be? God speaks of lovingkindness and forgiveness, then visits punishments on people to the third and fourth generations? That doesn't sound very kind or forgiving to me!" But they confuse forgiveness with pardon. Forgiveness clears away guilt and restores us to fellowship with our Father, but it does not do away with discipline or punishment. If a man cheats me at law, I may forgive him, but the government still sends him to prison for fraud. My forgiving him does not cancel his need to pay for his crime. But the governor may eventually pardon him, which does wipe away need for further punishment.

When my father caught my older brother and me in a sin, he would sit us down and say, "Hal and Jackie, I want you to know that your mother and I love you, and we forgive you, but now I'm going to have to discipline you." We were taught at "the seat of hard learning" that forgiveness restores relationships but does not do away with the need for discipline.

But to the third and fourth generations? Is that fair, when those children did nothing to deserve all that trouble? God is fair, but ever since sin entered the world, life on earth has not been fair. God designed the law of sowing and reaping to create blessings, so that as Adam and Eve did good things in the Garden of Eden, they would reap blessings, and the universe would upbuild itself in love. When sin entered the world, however, the very laws meant to bring blessing now worked impartially to return evil, as Paul explained in Galatians 6:7–9:

> Do not be deceived, God is not mocked; for whatever a man sows, this he will also reap. For the one who sows to his own flesh will from the flesh reap corruption, but the one who sows to the Spirit will from the Spirit reap eternal life. Let us not lose heart in doing good, for in due time we will reap if we do not grow weary.

Because we are corporate, the laws of God do not affect us alone. They bring either blessing or harm to everyone connected with us. "A good man leaves an inheritance to his children's children" (Proverbs 13:22). And iniquity (as we saw from Exodus 34:7) is visited "to the third and fourth generations."

God did not want evil to be reaped by innocent children but knew it would happen. Thus He made provision for Jesus to come, to bring not only forgiveness but redemption. On the cross the Lord Jesus reaped the harm all generations incur from the sins of their forefathers. This is the good news proclaimed by Ezekiel:

> "What do you mean by using this proverb concerning the land of Israel, saying, 'The fathers eat the sour grapes, but the children's teeth are set on edge'? "As I live," declares the Lord God, "you are surely not going to use this proverb in Israel anymore. Behold, all souls are Mine; the soul of the father as well as the soul of the son is Mine. The soul who sins will die. But if a man is righteous and practices justice and righteousness ... he is righteous and will surely live," declares the Lord GOD.
>
> Ezekiel 18:2–5, 9

Ezekiel goes on to say that each man shall die for his own sin and live by his own righteousness. But Psalm 14:3 (quoted in

Romans 3:12) declares that no one is righteous. We know, from this side of the incarnation, that only our Lord Jesus Christ is righteous. It is only by His grace poured out for us on the cross, and by His righteousness imputed to us (see 2 Corinthians 5:21), that we no longer have to reap the iniquity of our forefathers.

We can easily see in our own lives, regarding the choice whether to sin or to obey, the unfathomable goodness of God. By His Spirit, for example, He urges us to do a good deed. When we finally obey and do it, He lets us reap thirty, sixty or a hundredfold, as though doing the good deed were all our own idea. At the same time He works incessantly—through preachers, His Word, relatives, friends, whatever open doors He can find—to prevent us from doing something sinful. When we do not listen but commit the sin, He works even harder, through all the above and more, to induce us to repent and confess so that Jesus can reap in His own Person on the cross the evil we were due!

That is the grace we enjoy day by day: "If we walk in the Light as He Himself is in the Light, we have fellowship with one another, and the blood of Jesus His Son cleanses us from all sin" (1 John 1:7).

But now comes the mystery, regarding the sins of our forefathers that have not been brought under the blood of Christ. Although Paula and I have ministered to literally thousands of Christians concerning generational sin, we cannot explain why inherited evil does not end when we die to ourselves and are born anew in Jesus. It seems to me that when we receive Him as Lord and Savior and our sins are washed away, all inherited evil also ought to stop on His cross. But the fact is, Christians still reap in their own lives the evils their ancestors have committed.

I was ministering to a well-known Holy Spirit–filled pastor. His brother (even more famous) was also a Spirit-filled pastor, as were their father, grandfather and great-grandfather. Each of the brothers had lost his first son to tragic death. Their oldest brother, their father's first son, had also died early and tragically. Their grandfather's first son had died young, as had their great-grandfather's first son.

This pastor and I tracked through his generations, by the guidance of the Holy Spirit, and found a particular sin that had been reaped continually in the tragic deaths of first sons throughout many generations. When he repented, representing his family, and I pronounced forgiveness, we could and did claim that the pattern of death was now ended on the cross of Christ. The tragic deaths stopped.

How Generational Sin Descends

That family's problem was one of the most dramatic I have encountered. But about the issue itself I remain mystified.

Maybe it is similar to inheriting a parent's estate and having to pay any outstanding debts—but that does not cover all the ground. I cannot explain why, in the lives of dedicated and holy servants of the Lord, a pattern like that could continue unabated. God does not want His people to suffer, especially needlessly. But apparently in God's legal universe, some sins must be prayed about specifically, or else the reaping continues.

I have found through thousands of first-person accounts that there are three ways generational sin descends.

By Physical Genes

Many African-Americans inherit a tendency toward sickle-cell anemia. Most Native Americans inherit the inability to handle alcohol. Many of us complain about some ailment, such as our families' bad back problems. Job 17:5 says, "He who informs against friends for a share of the spoil, the eyes of his children also shall languish." Does this mean that all of us who have to wear glasses can blame our ancestors for taking bribes? Hardly. But even though it does not mean we can trace all eye troubles to this one cause, a little research into the family history might reveal clues that lead to healing—of eyes and of many other things.

By Modeling Others' Behavior

Generational sin also descends through the modeling of our parents, siblings, teachers, grandparents and others. We tend to become what they do rather than what they say. Good and

185

bad characteristics alike are passed down from generation to generation through modeling.

By Law

Romans 2:1 tells us that if we judge another, we are guilty of the same thing or something similar. Condemnatory judging causes us to become like whatever we are criticizing in another, unless grace intervenes. But most cogently by far, troubles descend by the law of sowing and reaping (see Galatians 6:7). We must understand the inevitability of this law. There are no exceptions. It is part of the dependability of God and His universe. Law is law. Whatever is sown must be reaped.

For this reason Jesus said, "Whoever in the name of a disciple gives to one of these little ones even a cup of cold water to drink, truly I say to you, *he shall not lose his reward*" (Matthew 10:42, emphasis added). God's computers do not crash; there is no way anyone can do a good deed and not receive a reward. Sowing and reaping was also the principle Jesus was referring to when He admonished us not to store up "treasures on earth, where moth and rust destroy, and where thieves break in and steal," but to "store up . . . treasures in heaven" (Matthew 6:19–20). We do that first and foremost by doing good deeds. Especially when we do good deeds and suffer for them, He tells us, "Your reward in heaven is great" (Matthew 5:12).

Forgiveness and redemption do not mean God looks the other way. *Every sin must be paid for.* Jesus did that for us on the cross—although in His wisdom He may allow us to reap a small portion of what we deserve in order to teach and discipline us, in order to write the lesson on our hearts (see Jeremiah 31:33).

But we cannot stop there. The descending of generational sins by law is compounded by the fact that Satan understands the principle of sowing and reaping. He knows that not only will our children and their descendants reap the good we have sown; they will also reap the evil. He also knows our ignorance about law, that we think we can just do this or that "little" sin and nothing will come of it! We do not realize there is no escape from consequences—except by grace.

That gives Satan inroads to tempt us. And regarding our own forefathers, the devil knows what weaknesses we have inherited in our flesh and how to set up circumstances that can match our worst tendencies. It means he can take hold of unrequited sins in our ancestry and send all kinds of troubles on us—bringing harm before grace can prompt repentance that would grant deliverance. He sends hundreds of his minions to track and plan how to make use of whatever evil is descended from our blood lines.

Examples from History

In 1869, when the Osage tribe was being moved from eastern Kansas into Oklahoma, white soldiers raped some of the women along the way. They did so calculatingly, knowing how fiercely Osage braves would defend their women. They wanted to lure the Osages into fighting in order to have an excuse to kill them, as happened later to a Sioux tribe at Wounded Knee. The elders were aware of this and forbade revenge. But this left "bitter root judgments"—those bitter judgments lodged in the heart against others, which sow seeds that must be reaped. Relatives and friends struggled to forgive, but a bitter root expectancy was left smoldering in Osage tribal hearts: White men will do great harm to Osage women.

In Osage County, Oklahoma, shortly after arriving there in 1869, council members decreed that any Osage could sell his allotted land, but that whatever might be found in the ground or in the air above would belong to the entire tribe equally, no matter who owned the land. The rolls were closed in 1907. Shortly afterward oil was discovered in Osage County—one of the largest oilfields in history. All enrolled Osages became wealthy instantly. Every three months large royalty checks came to each tribal member who held a headright in the nation. (Not every Osage had been willing to sign up.)

Because Osages knew little about handling money, white men moved in to swindle and cheat. The investigation of such swindling was actually one of the reasons the Federal Bureau of Investigation was formed. Unscrupulous white men, including drifters, alcoholics and malingerers, began to woo and marry young Osage women for their money. They drank heavily, beat their wives and probably even killed some of them in order to obtain their headrights. Again, bitter root judgments formed in Osage hearts: Worthless white men will harm Osage women.

In both cases, first with the soldiers, then with the swindlers, the Osages were innocent victims. But law is law. Those bitter root judgments set in motion forces that had to be reaped. I have discovered that what happened in other Osage families was, in many cases, worse than what happened in my own—but the pattern was the same.

My father was a good man, but by the time I was ten he could not support the family because of financial reverses and alcohol. We were raised on the food that came from my milk cows and garden, as well as Osage oil money, which at that time had dwindled to a hundred dollars a month.

My aunt married a doctor who, in the 1950s, made about thirty thousand dollars a year (equivalent to perhaps $150,000 today). But he drank, gave her no money to raise their three children and beat her—until she divorced him. She had inherited a one-half headright and used Osage money, as well as her skill as a music teacher, to raise their children. One of their two daughters married a violent alcoholic and divorced him, and the other did not marry at all until after Paula and I prayed and our entire family was set free.

Of my older brother's two daughters, the first married a "worthless" man and divorced him. The second has never married.

My younger brother has three daughters. Two married the same kind of "worthless" man and divorced. Only the Lord's grace keeps the first daughter married.

My only sister married an alcoholic who sat in front of the TV and drank himself to death while she earned the money to raise their three girls. Each of her daughters married the same kind of man and divorced him.

Paula and I have two daughters. Ami married a man who was unfaithful to her and molested their daughter. She divorced him. It was during our prayers for Ami that we discovered generational sin and how it works.

The Lord has stopped the pattern. Andrea has married a fine Christian man. Ami, too, has now married a fine Christian man who serves the Lord with her.

Now that the pattern is broken, each of my sister's three daughters has remarried well. My younger brother's daughters are beginning to find good lives as well. And my aunt's second daughter has married well, too.

It sounds phenomenal, doesn't it? But before Paula and I prayed, not one married woman on my side of the family escaped the pattern.

The longer anything of evil proceeds without repentance, the greater the reaping and the more persistent the pattern of evil.

The Spread of Harm

Innumerable harmful results may descend as a result of previous sin. (Note that judgments made in the Osage Nation as a whole were reaped by its individual families.) Tendencies to cancer, allergies, lung problems or circulation disorders may descend from sins in previous generations. The relationship between sin and disease is clearly documented in Scripture. Jesus said to the sick man, for example, whom He healed at the pool of Bethesda, "Do not sin anymore, so that nothing worse happens to you" (John 5:14).

While tracking troubles that descend through families, however, we need to be careful not to leap to conclusions. Not every present illness can be traced to ancestral sin:

> [Jesus'] disciples asked Him, saying, "Rabbi, who sinned, this man or his parents, that he would be born blind?" Jesus answered, "It was neither that this man sinned, nor his parents; but it was so that the works of God might be displayed in him."
>
> John 9:2–3

Some problems are caused by sins in our progenitors' lives and some are not. Some originate in our own lives or because we are members of a group involved in present sin. In Genesis 20 Abraham lied to Abimelech, king of Gerar, saying Sarah was his sister; and when the king took Sarah into his household, intending to go to bed with her, all the wombs of his household were closed. His wife and her maids were innocent, but they suffered simply because they were members of his household. God warned Abimelech, moreover, that unless he restored Abraham's wife, they all would die.

Tendencies to sexual perversion, homosexuality, frigidity, barrenness, tragic early deaths, a lack of boys or girls born into a family generation after generation—any of these can descend from ancestral sins.

Additional harmful reaping includes depression, bipolarism, mental imbalance, neuroses and psychoses, alcoholism and chemical addiction. I prayed for one woman and her Indian family. Her uncles were all hopelessly alcoholic. A year later, when I saw her again, she had just come from a family reunion. All her uncles had come to the Lord and had stopped drinking! Prayer is powerful.

Then there are separations and divorces. One man I ministered to was the third child of his mother's fifth marriage. His mother was one of twelve children; so was his father. Not one of those 24 had been married only once! Most had been married several times. He himself was on his third marriage and it was failing.

The list of woes is endless. You can find more information in *Healing the Wounded Spirit* and *A Comprehensive Guide to Deliverance and Inner Healing*. There I teach in full how to deliver people from generational, inherited patterns. Here let me only sketch it.

First, see the patterns; inquire into the family tree. Look for repeated occurrences in grandparents, parents, aunts, uncles, cousins and so on. List them. Pray, first giving thanks for all the good that has come from those forefathers. Then place the cross, through prayer, between your forefathers and the person (tribe, region, state, nation), declaring that all the destructive patterns inherited from the ancestors now stop on the cross of Christ. Name the patterns, believing that Jesus has died with them on the cross. Repent on behalf of those who have gone before, and for yourself. Receive forgiveness. Pray blessing, declaring that the very opposite of the harmful descendancy will now replace it. Give thanks. Reaffirm the prayer whenever you feel led, keeping at it for at least several weeks. Then give thanks, believing it is done.

How Nations Are Affected

Let's look now at ways generational sin affects individuals within their particular nations, and ways those nations—specifically religious, political and ethnic—are affected by the sins of their individual members.

Religious Generational Patterns

Paula and I have often been called on to look into the history of a local church because of a pattern of persecuting and casting out its pastors. Invariably this pattern starts in a bitter judgment made against a previous pastor many times removed from the present. We have sat in meetings in which one could almost see a satanic anointing come on certain church members, to the point that they demonstrated irrational thinking and spouted innuendo or outright slander—all the while apparently considering themselves righteous. Once generational patterns were revealed and repented of, and the blood of forgiveness applied, these same church members were apt to speak wisely and with forbearance.

In one church more than four successive pastors' wives had suffered debilitating illness and died or been killed in an accident. We found the cause in the rivalry and jealousy of a pastor's wife several pastors earlier. When we repented and prayed forgiveness, bringing that descendancy to death on the cross, the pattern stopped.

Observe that the pastors and wives were "innocent." They suffered by reaping the generational sins of their religious "nation."

Satan loves to blindside people, especially Christians, hitting them through generational patterns. He knows they may have

191

no idea why this awful thing has been allowed to happen. He hopes they will cry out against God and lose faith. Truly "My people are destroyed for lack of knowledge" (Hosea 4:6).

Political Generational Patterns

Paula and I know a number of believers in Germany who struggle to experience God in their spirits. To them the Christian faith is primarily mental. If they begin to experience rather than simply apprehend the Holy Spirit, their minds jump into the experience, analyze, box and kill it. They are like a young medical student who was doing fine with his fiancée until one night, as he was kissing her, she caught him holding her pulse and checking his watch! That is what the mind does to spiritual experiences.

Almost a thousand years ago Germanic people turned from experiencing God to thinking about Him. For four centuries, from A.D. 950 to 1350, the Eastern and Western wings of the Roman Catholic Church drifted apart from each other. The Eastern, Greek wing was moving toward piety and becoming more mystical than theological. The Western, Latin wing was becoming more theological, logical, structured and organized. In Germany the emphasis on the cerebral went further, until many came to believe that we are body and soul but that we do not have a personal spirit. Over the centuries this overly mental approach to anything religious became an entrapping, blocking stronghold. (I have encountered it many times when teaching in that country.)

In 1998, when Michael Ellis, one of our Elijah House counselors, was in Germany with Paula and me to do ministry, he reported that ninety percent of the people who came to him had the same problem: They could not experience God in their spirits or break beyond the confines of their own practiced mentality. They were experiencing the inheritance of evil in their religious nationality, accompanied by blocking spirits.

When Paula and I taught at the University of the Nations (one part of missionary training for Youth With A Mission, an international evangelistic organization), some Japanese people who took our course on Christian counseling complained of two conditions besetting them. First they struggled with performance orientation, a condition of striving to perform well enough to deserve the love of God and others. Regardless of how many times they heard the message of free grace, they were conditioned into continual dread of failure and fear of rejection if they did not do everything rightly.

The second besetting condition was worse. In centuries past, whenever a new emperor took office, he withdrew to a mountaintop to cohabit with the goddess of fertility for a month, in order to induce fertility among his people. He would experience sensations of intercourse with the "goddess"—actually, a demonic succuba spirit. The result has been a virulent descendancy of sexual infidelity and perversion among Japanese men.

Bruce Thompson, one of the leaders of YWAM, informed Paula and me that Japan is one of their most difficult mission fields, and that missionaries to Japan must be circumspect, because they may begin to suffer sexual problems in their own lives. A stronghold of sexual perversion lies over the nation. Through it Satan pressures moral people, tempts weaker ones and creates havoc in many lives.

For centuries England was the nation that ruled the seas. Her ships controlled the world's waters. But that meant a disproportionate number of her men were out at sea for months at a time. Their wives had to take over and run the households. Britain became a matriarchal society. Witness how often England has been ruled by queens rather than kings. Conservative prime minister Margaret Thatcher led the nation for eleven years.

As a counselor I can tell you that we minister to more cases of sexual frigidity in British women, and relational passivity in British men, than in any other nation. Matriarchalism has become a powerful stronghold there—and largely hidden. At this point in our ministry among them, few English women or men have been willing to acknowledge that the condition exists or wanted to do anything about it.

I could catalog peculiar traits in many nations of the world, but one is outstanding. Australians, like many Americans, are usually warm, open and outspoken. But that nation (as you probably recall) began as a British penal colony, criminal outcasts abused by some British guards and soldiers. One of the historical results has been a "down under" mentality, bitter root judgments and expectancies to be abused and regularly given the short end of the stick. In war this has meant that almost invariably they are assigned to suicidal tasks like Gallipoli.

At Gallipoli during World War I, in the ultimately disastrous Allied expedition to capture the Dardanelles Straits, Australians were ordered to charge uphill against entrenched machine guns, to protect British landings on the beach below. Repeatedly they charged heroically and were mowed down—after which it was discovered that the English had long since landed successfully and were sitting comfortably on the beach having tea.

In the Second World War Australians were assigned to attack entrenched Japanese positions in the jungle mountains of Borneo, in tropical heat and humidity, often through downpours and swarmed by biting insects.

Today, politically and economically, Australians still expect and often receive the same kind of treatment.

Ethnic Generational Patterns

Ethnic generational patterns may be the worst. The historic hatred between Hutus and Tutsis in Rwanda, for instance, resulted in the massacre of hundreds of thousands. The centuries-old racial and religious sins of the forefathers in Yugoslavia have been reaped in recent years in a holocaust of war, massacre, rape and devastation.

All over the world indigenous peoples—for example, the Kurds of southwest Asia—have been largely disenfranchised, sometimes enslaved, often used, misused and abused.

How to Start the Healing Process

In all of these—religious, political and ethnic nations—Satan has enjoyed a playing field orchestrating multitudes into senseless activities and reactions. The combination of corporate mental strongholds and generational sin has enabled the "world forces of this darkness" to rule almost unchecked.

Ignorance and apathy have allowed these patterns to continue far too long. This book is calling the citizens within or descended from each nation—religious, political or ethnic—to arise in Spirit-filled fervency and go to war. Christians can heal generational sin, dislodge corporate mental strongholds, heal and set the imprisoned free. How? Individuals and groups called and guided by the Lord can study the histories of families, churches, groups, cities, regions and nations, then pray through these histories in repentance and with expressions of forgiveness.

In 1997 I was speaking at a meeting along with Jean Steffenson, head of the Native American Resource Network (formerly called the International Reconciliation Coalition), which works to accomplish reconciliation and healing among the tribes. She is part Cherokee. Both of us were well aware that the Cherokee tribe had been moved during Andrew Jackson's presidency from Georgia down the "Trail of Tears" into Missouri, thus being relocated in Osage territory, where the two tribes slaughtered one another three times! I felt led by the Holy Spirit at the meeting to ask Jean if we could say prayers of forgiveness and healing as representatives of our tribes. She agreed.

Both of us thought this would be only a simple, ritualistic kind of asking for and speaking forgiveness. But when we prayed, something powerful happened. It was as if a bolt of light flashed out of heaven down through both of us and out into the world. I felt it coursing right through the generations, and I burst into tears, as did Jean.

Who knows what God accomplished that day, and continues to accomplish, because of our invitation through mutual asking of forgiveness? We know something mighty happened—and still does.

Prayer groups can examine their cities' history and pray through whatever sins are found, overcoming or upsetting resultant patterns of harm. No formula, no special training or way of praying is needed. Wherever sin has occurred, repentance and forgiveness are needed. Wherever animosities have existed, words of reconciliation—repentance and forgiveness—can be said by whomever the Lord prompts. Destructive behavioral patterns can be reckoned as dead on the cross. Usually a living participant or direct descendant can pray most effectively.

After studying Osage history, I walked in prayer through the events of our past with the Lord, repenting on behalf of my ancestors, receiving forgiveness and praying that any patterns—like the bitter root judgment about Osage women—be stopped on the cross of Christ.

What wonders might result if individuals or groups in every ethnic nation of the world were to respond in prayer? Germans could be set free from their analyzing mindset. In England matriarchalism could be reversed. Australians could leave behind the bitter root judgments that they are to be taken advantage of. Discrimination against African-Americans could be smashed once for all. And prejudice against Jews might lose its grip on the hearts of people all over the world.

Ever since Abraham fathered his first son, Ishmael, by Sarah's maid, Hagar, after which Ishmael was cast away, history has enacted repeated instances of rivalry and outright hatred between Arabs and Jews. Wars and terrorist activities have exploded down through the centuries. What if a sufficiently large number of messianic Arabs and Jews were called by God into a siege of prayers for repentance, forgiveness and reconciliation, and into warfare to bind the ancient strongholds of sibling rivalry, hatred and violence? Could the final battle of Armageddon be turned into an event that neither Satan nor the world expects? Could that possibly become a spiritual battle in which the fire of God falls to consume the armies of hatred within us all?

I do not say it will be so, and hardly dare to hope, but who knows what God might do?

Someday reconciliation will happen between Jew and Gentile, because "[Christ] Himself is our peace, who made both groups into one and broke down the barrier of the dividing wall" (Ephesians 2:14). Will that just happen, or will God's end-time prayer warriors have something to do with it?

I related in chapter 3 that well-intentioned missionaries have often confused Christianity with their own national cultures and consequently denigrated native cultures. Frequently they forbade native arts, songs, dances and regalia. Even though a European could die to himself in Christ and be reborn within his own cultural identity, natives were told there was nothing redeemable in theirs. To get saved they had to become "white," lost to the cultural heritage of their own souls.

But now the Holy Spirit is raising groups of native Christians who are rediscovering the glory God created within their own cultural heritage. One such group, which took much of its inspiration from John Dawson's works, is the World Christian Gathering of Indigenous People. Their first international gathering was hosted by the Maori Nation at Rotorua, New Zealand, in November 1996, led by Monte Ohia.

More than two thousand Christian natives attended from more than thirty countries and many more tribes. Sharing of hurt and affliction was part of each tribal group's presentation, resulting in much healing as many silent prayers were offered.

Day by day each group presented its own songs and dances, attired in its own unique regalia. Maori men did the *haka*—a dance, now redeemed, used originally to call forth spirits of war. With power and fervor they portrayed the death and resurrection of the Lord and His triumph over evil. The entire gathering rose spontaneously with shouts of joy as exhilaration and worship filled our hearts. What God had created was being resurrected, transformed and honored. Glory was being given back to Him.

The joy of the Lord cascaded through me in waves that smashed my heart into tears, and I cried out to God to continue to set His children free from bondages that we early Christians have created among them.

Two Mandates for the Church

What a wonder it is to see God move throughout the world to resurrect what Satan thought he killed! If the Lord's call can be heard by enough prayer warriors, the devil's field of division and animosity can be destroyed, and healing through understanding and acceptance can prosper.

Many prophecies have come forth that through His indigenous people around the world, God will begin the prophesied great revival before the Lord Jesus returns. Surely the calling to pray for the healing of indigenous nations outranks most others!

When the Lord first called Paula and me to begin the work of Elijah House, He gave us two scriptural mandates: Malachi 4:5–6, to unify fathers and children, and Matthew 17:11, to restore the Church.

1. Unifying Fathers and Children

Malachi 4:5–6 says:

> "Behold, I am going to send you Elijah the prophet before the coming of the great and terrible day of the LORD. He will restore the hearts of the fathers to their children and the hearts of the children to their fathers, so that I will not come and smite the land with a curse."

Attempting to fulfill this first mandate to heal families has consumed our prayers and energies for 25 years. Now the Lord has spoken to say that Paula and I have interpreted that text too narrowly. Fathers and children carry broader meanings as well.

Jews and Christians

The Jewish people are the fathers of Christianity. Unless our hearts are turned toward them, how shall we mature into who God has created us to be, and how shall we be blessed?

Many of the early Church Fathers wrote diatribes against the Jewish people who refused to convert. Historically Christians have often been part of pogroms against them. The Nazis who slaughtered the Jews wore the iron cross and most attended church. This shameful history needs to be redeemed through prayers of repentance and acts of contrition, accompanied by dialogue and shared works in love.

198

Roman Catholics and Protestants

Roman Catholics are the fathers from whom Protestantism sprang. Centuries of war, hubris on both sides, rejection and disparagement of one another's ways have disgraced the name of our loving Lord before the world. Our hearts need to be turned toward one another. The bells of unity must ring throughout the world.

Many devout Christians the world over have already responded to the Lord's call and have begun to pray fervently to dislodge Satan's devices of division and to work to establish unity. But the battle has only begun. I trust that the Holy Spirit will raise a multitudinous army that will not quit until its prayers are heard and the Lord's Body sings one great chorus of unity and love in action.

Indigenous Peoples and Colonists

Indigenous people in any country are the fathers, colonists the children. Hearts must be turned toward one another in repentance, forgiveness and reconciliation. All of this lest, in the warning of Malachi, the earth be smitten with a curse!

God's Mature Sons and Daughters Will Arise

Is not our work cut out before us? Who can miss the calling of the Lord once he or she understands the issues at hand?

The work must be carried out by all, but it is the fathers and mothers in Christ (spoken of in chapter 6) who must arise and take the lead. There will come a time when the nation of these mature sons and daughters of God will be revealed (see Romans 8:18–25). Many eschatological passages prophesy the birth of the state of Israel. More and more Christians are coming to see that these same passages refer as well to our own birth into what God wants in the end time—and why not? The two are made one, neither able to arise in fullness without the other, if we comprehend our Lord's nature and plan.

> "Who has heard such a thing? Who has seen such things? Can a land be born in a day? Can a nation be brought forth all at once? As soon as Zion travailed, she also brought forth her sons. Shall

I bring to the point of birth and not give delivery?" says the Lord. "Or shall I who gives delivery shut the womb?" says your God. "Be joyful with Jerusalem and rejoice for her, all you who love her; be exceedingly glad with her, all you who mourn over her, that you may nurse and be satisfied with her comforting breasts, that you may suck and be delighted with her bountiful bosom."

For thus says the Lord, "Behold, I extend peace to her like a river, and the glory of the nations like an overflowing stream; and you will be nursed, you will be carried on the hip and fondled on the knees. As one whom his mother comforts, so I will comfort you; and you will be comforted in Jerusalem." Then you will see this, and your heart will be glad, and your bones will flourish like the new grass; and the hand of the Lord will be made known to His servants.

Isaiah 66:8–14, emphasis added

Note first that it is when the Church learns to travail that the Lord's mature sons and daughters will be brought forth—in a hurry, all at once, in a day. And so will Israel.

Travailing does not merely mean weeping before the altar of the Lord. Rather it is connected to Paul's travail that "I am again in labor *until Christ is formed in you*" (Galatians 4:19, emphasis added). Paul is referring to literal labor pains, as in giving birth. The Isaiah prophecy uses the same metaphor, speaking primarily of burden-bearing—sharing our Lord's labor pains as He groans to give birth to His mature, end-time saints and to His own people generationally.

Observe also the progression. First God's own are to be nursed at the breast; then carried on the hip; then fondled on the knees, comforted as a mother comforts; and finally spoken of as His servants. The nurture and comfort that brings about maturity is to come through the Church. It is we who are to raise one another into maturity as one new man, as Ephesians 4:14–16 says so eloquently.

2. Restoring the Church

The second scriptural mandate Paula and I received when we first began the work of Elijah House was Matthew 17:11:

200

[Jesus] answered and said, "Elijah is coming and will restore all things."

For 25 years we thought of the task of restoring only from within our hope for the Church—and so have worked tirelessly for unity. But again the Holy Spirit has expanded our sight. He means, of course, first the nation of the Church, as a type of Elijah. But the Church is meant to be His means to restore His Kingdom. God will unite Jews and Christians (in heart if not in theology) and move to heal all the nations and the earth. But the Church must arise before all else can be restored. Here is where Satan's devices of criticism, Pharisaism, legalism, traditionalism, control and judgment must be defeated.

When Jesus said, "Elijah is coming and will restore all things," He was speaking of His Second Coming. That is the fundamental purpose of this book—to call the nation of the Church to the essential task of restoration. But first the Church herself must be set free, healed and restored to God's original purposes for her—not just to convert souls, though that will always be primary, but also to prepare the earth for Jesus' return and to clothe herself with holiness and maturity as a bride adorned and prepared for her husband.

Would we set free ethnic and political nations from generational bondages and corporate mental strongholds? Our own eyes are full of logs—telephone poles!—that must be removed through repentance and prayer.

God's call is for churches and prayer groups throughout Christendom to take on whatever projects of intercession for healing generational sin and breaking the power of strongholds that the Holy Spirit leads us into; and, in the process of serving, to nurture one another into the fullness of maturity He intends for all of us.

Praise the Lord, He is not coming back for a defeated and bedraggled bride! We shall be ready. Will we be found serving to heal and restore the nations when He arrives? My faith celebrates that we will.

ELEVEN

HEALING AND DELIVERANCE THROUGH SPIRITUAL WARFARE FOR THE NATIONS

by Cindy Jacobs,
Co-founder, Generals of Intercession

The subject of how to heal nations has been important to me since a remarkable time I had with God in 1985. On the third day of praying and fasting for the United States, I posed a question to the Lord: "Father, since Satan is not omnipresent or omniscient, how is he so effective in his war over the nations?"

The Lord spoke back to me a single word in a still, small voice: *Strategy*.

Eventually it became clear to me that the enemy has a strategy for every nation and ministry. I also recognized that his army does not rest from battle.

In response to my question concerning Satan's inroads, the Lord impressed me to gather His "generals" or leaders of intercession together. One of the assignments of those meetings was to ask God to forgive the sins of our nation. I am embarrassed to say that I had to ask Him, "What *are* the sins of my nation?" The Lord listed sins such as the Trail of Tears (the relocation of the Cherokee tribe into Osage territory, where the two tribes slaughtered one another three times!); slavery; the Japanese being put into internment camps; and other such atrocities.

At the time I received this vision, neither my husband, Mike, nor I dreamed it would lead to the founding of an international organization called Generals of Intercession. Nor did we know that prayer groups based on the principles God was teaching us would help bring healing to nations all over the world. We were just following God the best we knew how, one meeting at a time.

Have you ever noticed that life with God is always an adventure? Just when you think you can sort of handle the last assignment He gave you, He says, *Now do this*, and it is more than you begin to know how to do! It has always been that way with Mike and me. Healing nations is a big job, to say the least.

I know it sounds strange to state that believers are called to heal nations through prayer and intercession. In fact, to the best of my recollection, when the Lord first spoke to me in that vision, I had never even heard all those words used in the same sentence! But since I had been reared in a good, Bible-believing home, the first place I went was to God's Word. If I could find no Scripture passage that talked about the healing of nations, I would figure it was something that had come from eating too much pizza!

To my surprise and delight, however, I learned that the Bible does indeed make provision for nations to be healed:

> In the middle of its street, and on either side of the river, was the tree of life, which bore twelve fruits, each tree yielding its

fruit every month. The leaves of the tree were for the *healing of the nations*.

Revelation 22:2, NKJV, emphasis added

A related passage is Ezekiel 47:12 (NKJV):

"Along the bank of the river, on this side and that, will grow all kinds of trees used for food; their leaves will not wither, and their fruit will not fail. They will bear fruit every month, because their water flows from the sanctuary. Their fruit will be for food, and their leaves for medicine."

The next question I posed to the Lord was this: "Well, then, Lord, how do you heal a nation?"

Knowing that I am extremely simple (I have to have my son or husband help me with almost everything mechanical), God posed a question back to me: *Cindy, how do you bring healing to an individual's life?*

At the time I was praying regularly for people who needed personal healing and deliverance, so I understood what the Lord meant. And this is what I gleaned from applying principles of personal deliverance to nations:

1. Nations have sin.
2. Nations sin against other nations.
3. This sin, unless repented of, allows Satan to oppress the nations.
4. The sin of nations can also cause judgment.
5. It is up to the Christians who live in the nations to repent of the sin to stop Satan's legal right of oppression. We now call this "identificational repentance."

In 1985 Mike and I started having prayer meetings in which we repented for the sins of our nation, as well as for those between the U.S. and other nations. In 1986 we repented with Christian leaders in Tulsa, Oklahoma, for the atrocities of the Trail of Tears. That same year we went to Pasadena, California, and repented for our having put the Japanese in internment

204

camps during World War II. Later that year we flew to Vancouver, British Columbia, where we met with Canadian Christian leaders and repented to them for how the U.S. had treated them. In 1987 we met in England with British and European leaders for reconciliation for the way they felt we had abandoned them during the beginning of World War II.

Little did we know at the time how the kind of praying we were doing was linked to revival. For a while we had been able to make only isolated efforts in prayer. It was hard to comprehend the impact to the whole country. But a dramatic turn of events led to my being able to look at the history of a whole nation, to study it and to begin to teach intercessors how to begin to heal it.

What Happened in Argentina?

Mike and I were in Washington, D.C., in 1989 at a prayer summit. One of the speakers for the meetings was a professor who taught at Fuller Theological Seminary. Little did we know how meeting Dr. C. Peter Wagner would change our lives.

One day during lunch Mike and I began to get to know Peter and his wife, Doris. They seemed fascinated to hear that our call was to heal nations. And from that day we became not only friends but like family.

Sometime after that I learned that Peter and Doris, who had been missionaries to Bolivia, were discussing a former student of Peter's one day and the ministry that this world-class missiologist, Ed Silvoso, was having in Argentina. Ed was developing a model to reach a whole city (which has since become a part of city-reaching strategies the world over). Doris commented to Peter that the strategy had something missing. Not only prayer but spiritual warfare, she said, was needed bring healing to a city and nation. Doris also knew that Argentina was under a curse put on it by José Lopez Regá, a former prime minister who was a warlock.

Suddenly she brightened. "We know someone who brings healing to nations. Let's call Cindy Jacobs and get her and Ed to work together."

They called me on the phone. But looking at my calendar (and being the spiritual person that I am), I turned them down flat!

I should have known better. God and the Wagners are an unbeatable team. If I had known then what I know now, I would have responded, "Let me see how I can change my calendar."

Months later, in the fall of 1989, I was staying with Peter and Doris after a meeting in California and mentioned that I had a cancellation on my schedule for the following June. Because it was some eight months away, I thought I was perfectly safe. Things do not move that fast internationally.

Right? Wrong. As I said before, if I had known then what I know now, I would not even have thought that way.

They got excited about the opening and asked if I would go to Argentina. Doris said she would go with me—which sounded good, especially since she speaks Spanish.

"If Mike says it's O.K.," I replied, "I'll go."

I never thought Mike would agree.

The turn of events made my head spin. Peter called Mike, who said yes. Then Peter called Ed Silvoso, who flew in from San Jose the next morning to make plans. And the next thing I knew, I was scheduled to join Doris Wagner, Ed Silvoso and other leaders in Argentina, along with our good friends Dave and Jane Rumph, to help bring healing to this South American nation.

Doing Spiritual Mapping

Before going in June 1990, we asked several spiritual leaders to study Argentina. We now call this kind of study "spiritual mapping"—backing prayer with diligent research to discern connections between the physical history of a land and the spiritual issues to be prayed for—but in those days we did not know what to call what we were doing. We simply realized that Satan had built historic places of darkness that had caused that nation to resist the Gospel.

One of the cities in which Ed Silvoso was working, a major trade and shipping center on the Paraná River in northeast Argentina, was actually called Resistencia, or "resistance." One cult in the city worshiped San La Muerte—Saint Death. Life was so bad that they sacrificed to this idol in hopes of having at least a good death after a miserable life. If ever a city needed healing, it was this one!

Not only was the city of Resistencia in trouble, but the whole nation. The inflation rate was three thousand percent per year. Costs fluctuated so much in one day that products were assigned numbers rather than prices, with the actual prices contingent on the current exchange rate. Our friend Claudio Freidzon reported that one day he went to buy a sack of sugar, only to find that the price had jumped between the time he walked from the aisle to the checkout stand!

Identifying the Strongholds

As we studied the strongholds over the nation of Argentina to see how we needed to proceed with a prayer strategy, we asked the Lord two questions:

1. What is Satan's legal entrance to hurt the economy?
2. How do we close the door so the nation can be healed?

The issues were complex, of course, but one major problem was the alliance the government had made with witchcraft. José Lopez Regá, as prime minister, had built a statue honoring witchcraft, and later had cursed the country when he was put out of office. We knew this assignment needed to be broken. For this we would go to the nation's capital, Buenos Aires.

We found a number of other governmental strongholds affecting the nation and the economy while in Buenos Aires. During World War II, for example, the Argentine government had harbored Nazi war criminals, and many rumors circulated as to the amounts of gold that government officials had received for allowing the Germans to immigrate. This was serious. The Bible is clear that we are called to pray for the peace of Jerusalem (see, for example, Psalm 122:6 and Isaiah 62). I knew that repentance for sinning against Israel and the Jewish people would be a key to the healing of Argentina's economy.

Another major stronghold was the issue of the "disappeared ones," which started in 1983 when the government kidnapped people on their way home from work. These people would never be seen or heard from again. Reports suggest that thirty thousand or more died in this tragic way. This left a big wound in the heart of the Argentine people.

A root issue that had brought a curse on the land was the killing of the indigenous people by the Spanish *conquistadores* who conquered the land. These soldiers slaughtered many of the Indian peoples and confiscated their property.

The final national stronghold we had to deal with in order to bring healing to the nation was the sin of idolatry. The first commandment is clear as to what God thinks about our worship of other gods: "You shall have no other gods before Me" (Exodus 20:3, NKJV). It was evident, as I looked around the main plaza in Buenos Aires, that the Argentineans had definitely broken this commandment.

Preparing for Warfare

How did we prepare to do battle, once we actually arrived in Argentina?

First we asked the Lord where we should hold our prayer meeting. We met with different Christian leaders to strategize. They all agreed: The place to pray in Buenos Aires was the Plaza Mayo, the plaza in front of the Casa Rosada, or Pink House (the White House for the nation of Argentina). Lining the run-down plaza were buildings representing each of the strongholds that needed prayer.

We decided to meet at 7:30 A.M. so the plaza would be empty of the usual traffic that gathered later. We also reasoned that both the early hour and the cold temperature—remember, in Argentina in June it is winter—would protect us from gawkers or those who disapproved of what we were doing.

The group had to meet various criteria. First, they had to be free from known sin in their lives; second, they had to be unafraid; and third, they had to sense a leading from the Lord to be part of the team. We also recruited a team of intercessors who would stay and pray for us while we went out into the plaza.

Our little band included some of the greatest Christian leaders in Argentina. Eduardo Lorenzo, a Baptist pastor who is almost legendary in his country, was there to "cover" us with spiritual authority. Marfa Cabrerra, a pioneer leader who recently went to be with the Lord, helped translate and stand in the gap for her country. Other great leaders also joined us who have gone on to help change their nation in a big way.

Demolishing the Strongholds

That morning in June 1990 dawned clear and very cold—one of many times the weather has protected us intercessors from the preying eyes of people, even officials, who might want to imprison us or even beat us to death if they knew what we were doing.

Our first point of intercession for Argentina, during five hours of prayer, was to deal with the oldest sin—that of the killing of the Indians by the Spaniards, starting in the sixteenth century. Pastor Lorenzo, who is of Spanish descent, was willing to stand in the gap for his people, as Daniel did for the Israelites (see Daniel 9:2–5). The place we chose to pray was the Cabilldo— the first government house built by the Spanish on the plaza.

Pastor Lorenzo prayed and asked God for forgiveness for the confiscation of the land and the slaughter that his Spanish ancestors had perpetrated on the Indian people. We also asked God to reveal their plight to the congress of Argentina.

It interested me that a congressman "happened along" after we prayed and asked what we were doing. He told us he would take a report of our prayer meeting back to the Congress.

Next we went to the government building where José Lopez Regá had his office. This was a powerful and moving prayer. The leaders prayed and repented for the sin of witchcraft. One could actually feel the powers of darkness giving way as Pastor Lorenzo prayed with great authority. Then we proceeded to break the curse on the physical land and on the government, in the name of Jesus; and we asked God to restore the damage done to the land and to the government.

Another area of intercession that day regarded the "disappeared ones." We prayed at the War Department, where the decisions had been made to order the killing and kidnapping of people who were often innocent. This prayer paved the way for the healing of the broken heart of the nation, just as for the broken heart of an individual. People's hearts were indeed opened to one another, and forgiveness flowed.

Recognizing the need for the land to be prayed over and redeemed (see Deuteronomy 21 and 2 Chronicles 7:13–14), we prayed and broke the curses that came on the land itself from the shedding of innocent blood.

Another strategic place to pray was at the government buildings that had housed officials who agreed to harbor Nazi war criminals in exchange for gold. We prayed repentance for the greed of the nation, for not blessing the people of Israel and for outright anti-Semitism.

At this point we sensed the Lord saying that He was going to change the guard in the government.

Beloved, not to get weird, but when we talk to God, He talks back! I have walked out of buildings with intercessors all over the world to bells ringing and rainbows splashing in the sky over my head. And at this point during our prayers at the Plaza Mayo, just after the Lord indicated that He was going to change the guard in the government, we saw, to our surprise, the changing of the *presidential* guard right before our eyes! Then, as we prayed for the president of Argentina, we looked up and saw the flag being hoisted up—a sign that the president had just come into the Casa Rosada.

I hope I do not need to tell you that we did not try to time these events or make them happen. They just did.

Our last prayer was of repentance for the worship of idols, which we did very discreetly. Major leaders repented and asked God to restore the land. And at this point in our prayers, the bells began ringing in a nearby cathedral. We had hardly noticed the time, but we had been praying for five hours. Our feet felt like blocks of wood from the cold, and we were tired and hungry. But now we listened in surprise and delight. It was like God saying *Amen!* to the morning.

What Has Happened Since

What were the results of our prayers?

First of all, I wish you could see the Plaza Mayo as it looked then and compare it with how it looks today! At the time we prayed, the plaza was run down, with just a few green shrubs and broken fountains with peeling paint. The Casa Rosada needed painting and restoration desperately. Later that day, when we intercessors stood in front of the Casa Rosada, I asked the Lord to give us a sign from heaven that He was going to restore Argentina from the bottom to the top. We asked Him to have the Casa Rosada completely refurbished.

On our very next trip to Argentina, one of the teams of Harvest Evangelism (which intends to see all of Argentina transformed by the Gospel) picked us up at the airport and excitedly showed us the headline from a recent Buenos Aires newspaper: *Casa Rosada Being Restored from the Basement Up.* We knew we had our sign from the Lord. He was (and is!) restoring Argentina.

Since we broke the curses from the shedding of innocent blood, we have seen a wonderful change in the physical land of Argentina. One way we knew our prayers had been answered was through the report of the Agriculture Department that the land suddenly started to produce and no one knew why. Land that had yielded poor crops became more fertile, without any external improvements being made to the earth. The land had ceased mourning (see Hosea 4:1–3).

Also recall that we asked God to reveal the plight of the Indian people—who had been slaughtered generations before by the Spanish—to the congress of Argentina. We have no way of knowing, of course, whether that congressman who "happened along" took a report of our prayer meeting back to his colleagues, as he said he would; or whether there was a cause and effect between our prayers and what happened later. But I believe it was a direct result of our repentance, and that of others, that the Congress gave hectares of land to the native peoples as restitution. This was absolutely historic!

And, finally, the inflation rate dropped over the space of two years from three thousand percent to one and a half percent. Unbelievable! When we first went, the Argentine currency was ten thousand *australes* to one U.S. dollar. Some joked about coming to Argentina so they could be millionaires. Later an article in *The Wall Street Journal* reported that "there is a revival in the economy of Argentina, but nobody knows why."

We know why: God heals nations.

Isn't it clear to you, as you read this testimony, that history indeed belongs to the intercessor? When God wants to make a change in history, He has His people pray. He wants to heal nations through you and through the prayer leaders of your church, and He wants to transform your city through intercessory prayer. Why? Because thousands of souls captured in darkness can and will emerge into the glorious light.

That is really what this is all about, isn't it? Nations are made up of people who cannot see and who are bound by everyday struggle and oppression.

Not only did the nation of Argentina enjoy better crops and a stronger economy, but the Indian people started getting saved in large numbers. New churches have been planted and people are getting saved in outdoor campaigns.

As you read this, believe God to change *your* nation, too, no matter how wicked or fallen. Gather a group of intercessors at your church and seek the Lord's face for a strategy. If you persevere, you will be amazed at the results. Keep praying until you see a change!

TWELVE

SETTING EARTH FREE FROM ITS TWO GREATEST STRONGHOLDS

Two entirely divergent worldviews grip all mankind. These are more than philosophies; they are ways of thinking so deeply imbibed in the childhoods of most Westerners that they may never have become consciously developed. Some nations, whether ethnic, political or religious, seem to be affected by one or the other more strongly, and some less. But in Western society and culture all of us drank both worldviews into ourselves.

Because these mindsets became part of us without our ever having thought them through, they are divergent ways of feeling, sensing and reacting that *affect* our behavior, apart from our conscious awareness At times they even *control* the way we think, feel, act or make decisions.

These two worldviews, one built on the other, have become extremely powerful corporate strongholds that control multitudes in every kind of nation. These strongholds are an antichrist approach to life, yet many well-meaning Christians believe and act within them.

Before I define any further, test yourself by answering the following:

1. Is spirit transcendent and pure, whereas matter (material reality) is impure?
2. Is praying spiritual, and eating a meal only natural? Is eating spiritual only if you are partaking of the Eucharist or if your thoughts are right? Or is it both spiritual and physical to pray, and spiritual and physical to eat a meal?
3. Is worshiping in church spiritual, while turning a lathe or punching a keyboard is only secular? Is it spiritual to labor, or does it depend on the kind of work?
4. Is it spiritual for married people to pray together but unspiritual to make love? Or is it spiritual as well as physical to make love to your spouse?

I am *not* asking whether your attitudes are "spiritual" or carnal! The question is whether actions can be intrinsically only "natural"—and, as such, perhaps, basically carnal or impure—or are our actions at all times both spiritual and natural? Are there some things we feel and think and do that have nothing of spirit in them, and thus are only natural or secular?

Or does everything we feel and think and do have spiritual ramifications as well as physical, however carnal or even sinful?

Most of us today, I trust, would answer that everything we do is both spiritual and physical—that nothing is not spiritual as well as physical. But when Paula and I first began in ministry, most of the believers to whom we asked this question divided the spiritual realm sharply from the physical. For them the secular world had nothing of spirit or life in it. It meant that people lived all week in the natural or material realm, whereas only in prayer or at worship on Sundays did they participate in anything spiritual.

We tend to think of anything that is recognizably spiritual as good and of God. But Satan is a spiritual being and so are demons.

All things have spirit in them. "[There is] one God and Father of all who is over all and *through* all and *in* all" (Ephesians 4:6, emphasis added). The Church has always believed not only in God's transcendence (that He is over all), but also in His immanence (that He is present, by His Spirit, in all things). The earth was defiled by mankind's sins (see Genesis 3, especially verses 14–19; and Genesis 4:11–12). But the blood of Jesus has cleansed the earth (see Acts 10:15).

As we will see, Christians have been made afraid to think of God's Spirit flowing in and through all things, sustaining all of life, for fear of being called pantheistic or spiritistic.

Perhaps we need a definition of *spirit* and *spiritual*. But who can define *spirit*? It is, in this context, the energy or vital life that flows in and through all things. In all creatures that have "life and breath and all things" (Acts 17:25), it is spirit that sustains life. When the spirit departs, life is gone, even as Jesus on the cross "bowed His head and gave up His spirit" (John 19:30). A person has a personal spirit that departs at death. Animals have their own kind of spirit. But all of creation has spirit flowing in and through it—not personal and distinct, as in humans, in whom God has breathed His own breath (see Genesis 2:7), but general and pervasive, in and through all.

The Two Worldviews

Today, by the grace of God, some have begun to break out of the delusional grip of the two worldviews I am about to describe. But the nations of all mankind, as well as much of the Church, are still dominated and corrupted by these strongholds. *Freeing the earth of them is a major part of the healing of the nations.*

What are these philosophies?

1. The Spirit-Matter Split of Platonism

In 333 B.C. Alexander the Great, king of Macedonia and a disciple of Aristotle, conquered Asia Minor, Syria, Egypt, Babylon and Persia. From that time on, the area was dominated by Hellenism. Greek thought, culture and language became the "in" thing. The New Testament itself was written in *koine* Greek, a simplified variation of classical Greek. During the Hellenistic period, Greek philosophy, and particularly Platonism and Neoplatonism, filled the minds of the intelligentsia and filtered into the thinking of common men and women. It still does today.

One of the hallmarks of the philosophy espoused by Aristotle's teacher, Plato, was dualism—spirit up there, matter down here. That Greek philosopher of the fourth century B.C. regarded pure spirit (including the ideals of beauty and truth) as good, and matter (including flesh) as evil and debased. The goal of every person's life was to free his spirit from the corruption of the flesh and soar in the pure realm of the spirit.

How closely this resembles Christian teaching! But we must remember that Plato spoke of the flesh as our bodies, whereas Christians use the word *flesh* differently. Sometimes *flesh* refers specifically to our bodies, as when Paul said, "No one ever hated his own flesh" (Ephesians 5:29). But at other times *flesh* means the practiced ways of iniquity built into our patterns of thinking, feeling and acting, as when Paul called on us to "cleanse ourselves from all defilement of flesh and spirit" (2 Corinthians 7:1). These altogether different ways of using the word *flesh* have created confusion in many, so that when they hear that we are to hate the flesh, they find it difficult to think of anything but hating our physical bodies. The docetic stronghold, of which we will now speak, has made use of that confusion to hurl many into difficulty.

2. The Matter-Is-Evil Deception of Docetic Gnosticism

The word *docetic* comes from the Greek word *dokeo*, which means to seem, or to appear. Docetism originated in Hindu theology, which permeated Asia centuries before the birth of Christianity. The Veda ("sacred knowledge") of Hindu religious literature taught that spirit is pure and transcendent, far above all matter. The soul of each individual has originated in a transcendent spiritual principle (*Brahman*), but when we "fell" into incarnation, we became defiled. It is necessary, therefore, for the soul to progress through a long cycle of sufferings and deaths and rebirths through reincarnation, depending on the ethical quality of actions (*karma*) in the preceding life, until it escapes the body altogether in spiritual release (*moksha*) and the experience of eternal transcendence and bliss.

A worldview similar to this and to Platonism colored the nations that surrounded Israel in the first century after Christ—that earth and matter are defiled, corrupt and evil. This was not Hebraic-Christian theology. God said to Peter in his vision on the rooftop, "What God has cleansed, no longer consider unholy" (Acts 10:15). But in the early centuries of the Church, a stronghold of what I am calling docetic Gnosticism took hold of many disciples. Some were scandalized that the very Son of God would be born as a baby, fully human, needing His diapers changed and to be suckled at the breast in all that "uncleanness."

Gnosticism—from the Greek *gnosis*, knowledge revealed to a special few—regarded pure spirit as good but trapped in matter, which was evil. Salvation consisted in freeing the spirit from matter. Teaching the truth to initiates would emancipate them from the prison of matter and return them to the realm of pure spirit.

So Jesus, they decided, had not really been incarnated; He just *appeared* to have a body, floated around for a while and went back up to heaven, where He was pure spirit. The Redeemer of the world must have nothing of the taint of flesh about Him. Like Platonism, docetic Gnosticism represented antipathy between spirit and flesh.

Most twentieth-century believers recognize instantly that such views run counter to Christian doctrine. Matter, and thus earth, are not unclean. We did not "fall" into incarnation; it is a privilege and blessing to be human. "You have made [man] a little lower than God," exclaims the psalmist, "and You crown him with glory and majesty!" (Psalm 8:5). We do not wish to escape from our bodies; we want to be perfected within them, and will be raised in new and glorified bodies. We are not to resign from all that is human, or even fleshly, but to overcome and transform all into the likeness of our Lord Jesus Christ.

All Christians, it would seem, ought easily to discern docetism and be free of it. The apostle John warned clearly against it:

> Beloved, do not believe every spirit, but test the spirits to see whether they are from God, because many false prophets have gone out into the world. By this you know the Spirit of God: every spirit that confesses that Jesus Christ has come in the flesh is from God; and every spirit that does not confess Jesus is not from God; this is the spirit of the antichrist, of which you have heard that it is coming, and now it is already in the world.
>
> 1 John 4:1–3

But remember that a corporate mental stronghold is not an inert philosophy on a dusty page; it is a living and active power in the mentality we share with others. It can grip, overpower and control—even though we know the Lord. A corporate mental stronghold can slip into our thinking unawares, because it came into us through the culture while we were children. This is why Paul warned believers not to be overcome by the world "but [to] be transformed by the renewing of your mind" (Romans 12:2).

A Christian View of the Creation

The history of docetic Gnosticism among mankind is ancient, its influence powerful. It is wielded by principalities and world rulers of darkness whose aim is to entrap and dominate all men and women. It has many sly, practiced ways to worm below the level of conscious thought into our feelings, thoughts and actions.

The base of docetism, deeper than Hinduism alone, was ingrained in the creation stories of all the nations.

Babylonian theology said that Marduk, their chief god, had fought with his mother, Tiamat. (Notice the difference between that and the relationship between Jesus and Mary!) Marduk stuffed the four winds into Tiamat's mouth, whereupon she bloated and died of gas poisoning. Marduk slit her belly and lifted up the top half, which became the heavens. The blood and guts running out at the bottom became the earth. With such a story of creation, how could people ever respect the gods—or God—and the earth?

Egyptian mythology said that a mud flood occurred, forming mud hillocks in its midst. On one of these a man arose. One version says he spat, and that act was creation; we are the spittle. The other says he masturbated, and we are the sperm. Yuck!

Contrast that to what the Holy Spirit said, through the writer of Genesis, about the act of a loving and holy God:

> God said, "Let there be light"; and there was light. God saw that the light was good; and God separated the light from the darkness.
>
> Genesis 1:3–4

For six days our loving heavenly Father spoke creation through His Son, who was to become our Lord Jesus Christ, and each day He saw that it was good. On the sixth day He created man and woman.

> And God saw all that He had made, and behold, it was *very good*.
>
> verse 31, emphasis added

What a glory!—and how drastically different from the myths and theologies that surrounded Israel. Here was no defilement. The earth is clean and good. From the dust of that cleanness, God formed man and breathed His own holy breath into him. Here was no "fall" into incarnation, but a holy creation for holy purposes.

But the holy revelation of God's creation was carried by a fragile and sinful people into a land already pervaded by the corruption of many strongholds of deception. They could not maintain the purity of it, before or after Christ.

How Do We Relate to Creation?

The Greeks taught that spirit is ethereal and transcendent, and that matter is solid and contains no spirit. Anything that

219

does not move or breathe has no life or spirit in it. *But this philosophy runs counter to the Hebraic approach to life and creation that came from revelation from God.*

The Lord's reproach to Cain, for example—"The voice of your brother's blood is crying to Me from the ground" (Genesis 4:10)—was, to the Hebrews, neither poetic nor figurative speech. It meant what it said. Abel's blood truly had a voice.

Scripture makes more allusions that actually personify the ground:

> "Now you are cursed from the ground, *which has opened its mouth* to receive your brother's blood from your hand. When you cultivate the ground, *it will no longer yield its strength to you.* . . ."
>
> Genesis 4:11–12, emphasis added

> The pastures of the wilderness drip, *and the hills gird themselves with rejoicing.* The meadows are clothed with flocks and the valleys are covered with grain; *they shout for joy, yes, they sing.*
>
> Psalm 65:12–13, emphasis added

> "For this [the sins of mankind] the earth shall mourn."
>
> Jeremiah 4:28

Unfortunately many Christians have been trained to think in Aristotelian terms. (He codified and expressed logically what his teacher, Plato, taught—a split of life into spirit and matter, separated from one another.) Such Christians can only think of these and the hundreds of other biblical references to nature as metaphorical. But Hebrew people thought of all aspects of nature (as we will see later in this chapter) as having their own form of intelligence, will and desire. Our model for truth is Jesus, who spoke to a fig tree and the winds and waves, obviously expecting that they would hear, understand and obey.

I realize that this way of thinking upsets the minds—and the theology—of many. I don't profess to understand it all myself. What I am saying is that if the nations are to be healed, all of us will have to undergo a paradigm shift in our thinking.

The fullness of thought in this area has not yet been developed. I am simply opening a field of inquiry, and calling for prayer, that we may grow together in rediscovering how Jesus thought about and related to nature and to all of His creatures.

To those trained in God's way of thinking, everything He has created possesses life and spirit. All creation, therefore, actually possesses its own desire, will and intention. Listen to Romans 8:19–21:

> The *anxious longing of the creation waits eagerly* for the revealing of the sons of God. For the creation was subjected to futility, not willingly, but because of Him who subjected it, in hope that the creation itself also will be set free from its slavery to corruption into the freedom of the glory of the children of God.
>
> emphasis added

Can anyone fail to hear the emotion, desire and hope resident in the creation with the words *anxious longing* and *waits eagerly?* The King James Version says the creation waits with "earnest expectation." According to the Revised Standard Version it waits with "eager longing." In the Phillips translation, "The whole creation is on tiptoe."

Is this metaphorical only? I don't think so. Some expressions, of course, are only poetical. Rivers cannot actually "clap their hands" (Psalm 98:8) and I doubt that meadows and valleys can actually sing together (see Psalm 65:12–13). But the meaning behind such metaphors is the same as Jesus' expression, "I tell you, if these become silent, the stones will cry out!" (Luke 19:40).

Besides the primary meaning of that verse in Luke, Jesus was also saying that nature does truly have a voice:

> The heavens are telling of the glory of God; and their expanse is declaring the work of His hands. Day to day pours forth speech, and night to night reveals knowledge. There is no speech, nor are there words; their voice is not heard. Their line has gone out through all the earth, and their utterances to the end of the world.
>
> Psalm 19:1–4

The observation in Romans 8 that *the creation was subjected . . . not willingly* (or *not by its own choice*, NIV) suggests, moreover, that nature does indeed have a will of its own. We know

221

from the Genesis account that nature was filled with the glory of God. But when man fell, as I infer from Romans 8:19–21, the Lord had to "turn down" the powers He had created in men and women. (My own assumption is that before sin entered the world, one man or woman alone wielded more power than a hydrogen bomb!) God also had to turn down the power in nature until redemption and transformation could restore the heart and consequent righteousness of mankind, so that creation could be safe once again to express all God intended it to become.

What are the full implications of this expression? As I said before, I have no idea. I do not know what powers God intended originally, and will restore, for men and women and for the creation itself. But ever since the Fall, Satan has been trying to release locked-up powers—through alchemy, magic, sorcery, Satanism, New Age concepts, channeling, whatever might give back to man the powers God turned down. (This concept can be found expressed eloquently in Watchman Nee's little book *The Latent Power of the Soul.*)

Many Christians, unfortunately, have become so steeped in Greek philosophy, and so seduced by docetic Gnosticism, that whenever their brothers or sisters begin to rediscover the implications of biblical truth about nature—that, in the words of the apostle Paul, it "will be set free from its slavery to corruption into the freedom of the glory of the children of God"—they are immediately labeled (actually, libeled) "New Age" and heretical.

Approaching Nature as Jesus Did

So many people registered for a conference in California that the meeting place was moved from a small host church to a large sanctuary in a nearby church building. I spoke as requested on the subject of this chapter—that matter was not created base, split off from the ethereal and transcendent, but was declared good by God at creation; and that the creation will be restored into the glorious freedom that the children of God will also enjoy. I spoke of the Platonic-Aristotelian worldview that keeps us from thinking as Hebrews did, and called for prayer to reveal how God wants us to think about and relate to nature, and to each other as human beings in physical bodies.

222

A young associate pastor rose with some heat. "We do not believe this!" he exclaimed. God created the universe, he explained, and now sat apart from it, watching it run down like a clock until the Lord Jesus returns to redeem and restore it.

This idea harks back not only to Platonic philosophy and Gnosticism, but specifically to the deism of the late seventeenth and early eighteenth centuries. The very presence of the universe implies a Creator, taught the deists, just as the appearance of an intricate watch would imply a watchmaker. They thought that the divine Watchmaker had created the universe to operate according to certain moral principles, then sat back from it.

I apologized to the young pastor, saying that had I known this was their theology, I would have changed the subject and not espoused my point of view publicly. But in private I grieved for that church and its pastoral staff, who apparently all held the same position. Not even the Holy Spirit, in their view, had an ongoing role to play in the created order. We had only to watch the world wind down and await Jesus' return.

Sad to say, I am afraid this point of view represents the majority, not the minority. Many arms of the Church have long been captivated by the strongholds of Platonism and docetic Gnosticism to desire only to flee this sinful world. Paul warned us that such philosophical deception could take place:

> See to it that no one takes you captive through philosophy and empty deception, according to the tradition of men, according to the elementary principles of the world, rather than according to Christ.
>
> Colossians 2:8

One of the great ironies of Church history is that the Christian missionaries who brought the Gospel to native peoples around the world often derided their beliefs as superstitious, spiritistic, pantheistic or something of that sort. The concepts of many natives were a mixed bag, of course, containing both error and idolatry. But the greater delusion was often on the part of the missionaries, who were teaching a spirit-matter split to people whose views were often purer and nearer the truth of Romans 8 than those of their teachers!

Here is one place where the rediscovery of biblical truth is needed desperately. The Western materialistic worldview has, for the most part, overcome the world. Native peoples the world over have been made to feel ashamed of their more spiritual approach to nature. In most places today men and women do not approach nature as Jesus did. He spoke to the winds and the waves and they obeyed Him, whereas *we treat all of nature as though it consisted of mere insensitive objects, to be handled as we see fit, with no concern for what nature itself might feel or intend, and no awareness that the creation might possess any feelings or desires of its own.*

In many places on earth, devout natives asked God (by whatever name they knew Him) for the life of the animal they hunted, and apologized to it for taking its life. Influenced by dualistic philosophy, we scoffed at this as superstitious pantheism. Derision has created a great rift between natives and Westerners, and such mistaken beliefs have caused us to greatly wound nature. As I said earlier, if the nations are to be healed— remember, 2 Chronicles 7:14 says that if we repent, God will heal our land, including the physical earth—Western mentality will have to undergo a paradigm shift, a revolution, an "upset-the-fruit-basket" that is no game. God requires serious repentance and biblical revelation for the earth and mankind.

The way we think about and relate to nature must change. Our Lord wants to take us on a walk to Emmaus to reveal what has always been in His Word—not only about Himself, but about how He wants us to relate to His creation. We are exhausting earth's resources exponentially as the world's population explodes. But what if enough Christians could catch hold of this message, and begin to explore how to heal nature?

A Call to the Adventurous in the Lord

Could we be approaching that time when the sons of God are to be revealed, who will set the creation free from its bondage to decay? Could it be that nature could be so healed that it would yield its increase to mankind again? Is it possible, since the power in a tiny atom can be released to destroy entire cities, that Jesus, the Lord of creation, was able to release the power He has created in a few loaves and fish to feed thousands? Could the redemption of creation create "green belts" that could feed the world, no matter how many might inhabit it?

Think of the possibilities! My intention here is not to do the healing. It is to spark a revolution of thought and prayer, to call forth an adventurous company that will assail heaven for the truth about creation—and find it already expressed in the Bible. My intention is also to challenge scientists who will detest and break the walls of scientific superstitions concerning nature, like the Darwinian theory of evolution, and venture beyond "acceptable" parameters of thought to hear the waves of God's revelations pounding on the shores of their minds.

I confess I do not know how such revelations will change our thinking and behavior. Will we say hello to a tree? Yet our Lord Jesus spoke to a fig tree (see Matthew 21:19). Will we talk to hurricanes? Jesus addressed the wind and waves (see Mark 4:39). Will we think twice about how and why we hunt? Might farmers pray to release the power of their fields and plants?

Were we not still immersed in a dualistic spirit-matter split, we would not be surprised at the references in God's Word showing that nature reacts to what we do and is hurt by our sin. Here are three such passages:

> *The earth mourns* and withers, the world fades and withers, the exalted of the people of the earth fade away. The earth is also polluted by its inhabitants, for they transgressed laws, violated statutes, broke the everlasting covenant. Therefore, a curse devours the earth, and those who live in it are held guilty. Therefore, the inhabitants of the earth are burned, and few men are left. *The new wine mourns, the vine decays.*
>
> Isaiah 24:4–7, emphasis added

> The land mourns and pines away, Lebanon is shamed and withers; Sharon is like a desert plain, and Bashan and Carmel lose their foliage.
>
> Isaiah 33:9

> As for the prophets: my heart is broken within me, all my bones tremble; I have become like a drunken man, even like a man overcome with wine, because of the Lord and because of His holy words. For the land is full of adulterers; *for the land mourns because of the curse. The pastures of the wilderness have dried up.* Their course also is evil and their might is not right.
>
> Jeremiah 23:9–10, emphasis added

Could there be a clearer revelation of the relationship between mankind's sins and earth's reactions? This is neither New Age mysticism nor philosophical speculation. *God's own Word declares most clearly how our actions affect nature.*

Do we think we know better than God, that we hold onto a materialistic worldview and label as New Age those who, speaking like Isaiah and Jeremiah, assert that the land is mourning? How long will we hang onto what is not God's Word? Satan is a hypnotist. For centuries he has used the strongholds of Platonic philosophy and docetic Gnosticism to captivate our minds and keep us in slumber. It is time to awaken from sleep.

Nature Is Waiting for Us!

Recall what we discussed in chapter 2—that people affect lands, but lands also affect the people who live on them. God will heal the land, or else corruption and wounding will seep back into our lives. Recall, too, from Romans 8:19 that the creation waits with "earnest expectation" or "eager longing." It waits "on tiptoe."

What is it waiting for? "For the revealing of the sons of God."

Dear brother or sister, please disabuse your mind of the fear of being involved in New Age ways (or of being called that!) and realize that there is indeed a relationship between mankind and nature. *Nature cannot be restored to wholeness until humankind is, and the creation waits with bated breath for its own liberation at the hands of men and women.*

Why is our liberation so important to us and to nature—and why so important to the devil? Because Satan does not want

226

us to be whole. He knows that we and the creation are intertwined. He also knows his time is short. But if he can keep us under the thrall of dualistic philosophy, fleeing whatever is construed as New Age, mystical or pantheistic, he has postponed just that much longer his inevitable journey to the lake of fire.

This is actually old territory—as old as creation itself—but new in many ways for our minds and hearts. We will have to shuck any comfortable husks that have shielded us from revelation. But understanding the connection between our own redemption and that of nature will be like coming home to what our spirits have known all along. Satan and our fearful hearts have painted such "new" revelations as awesome and daunting—but we must change.

It will take courage. The Holy Spirit is raising a corps of prayerful people who will not be daunted by the inevitable name-calling. "New Agers," "worshipers of mother earth," "worshipers of Gaia," "followers of delusion," "spiritists," "pantheists"—any title will do so long as it prevents us from learning how to relate to the creation as God has ordained we shall. The fearful always want to keep knowledge and experience in safe, familiar, manageable boxes. They are offended by any Copernicus or Galileo who dares explore beyond the supposedly safe world of the known. There will always be scribes and Pharisees who appoint themselves guardians of biblical truth and who fasten their limited view of reality on everyone else, actually persecuting Jesus and His prophets.

Will the Lord's latter-day disciples hear and respond? How desperately they are needed! Can scientists and heavenly minded prophetic types find common ground and work together to discover how mankind should relate in a godly and more appropriate way to the earth? Many species are already extinct and more are disappearing every day. Can we revive an appreciation of God's creation in a greedy society that wants to use and exploit resources, no matter what?

Such a revolution is already underway. Many wise and thoughtful leaders in the business community are working tirelessly to relate to nature in ways that cherish and preserve its riches. Believers, of all people, need to applaud and support them in prayer and in every other way.

But these efforts alone are not enough. We need to let God's Word launch a massive assault on our own minds before it is too late. Dualism and docetic Gnosticism must be defeated. Those ways of thinking are not the biblical way and must find their death, in all of us, on the cross of Christ. *We must rediscover how our Lord Jesus, who created all that is, wants us to relate to His creation.*

Granted, that is an inexpressibly vast task! But mindsets do change. People stopped thinking that the sun revolved about the earth when enough facts controverted that old way of thinking and brought it to death. In this generation can we bring to death our wrong, insensitive, exploitative ways of relating to God's creation? I believe we can. But I know it will require massive intervention from heaven, and that happens only when enough people cry out to God in prayer.

A Biblical Response to the Strongholds

We saw earlier that in that tiny speck of land called Palestine, God prepared the mental ground for the coming of His Son. There He nudged the truths of His creation to the subjugated few to whom Jesus would come.

We have also seen that the newly born Christian faith, in the first few centuries, was surrounded by a populace dominated by Greek thought and defiled by docetic Gnosticism. Worse, new Christian disciples carried in their subconscious minds, like a hidden virus, the tenets of both philosophies. From the moment of its inception, Christianity was engaged in mortal spiritual warfare, as Satan's principalities and world rulers of darkness played on corporate mental strongholds that remained inside us, and in the world around us, to seduce, corrupt and destroy the deposit of faith.

In response the Lord raised up a company of Christian apologists who defended the faith, as Jude exhorted that they should:

> I felt the necessity to write to you appealing that you contend
> earnestly for the faith which was once for all handed down to
> the saints.

Jude 3

Many of the messages of the first-century apostles' letters,
which became the Bible, were written to contend against
(among other things) the strongholds of dualism and the emerg-
ing docetic Gnosticism. The Greeks had already been seduced
into believing that the mortal body is something to be sluffed
off so we can return to being pure spirit. (So Socrates must
have thought when he drank the poisonous hemlock.) To the
Greeks of New Testament times, some four centuries later, the
idea of being resurrected in the body was anathema. Horrors!
The very idea of death was to escape the body, and now here
were these Christians telling them to rejoice that they would
be right back in it again?

The Greeks in Corinth, scandalized by "defiled" human flesh,
wanted to say that in the resurrection, ours would be some kind
of *spiritual* (as opposed to physical) body, with no physical
dimensions. Against this false way of thinking, the apostle John
wrote the first chapter of his gospel. Once we understand what
lay behind John's words, the first few lines become the ringing
rebuke and thunderous declaration of truth they were meant
to be—and were known as in those days. Recall the philosophical backdrop of the first century and listen anew to the
apostle's resounding assertions:

> In the beginning was the Word, and the Word was with God,
> and the Word was God. He was in the beginning with God.

verses 1–2

John was stepping into current Hellenistic philosophical ter-
minology and claiming the Greek word *logos*, "word," for Christ
Jesus. The Logos was not a corrupt "Demiurge," as the Greeks
said, a half-god who created a defiled world and encased the
souls of men and women in debased human bodies. Nor was
the Logos, who became incarnated as Jesus, a lesser god or a

being created later. Nor did He only appear to have a body. No, Jesus Christ, the Logos of God, incarnated in human flesh, was in the beginning with God. He is God Himself. The Logos is no Demiurge or some lesser god. Jesus Christ is fully man, neither separate from God nor defiled, and one with the Father, fully God in Himself. Extraordinary!

> All things came into being through Him, and apart from Him nothing came into being that has come into being.
>
> verse 3

No corrupt half-god created anything. Everything was created by our Lord Jesus Christ. Nothing was created by anyone other than by Him who was from the beginning—the Logos of God Himself.

> In Him was life, and the life was the Light of men. The Light shines in the darkness, and the darkness did not comprehend it.
>
> verses 4–5

The marginal note for the New American Standard Bible suggests, as an alternative to *comprehend, overpower*. The Revised Standard Version says, "The darkness has not overcome it"— a more correct rendering, perhaps, of what is meant by *comprehend*. Greek philosophy and docetic Gnosticism would maintain that being encased in flesh had defiled the Logos; but John declared forcefully that our Lord Jesus Christ, while fully flesh, was not defiled or overcome by anything!

"In Him was life," not a mixture of life and death. "And the life was the Light of men," not a confusion of light and darkness. In one of his letters John said it most clearly: "God is Light, and in Him there is no darkness at all" (1 John 1:5). Our Lord Jesus Christ is life, and not confusion, to every man and woman.

What a resounding declaration these words are! And what a comfort to a fledgling Christianity struggling to ascertain and hang onto the true deposit of faith.

The apostle followed his opening declarations in John 1 with a final assertion that would have appalled the Greeks:

And the Word became flesh, and dwelt among us, and we saw His glory, glory as of the only begotten from the Father, full of grace and truth.

verse 14

Full of grace and truth, not half-full. *Became flesh,* not "appeared to be flesh." Jesus did not become something like water sloshing in a bottle, to be poured out at death. He was fully incarnated, truly God and truly man. *We saw His glory.* This is no theory, no figment of someone's imagination. This is historical fact—reality. John said he saw it himself.

Our Lord Jesus Christ was not apart from and in opposition to some kind of half-god, nor was He created later on; He was God from the beginning, and now He has been begotten of the Father as a human being like the rest of us, except perfect and undefiled by Adam's sin.

On the Day of Pentecost, when the Holy Spirit was poured out, three thousand people were converted. These people came from all over the Middle East, infected and infused with docetism and Greek philosophy. It would take a long while for them to be transformed by the renewing of their minds. (It is just as long and needful a process for us today.)

What followed, therefore, was a period during which, in council after council—Antioch, Nicea, Alexandria, Ephesus— the early Church had to hammer out what is and what is not the true faith. Who was the Person of Jesus Christ? Did He only appear to take on human flesh, or was He fully human (and not fully God)? Was He of the same being with the Father, or of only similar substance?

It was not a purely mental battle, as though if settling the facts of dogma would straighten everything else out. It was a spiritual battle.

At the Council of Nicea in 325 A.D., called to quell a growing controversy over the nature of Jesus Christ, warfare raged. Athanasius, a young ascetic from Alexandria and champion of the faith, wanted the new creed to state that Jesus was *homo* (of the same) *ousios* (substance) with God the Father. Such a statement would declare that Jesus is of one nature with God. Arrayed against him were Arius, an eloquent presbyter in the Alexandrian Church, and his supporters—along with the strongholds of Platonism, docetism and Gnosticism and their demonic world rulers. The Arians wanted the creed to say that Jesus was *homoi* (of similar) substance with God, similar but not the same. Those corrupted by docetism could not comprehend that a good and holy God could allow Himself to be incarnated, the body being defiled, no matter how divine Jesus might be.

Homo or homoi? All of Christendom, it is said, hinged on one Greek letter, *iota*. The average Christian layman at the time, if aware of this controversy, probably thought it was semantic nitpicking. But more informed believers were praying passionately that truth would prevail.

Praise God for His providence! The view of young Athanasius carried the day, and the true deposit of the faith was preserved. So it is that the Nicene Creed, recited in many churches every Sunday, reads:

> I believe . . . in one Lord, Jesus Christ, the only begotten Son of God: begotten of the Father before all worlds, God of God, Light of Light, very God of very God, begotten, not made, being of one substance with the Father.

Ripping Out the Morning Glories

It was one of my jobs in the garden as a child to weed out the morning glories. Nothing could have been more misnamed! Though a beautiful flower, it was a weed. Its roots ran underground, spreading through much of the garden. I would cut it down time after time, only to see it spring up again here, there, everywhere. Furious, I ripped up vast networks, finding and pulling out its spreading root system, upsetting many good plants in the process. But it would pop up again relentlessly anyway.

The strongholds of Greek philosophy and especially docetism—that Christ only appeared to be a man—have proved to be like that weed. Throughout the conciliar period of the first four centuries, and even to this day, they have cropped up continually, defiling and seducing Christians, and through them, the world.

How does docetism, though defeated doctrinally, still corrupt Christianity and the world today? In four ways: through compartmentalizing sexual passion; through dehumanizing life and relationships; through skewed thinking; and through compartmentalizing all of life. Let's look at each of these in turn.

1. Through the Compartmentalization of Passion

Plato's idea of the split between the spiritual and material realms came through Christian theology into the Western Church, and with it a split of life into compartments, spiritual and secular. Then the pernicious, persistent weed of docetism wormed its way into the culture and even the theology of the Western world. The religious, ethnic and political nations of the Western world were defiled by both strongholds.

The nineteenth century was dominated by a mindset that grew out of docetic Gnosticism. Elizabethan England especially, and all her colonies, were diseased by it. Sex, among both Catholics and Protestants, was proclaimed nasty. Married couples were supposed to have sexual relations only to produce children. If you enjoyed sex, you were guilty of unchristian passions and were to confess to your priest or pastor. If an Englishman made love to his wife and she responded passionately (which was actually quite appropriate and holy), he might apologize profusely the next morning. She could be sure he would never again arouse her passions like that (although he might maintain a mistress with whom he felt free to be as passionate as he wanted!).

Paula's great-grandmother, who gave birth to nine children, proudly proclaimed to her dying day that her husband had never seen her naked.

I watched a woman on a TV talk show, by contrast, who practiced adultery openly and testified proudly that she was a devout Christian. Her God wanted her to be happy, she said, and what she did with her body had nothing to do with her spirit or her faith. Life for her was compartmentalized. She took care of God

233

on Sunday, and the rest of the week was hers to do with as she pleased.

The founders of one denomination of the Church believed and stated that the body itself is evil. This is precisely the heresy of docetic Gnosticism! We are under the drag of original sin, but our bodies are temples of the Holy Spirit (see 2 Corinthians 6:16). Yet these founders thought themselves Christian and supremely righteous in their beliefs.

What that heresy has done to the life of their denomination has been horrendous! I have checked with other counselors, who all agree with me. In that branch of the Church there is more adultery by far than in any other! Why? Because when some leaders began to make love with their spouses, they felt guilty and suppressed their natural feelings. Suppression acts like holding a ball under water. When released it whooshes to the surface and spurts into the air. Their suppressed sexual drives eventually could be checked no longer and found expression illicitly. I knew this from having heard some say so in counseling sessions—which then required much teaching and many prayers for healing.

For more on this, see my book *Why Some Christians Commit Adultery*.

2. Through the Dehumanization of People

As we document how docetic Gnosticism has corrupted Christians and the world, let's take it one step further. The same compartmentalization of life that lets us think we can do things with our bodies that do not affect our spirits also acts to dehumanize and devalue all other actions and relationships. Murder is now commonplace; we see reports of it every night on TV. Why? Because when the stronghold of lawlessness (which we described in chapter 5) couples with docetism and the compartmentalization of life, people become mere objects. A human being is reduced to an "it" that has no intrinsic value and can be taken out. If a person is regarded only as a body (defiled and therefore worthless), why not kill it?

Conscience, destroyed by the stronghold of lawlessness, is thus further dissolved. When people are dehumanized, we are free to do to others whatever we think profits us. Callousness becomes the norm rather than the exception. This is why mobsters can calmly order hit men to "waste" their rivals, and then attend mass on Sunday as though they were devout followers of Christ. Or why Serbs can pillage, rape, destroy and murder—and boast proudly of what they have done.

Life has been compartmentalized. Matter has no spirit; it is only something to be used. The body is evil, while the spirit is saved to go to heaven . . . and what happens from week to week has little to do with anyone's spiritual condition. Consequently Nazis could oversee Jewish death camps, preside over unspeakable genocide, attend church and wear the iron cross all the while.

3. Through Mental Abnormality

We have discussed our need to let God renew our minds according to His Word. There is no need for the mind to be renewed if the first one is not sick. *But indeed the entire world is mentally ill!* Truly the nations are sick in the head. Only in Christ are we restored to sanity, and that only as we let Him transform us by the renewing of our minds (see Romans 12:2; Ephesians 4:23).

Look at the massacres that have taken place in northern Iraq, Rwanda, Bosnia, Kosovo and all over the world. So-called ethnic cleansing takes place when disrespect for the unity and holiness of spirit and body as one in every person has allowed men to treat others as mere objects. This can happen only where lawlessness has released the evil in human hearts and life has become fractured by the docetic heresy.

When the love of God rules our hearts, by contrast, instinctively we cherish the whole being of every other person. Even adherents of the docetic heresy—whether or not they call it by that name—find it hard to treat others as objects where love rules. This is why raising a company of prayerful lovers of the Father is so crucial. Their presence must counter the serpent's flood that bids to sweep away not only the Church, symbolized by the woman (see Revelation 12:15), but the world as well.

4. Through the Compartmentalization of Life

People have asked me, "John, what can I do at work that is specifically Christian?" The question reveals the depth of their confusion! Satan has convinced these men and women that work in so-called "secular jobs" does not have His Spirit in it. But believers themselves are God's vessels. There is nothing of goodness, whether through simple labor or in interpersonal relationships, that is not Christian, simply because *we* are Christian. Sons or daughters of God are redolent with His Spirit. Whatever good we do, God does through us. In God's sight life is not separated into "secular" or "holy." All of life is holy when God's presence flows through one of His children.

Three psychiatrists asked me during lunch at a teaching seminar, "How can we get God and His Spirit into our practice?" My mouth fell open in shock. The minds of these trained men had been taken captive by the stronghold of docetism. God and His Spirit met them on Sundays or in private devotions, but they had no awareness that He was already in everything they did as they listened, opened their hearts in compassion and gave counsel and medication. Life for them had become compartmentalized, and the docetic heresy told them there was nothing of holiness or the Spirit of God in what they did; they were simply performing their own human work as doctors. What a deception, and what a tragic loss!

There is nothing good we can do outside God's Spirit. We may not recognize Him, or allow Him sufficient access to our lives, or grant Him permission to operate more fully through us, or give Him the credit He is due, but these hindrances in no way prevent His Holy Spirit from flowing through every righteous deed we do. Every Christian is a sacrament in action—an act of God's grace done for others in every moment of life—when we allow Him to live His life in us. *For Christians filled with the Holy Spirit, there is no secular life apart from God. All of life is holy.*

Mow a lawn; God is working with you. Wipe a dish; so is God. Hoe a row; your sweat is His as well. Type a sentence, send an e-mail, read a book. Do you think God is nowhere around? You can do nothing apart from Him. God's Spirit is not off somewhere in the heavens, detached and uninvolved. He is everywhere, and committed in every detail of our lives to love and watch over us. He withdraws from every sin, to be sure. But we cannot even participate in sin apart from His sight.

Most of the Church and the World . . .

Much of Christendom does not think this way. Most in the Church and many more in the world are controlled by both Platonic philosophy and docetic Gnosticism.

The harm this does is immeasurable. Political and ethnic nations could not be hurled into war if they were suffused with the realization that every person is indeed a holy other, an eternal spirit to be cherished and protected.

Leaders of political nations would find their consciences violated if they realized that expediency or opportunism (the political term for *might-makes-right*), disrespects and disbelieves the holiness of others in every daily action.

Ethnic nations would find themselves shedding hatred and vengeance-taking if their spirits were tuned in by empathy into the suffering hearts of those they perceive as their enemies. But docetism causes them to think only of the objectionable behavior of others rather than the heart suffering that weakens others and drives them into sin. When people are dehumanized by docetism, compassion fails.

Religious nations could not help but lay down their childish suppositions of who God is, and right and wrong theology and practice, and choose to love one another if their hearts were not corrupted by Platonic philosophy and docetic Gnosticism.

Isn't it ironic that all over the world, native peoples uncorrupted by the West still meet others with their spirits, embracing, empathizing and "reading" them for better communication, whereas some Christians who have come to teach them a "better" way meet first only mentally, analyzing and treating them as objects of impersonal scrutiny before opening their hearts?

We could not so depersonalize people if we thought as Jesus thinks, meeting others first spirit to spirit. Paul wrote, "From now on we regard no one from a worldly point of view. Though we once regarded Christ in this way, we do so no longer" (2 Corinthians 5:16, NIV). But the Greek philosophers and docetic Gnostics have so compartmentalized life for us that we do not meet others whole-person-to-whole-person. We meet "I-it." God would have us meet "I-Thou."

What Is the Antidote?

There is no antidote other than Jesus. He is the only Way, the Truth and the Life. The question is, "How can we get *to* Him, and the truth *from* Him, apart from the mental trammels that have governed the way we see Him?"

> Beloved, now we are children of God, and it has not appeared as yet what we will be. We know that when He appears, we will be like Him, because *we will see Him just as He is*. And everyone who has this hope fixed on Him purifies himself, just as He is pure.
>
> 1 John 3:2–3, emphasis added

Did you catch it? We do not yet see Jesus as He is. Why not? For many reasons, but two of the most cogent are Platonism and docetism.

Did you catch the answer? The person who has this hope fixed on Jesus "purifies himself, just as He is pure."

This does not mean we should become self-centered Pharisees trying to be righteous and holy every moment. Notice the words *just as He is pure*. How was Jesus pure? Not merely by sinless obedience to the laws of God. More than that, He modeled for us what holiness under the New Covenant is.

Old Testament holiness lay in striving to live up to the laws of God in order to make it to heaven. It was necessarily self-centered and selfish and often bred judgment from others. Old Testament holiness could be likened to a tractor washed and polished and sitting in a field, doing no good for others but surely looking good!

New Testament holiness is Jesus becoming our sin and dying with it. New Testament holiness is love hanging on a cross. New Testament righteousness is serving others unmindful of ourselves. New Testament purity is that same tractor, pulling a plow to feed others and getting dusty and dirty in the process.

In the way of Jesus, holiness takes on an almost opposite definition from that of the Pharisees. Those religious leaders underwent 450 ablutions a day, trying to remain clean and holy before God. But Jesus allowed Himself to be defiled by the touch of a wicked woman, knowing it would bring healing and forgiveness to her heart. God made Jesus, "who knew no sin to be sin on our behalf, so that we might become the righteousness of God in Him" (2 Corinthians 5:21).

Getting dirty in service to others—in addition to remaining pure morally—is what New Testament holiness is all about. Holiness is love in action. Jesus tells us our righteousness must "[surpass] that of the scribes and Pharisees" (Matthew 5:20), which means not striving more than they to live up to all the rules, but laying down our lives for others in the love of God.

Historically every time a great revival has converted many, the Holy Spirit has issued a clarion call for holiness. Unfortunately the Church has most often run back into striving for Old Testament holiness, and the resultant Pharisaism has killed the anointing of the revival. *We are at precisely that point again in history.* A great wave of the Holy Spirit has been rolling over the Church. The long-prophesied great revival is on us and the call for holiness is sounding.

Oh, that this time we might graduate from the school of the law into the holiness of our Lord Jesus Christ!

We Need to Be Crucified

Purity does not come without death. Anything in us apart from the likeness of Christ must find death on His cross, not merely daily but moment by moment. Consider two passages in Galatians. One says that "those who belong to Christ Jesus have crucified the flesh with its passions and desires" (Galatians 5:24).

This suggests that crucifixion is something we do to ourselves. The other passage says, "I have been crucified with Christ" (Galatians 2:20). This suggests that crucifixion is something done to us. Here is the point: There cannot be one without the other.

If we set out to crucify ourselves, we will always be subject to pride that we did it. There is no escaping from self that way. Only when God's Holy Spirit slays us is boasting excluded, so that we boast only "in the Lord" (1 Corinthians 1:31). But our Lord will not crucify us without our permission and participation, so Galatians 2:20 cannot happen without Galatians 5:24.

We must move ourselves into position so He can crucify us. How? Here lies the crux of this entire chapter—indeed, of this book. *It is only when we forget about ourselves and obey God's call to serve others that we give Him permission to put us into circumstances and situations that crucify our old nature. It is only as Jesus' love pours through us for others that resurrection life overcomes what we have been and transforms us into His likeness.*

If we set out to perfect ourselves, we are doomed to failure. But if we set out to serve God in obedience, He crucifies us and makes us new and holy creatures in Him. "As He is pure"— harking back to 1 John 3:3—means, "As Jesus lives unto the Father," in loving service to God for the sake of whomever God calls us to love and serve.

In chapter 7, "Transforming Prayer for the Nations," we developed what it means to lay down our lives for others. Reread that chapter. Platonic and docetic strongholds cannot be defeated by debate or simply by being exposed in books like this one. Their hold on mankind can be broken only if enough Christians are willing to lay down their lives in intercession and burden-bearing prayer.

We must come into a pure and perfect hatred of "what is evil" (Romans 12:9, RSV). Not, "Hate *who* is evil." Not hate in any wrongful way. Only when our Father's perfect love infuses our hearts and causes us to siphon death out of others to our Lord's cross—only when we experience with Him the desperate cost of sin—do we come into a perfect and righteous hatred of it. This kind of hate is born of love. It is our Lord's anger at what destroys His children.

If we are impelled by our Father's love to draw death through ourselves to our Lord's cross, and allow Him to flood His life back through us to resurrect His own (see 2 Corinthians 4:10–12), then we learn to love as Jesus Christ loves and hate what He, in His purity, hates.

The world must be broken out of the evil grasp of Platonic and Gnostic strongholds. God our Father must find a people willing to serve beyond the familiar, beyond the walls of Christianity, for an uncaring, unloving world that does not deserve His love but will receive it anyway (as we have ourselves!) if enough of the Father's own will respond to His call.

God our Father seeks to extend mercy to the nations, until He can present them as gifts to His Son. If we ask why He has not done so already, I am afraid the answer is that He waits on high to have compassion on us (see Isaiah 30:18); because He waits for us. Many individuals pray fervently every day. But so far that has not been enough. I believe His response awaits two factors. One, that we understand many things and pray accurately in His wisdom. For this reason I (and many others) write and teach. Maturity beyond our current level may be required. Two, unity. We have been, as I said at the beginning, too isolated, too singular. God wants an army.

Have you ever sensed a nudge to be a missionary? Do it first from your rocking chair, in longsuffering, patient, burden-bearing intercession. Millions walk haltered to their death—not just physically, but to the second death. If enough of us cry out to the Father in repentance and loving prayers for the lost of the world, God, who so loved the world that He sent His only Son, will break the chains that lock the masses in thrall.

Platonic philosophy and docetism cannot survive where a people truly and righteously hate those strongholds and what they stand for. They cannot continue to shackle victims whose hearts are being freed by those whose burden-bearing natures draw the poison to the cross. Lies cannot prevail where He who is the truth is manifested through the love of an army, all laying down their lives as He did.

We can win this war. We do not have to stand by helplessly as multitudes are hurled at one another in war and killing. We do not have to grieve without effect as our children and our neighbor's children are sucked down the drain of immorality, especially sexual. Opportunism in the nation of politics does not have to go on reigning over the minds of public servants, presently prevented from thinking of people as people by strongholds they do not even know exist. In the nation of the Church, hubris, Pharisaism, liberalism and modernism can die if our Father's love is allowed to pour through enough willing hearts.

Our Father has not abandoned us to what we deserve. The flood of His love is greater than that of Satan. He is calling. He wants hearts through whom He can heal His tattered and broken earth. That is holiness. That is purity. The reward? We get to see Jesus as He is.

Fix that hope on us, Lord.

THIRTEEN

Seven Principles of Inner Healing for the Nations

In the preceding chapters we have opened new vistas of inquiry, explored vast revelations of possibilities, called for the raising of armies, taught about burden-bearing intercession as crucial and, I hope, enlisted prayer warriors. Nothing has been tied up, however, in a nice, tightly wrapped package. Nothing is complete—on purpose. Everything we have talked about remains open-ended, inviting all of us into what is often unexplored, unwrapped territory. Our message: God is calling us beyond the familiar into raw and what often seems to be foolish obedience, like the man told to do the very thing he could not do—stretch out his withered hand (see Matthew 12:13).

But lest the invitation seem to be presumption, or carnal foolishness, there are some unchanging principles, like a bank of lights along a darkened road. Let's conclude, then, with a summary of all we have said, formulated in seven principles that will always remain constant.

1. Change Requires Sanctification

The first principle of inner healing for the nations is that *little lasting change occurs unless people are sanctified and transformed in their hearts*. Good change happens from the inside out, not from the outside in. Changes in governmental structure may help, but no form of government can bring about an enduring, healthy environment for living. The sinful drives of mankind, unless corralled, will ultimately destroy any government and its society.

Attempts at teaching and at changing behavior *before* sanctification has transformed the heart only make the sinful nature more clever in denial and manipulation. But after sanctification and transformation have altered—and "altared"—the heart, self-discipline, teaching and behavior-changing methods may be greatly beneficial. Nor can laws and regulations transform nations. To a people whose desires are running rampant, these become hated and repressive instruments. But to those whose hearts have been purified, laws and regulations are beloved ways of life.

2. Repentance Is Vital

Repentance is a first and necessary step for wholesome change of any kind. Nothing of lasting value can be done for the nations unless hearts are changed. That is why the first chapters of this book call repeatedly for repentance. This first step cannot be overlooked or bypassed.

Repentance is turning heart and mind and activity from what was, to what is to be. Repentance is a gift from God, born of love for Him until we cannot stand to continue to hurt Him and others we love through sin. A corollary principle is that God's kindness is meant to lead us to repentance (see Romans 2:4).

Applied to the nations, this means our Father is raising a corps of people whose hearts, infused with His love, embrace the unlovable. (The company of the Father's own is described in chapter 6, "Whose Job Is It to Heal the Nations?") "Love never fails" (1 Corinthians 13:8). Enough prayer warriors must arise, their hearts of love uniting with the hearts of others, and their burden-bearing natures siphoning harm out of their nations' troubled hearts, until the citizens of those nations—political, ethnic or religious—*want* to change and are empowered from within to do so.

The healing and salvation of the nations depend on the arising of that army of lovers who know how to pray.

3. Prayerful People Can Repent for Others

A third principle is that *prayerful people can at first identify with—that is, become one with—others, and repent in, as and for them.* Eventually each person must do his own repenting (see Galatians 6:5), but in ministry for others, there is a "priming principle."

When I was a child on the farm, the leather in the pump of our well would often dry out, preventing the pump from drawing water. We would pour water in to soften and expand the leather, priming the pump, until it filled the surrounding pipe and formed airtight suction. Then it worked fine. Just so, identificational prayers soften and swell hearts until they begin to function. Our prayers to repent on behalf of others pour the water of God's love into them, until they in turn begin to pour God's love out for others.

Or we could say there is a "cranking principle." Early autos did not have starters. One had to insert a crank and turn vigorously until the car engine caught and ran on its own. In the same way, prayer warriors can become God's "cranks" until, having been started by the prayers of others, people can function in blessed ways on their own.

Make what you will of being a "crank"—"angry," "crazy," "turned around," "going in circles." Have fun with it! But remember, God wants all the above, a person who is different—angry at sin, crazy in the world's eyes, listening to a different drummer than the world follows, turned around from the world's ways, going in a different direction, going in the Lord's circles, not square with the world. It is that sort of person—His sort—who stirs things up, who makes things happen. Floods of love carve out and follow different river banks than the world has ever known.

God's kindness touches hearts and facilitates repentance and change when, by the faithful prayers of the Father's army, hearts are infused with His love. A saint in C. S. Lewis' book *The Great Divorce*, speaking to an observer riding on a bus to heaven and hell, tells him that if there is a spark of the real anywhere in an individual, they will find it and fan it to life. Somewhere in every person is a spark of God's image—the breath of His life that, however twisted, corrupt and dead in sin, is still capable of redemption.

Resurrection is the work of the Father's own. They must love both unbelievers and believers to life with the love of Jesus until they repent, change and become the Father's own, mature in Him.

4. The Old Ways Must Die

A fourth principle is that, since death precedes life, *the old ways must die before the new can replace them*. Jesus' death on the cross has accomplished that once for all, for all of us. The problem is, how to apply His death to the deep reaches of the heart, where practices in the old nature are born and empowered?

Again, the Father's own can begin but not end that process for the nations. Our task is to study the history of any nation—political, ethnic or religious—and to repent specifically for its sins. *We are to uncover and call for the death of our nations' practiced ways on the cross of Christ.*

A number of those old ways have been enumerated in previous chapters—the practiced ways of hubris and cultural naïveté, for example, that have defiled missionary efforts in the "nation" of the Church throughout the centuries. The Osages and many other Plains tribes practiced stealing others' horses as part of the game of life, and for *o'don* (honors in the tribe). America practiced slavery and reaps ill from it to this day. Occultism (including Freemasonry) has beset nation after nation.

Research into the history of the nation for which you are called to pray should reveal not only the practiced ways that need to die, but their causes in the sins of the people. Death cannot happen before repentance for sins has cleared the way.

Repentance for sin and *prayers that reckon practices to death on the cross* are two of the most important actions that must be done if the nations are to be healed.

Such repentance and prayers can be done for unbelievers and even for those who believe in other gods. Recall that not everyone Jesus healed was a disciple of His, or even a devout Hebrew (e.g., the Syrophoenician woman of Mark 7:26). In the end, of course, our Lord wants all to be converted and to know Him as Redeemer, but in the meantime people's lack of desire for Him does not inhibit the reach of His love or altogether prevent the power of His redemptive actions in their lives. *Our loving Lord heals and transforms because that is His nature, and He wants a flock of believers who apply His redeeming grace wherever hearts allow.*

Repentance needs to be concrete and specific. Studies of history, whether in individuals, groups, cities, regions, states or nations, can reveal the specific acts in history that God wants to address and heal.

I have mentioned that I have researched the history of my own Osage ethnic nation and walked through its history with healing prayers. To some extent I have done the same for America, Germany and England. But these works have barely begun what needs to be done—a mere drop in a sea of need. *Imagine how powerful and transforming when hundreds or thousands of prayerful people respond to the Father's call and begin to track the history of their political, ethnic or religious nations, repenting specifically for sins and reckoning resultant practiced ways to death on the cross!*

Remember, the Father's call is essential. He is the General on the field and retains specific tasks for each of us. Rushing in presumptuously just because an idea grabs hold of us is nothing but dead works. But oh, what wonders will be accomplished when multitudes of prayerful people respond and obey God's call for the healing of the nations!

5. Inner Healing Requires Persistence

Inner healing of any kind for individuals, groups, cities, regions, states or nations requires persistence. There is no escape from

247

longsuffering. We who have become conditioned to instant-on TV and microwave meals would like to cook up healing in a flash of prayer. One New Testament admonition is not very popular with our generation: "We desire that each one of you show the same diligence so as to realize the full assurance of hope until the end, so that you will not be sluggish, but imitators of those who through faith and patience inherit the promises" (Hebrews 6:11–12).

Prayer for physical healing is sometimes rewarded with instant, visible, miraculous change. Rare as this is, it nevertheless engenders great increases of faith and creates increased desires to pay whatever price for more of God's intervention. But when praying for the healing of any kind of nation, you may have to pray for months or even years before any results begin to appear. It can seem like pouring time and energy down a bottomless hole. Discouragement stalks every prayer warrior who tackles such projects for the Lord.

Remedies? I suggest taking hold of a good concordance at least once a month, looking up and reading the promises of the Lord. Second, make a practice of reading the lives of the saints. Many spent themselves in exhausting labor and persecution for years on end before the people they were praying for and serving began to change. Best of all, spend time just letting our wonderful Father love and refresh you.

6. Celebration Enhances Change

Celebration and thanksgiving, especially before evidence of victory begins to appear, make possible change for the better. The psalmist wrote, "He who offers a sacrifice of thanksgiving honors Me; and to him who orders his way aright I shall show the salvation of God" (Psalm 50:23). And the writer to the Hebrews called faith "the assurance of things hoped for, the conviction of things not seen" (Hebrews 11:1).

Thanking God in advance demonstrates faith. It assures God that you believe in what He is doing through you, and it says to Him, "Risk sending Your angels to war for us. I will not let

You down by quitting too soon or by not believing that Your redemption is going to happen."

Celebrating and thanking God when victory begins to arrive says that you give God glory and will not quit until the full work is done.

The enemy always wants to counterattack. He loves to approach those to whom victory is coming and lay temptation in the new, raw track, to see if he can seduce us back to the old track before the new has found time to seat itself. He wants to resurrect sinful ways before the new has become an accomplished habit, to cause us to slide into the old and conclude, "The prayers didn't work!"

The arrival of the first instances of victory signal us to more fervent prayers than before—for a while. That may be followed by a time of drought. Nothing good seems to be happening. But persist. Don't give up. There will come a time when new ways have so displaced the old that more and more people will sense danger and flee from evil, redoubling efforts in the new ways. A time will arrive when rest and peace settle in. "After you have suffered for a little while, the God of all grace, who called you to His eternal glory in Christ, will Himself perfect, confirm, strengthen and establish you" (1 Peter 5:10).

The good news for people whose hearts are turned outward for the sake of others is that they receive this promise not merely for themselves but for the sake of all for whom **they** have been praying. After we have persevered and suffered (mainly in burden-bearing) in longsuffering, persistent prayer, others will be perfected, confirmed, strengthened and established. Isn't it true that we can only rejoice in our own salvation for a little while, but we can rejoice forever in the salvation of those for whom we have labored?

7. The Labor Is the Lord's

The seventh principle of inner healing for the nations is that all this labor for the sanctification and transformation of hearts is not ours, and it never was. It is the Lord's labor for the lost of the world whom He loves and for whom He died. Isn't it good to know we are serving in the center of the Lord's will? And how relieving and refreshing it is to know we are only instruments in the hand of the Master. If results do not seem forthcoming, so what? It is His responsibility, not ours, to bring forth victory, and His timetable, too. Ours is only to obey.

Remember the end of the Book. We win!

Index

In 1974 John Loren Sandford, together with his wife, Paula, founded Elijah House, an international writing, teaching and counseling ministry headquartered in Post Falls, Idaho. Its mission is restoration and reconciliation. With numerous full-time staff and counselors and a long waiting list, Elijah House treats marriage and family problems, abuse, multiple personality disorders, schizophrenia and depression. There are now five international Elijah Houses—in Canada, Australia, New Zealand, Austria and Finland.

John Sandford, a Congregational pastor for 21 years, travels worldwide with Paula. Together they conduct seminars on marriage and family, inner healing and transformation, prayer, the gifts of the Holy Spirit, burden-bearing and intercession, small group ministry and leadership training. Active in the renewal and reconciliation movements, the Sandfords have taught and counseled many Christian leaders and make frequent television appearances.

John and Paula have co-authored four books: *The Elijah Task, Restoring the Christian Family, The Transformation of the Inner Man* (which has sold almost two million copies) and *Healing the Wounded Spirit*. John, with help from their son Loren, wrote *The Renewal of the Mind* and *Why Some Christians Commit Adultery*; and with their son Mark, *A Comprehensive Guide to Deliverance and Inner Healing*. Paula wrote *Healing Victims of Sexual Abuse* and *Healing Women's Emotions*. With Paula's brother, Lee Bowman, they wrote *Waking the Slumbering Spirit* and *Choosing Forgiveness*. *The Healing of the Nations*, by John, becomes their twelfth.

John and Paula have six children, twenty grandchildren and six great-grandchildren.